BODYTALK

University of Pennsylvania Press
NEW CULTURAL STUDIES
Joan DeJean, Carroll Smith-Rosenberg, and Peter Stallybrass, Editors

A complete listing of the books in this series appears at the back of this volume.

BODYTALK
When Women Speak in Old French Literature

E. Jane Burns

University of Pennsylvania Press

Philadelphia

Library of Congress Cataloging-in-Publication Data

Burns, E. Jane, 1948–
  Bodytalk : when women speak in Old French literature / E. Jane
Burns.
    p.   cm. — (New cultural studies)
  Includes bibliographical references and index.
  ISBN 0-8122-3183-X. — ISBN 0-8122-1405-6
    1. French literature—To 1500—History and criticism.   2. Women
and literature—France.   3. Body, Human, in literature.   4. Speech
in literature.   I. Title.   II. Series.
PQ155.W6B87   1993
840'.9'353042—dc20   92-38403
                                                            CIP

This book is dedicated to all my aunts:

Alice Elmas Marootian Asoian
Zabelle Dorothy Marootian
Seda Garapedian Marootian
Anna Charlotte Dilworth Flanagan
Amelia Marguerite Dilworth Mackie
Luvilla Belle Dilworth Reichhardt
Marjorie Ellen Dilworth Murdock

Contents

viii   Contents

Acknowledgments

Many voices have shaped the "body" of this book. I would like to thank Bonnie Krueger, Linda Lomperis, and Elizabeth Robertson for long and productive phone collaborations. More locally, insightful comments on various drafts of this project have been provided over the years by Judith Bennett, Helen Solterer, Elizabeth Clark, and Sarah Beckwith. Special thanks to Mary D. Sheriff for generously adding the perspective of a non-specialist reader and to members of the North Carolina Research Group on Medieval and Early Modern Women who nurtured this project in its infancy. I derived enormous benefit from careful readings by Norris Lacy, Nancy Regalado, and Joan Ferrante. Joan DeJean's incisive suggestions proved crucial in shaping the book's final contours.

Thanks to Jerry Singerman, an editor extraordinaire, and to Merrimon D. Crawford, Marlyse, Bach, and Laine Doggett for special editorial help.

I owe a great debt to the Institute for the Arts and Humanities at the University of North Carolina, Chapel Hill, and to its director, Ruel Tyson, whose generous support enabled me to bring this project to completion.

Extra special thanks are due to Fred Burns and to Ned.

A portion of Chapter One first appeared as "Knowing Women: Female Orifices in Old French Farce and Fabliau," *Exemplaria* 4, 1 (1992): 81–104, Copyright Center for Medieval and Early Renaissance Studies, State University of New York at Binghampton; reprinted by permission. A portion of Chapter One also appears in "This Prick Which Is Not One: How Women Talk Back in Old French Fabliaux," in *Feminist Approaches to the Body in Medieval Literature,* ed. Linda Lomperis and Sarah Stanbury (Philadelphia: University of Pennsylvania Press, 1993), Chapter 9, pp. 188–212.

A portion of Chapter Five first appeared as "How Lovers Lie Together: Adultery and Fictive Discourse in Beroul's *Roman de Tristan,*" *Tristania* 8, 2 (1983): 15–30; reprinted by permission.

Preface

This book is about female bodies and what they say in Old French literary texts authored by men. My interest in the topic is not purely literary or theoretical but also personal and political. Directly implicated in this project is the complex relation between the fictive bodies and voices of medieval literary heroines and the problematic positioning of the historical bodies and voices of contemporary feminist academics working in the field of medieval studies. I hope, however, that the pages to follow will also speak to the concerns and experiences of feminists more generally—those who live, work, and speak from the female body and others interested in learning more about that culturally charged process. Part of my agenda here is to demonstrate how feminist medievalists have common ground with scholars working on the woman question in later literary periods and to convince non-medievalists of what they stand to gain by reading these early texts. In addition to giving practitioners of feminist studies a glimpse of the rich literary resources to be found in selected texts representing women from the twelfth through the fifteenth centuries, I want especially to show how a familiarity with medieval texts can provide a wider historical framework for the issues of female sexuality, subjectivity, speech, and the body that so crucially inform current feminist debate.[1] Whereas many Old French texts stage these issues in compellingly modern ways, they also offer historically specific accounts of the founding moments of Western conceptions of love, desire, and sexuality.

Before starting this book, I had quietly observed for more than a decade the varied ways in which female voices speaking in the academy—as professors, advisors, and administrators—were so often interpreted by their listeners specifically in terms of the woman's body that articulated their words. At the same time I heard repeatedly from some men and some of the women in question claims of unproblematic female agency—these women had "made it" in academe, they were doing "what they wanted" pursuing the career "of their choice." They had a voice in the university, it was claimed, a fully acknowledged presence, "too influential a voice" some even charged. And yet incidents of sexual harassment persisted, as they do still today—moments when the female "presence" in the academic work-place is shockingly reduced to a mindless body. And pregnant professors repeatedly confess feeling discomfort as their bellies swell in the halls of learning. If pregnancy somehow makes the female anatomy all too present for many colleagues, calling into question the viability and "professional" status of the woman academic, cases of sexual and gender harassment re-inforce the message that women are bodies first and thinking beings only secondarily. The most egregious incidents of sexism in the institution seem always to remind us that our professional voices can only be heard through the filter of our gendered anatomy.

I do not derive from these sobering observations a sense of the im-possibility of female agency in speech, a feeling that women can have no voice. On the contrary, what has fascinated me most about the institu-tional positioning of academic women over the years is the extent to which our voices as teachers, readers, and interpreters of texts can so often be both our own and simultaneously constructed by the institutions and au-diences within and before which we speak. It is this double positioning of the contemporary female split-subject that initially spurred my investiga-tion into the highly stereotyped "female subjects" of Old French literary texts.

From the excessively beautiful lady of courtly romance to the lascivi-ous shrew of Old French fabliau and farce, medieval portraits of femininity appear to be thoroughly the product of male imagination and fantasy. But are they nothing more than that? As a teacher of texts from the early pe-riod of Old French literature (the eleventh through thirteenth centuries) with few female authors available for inclusion in my course syllabi—the women troubadour poets (*trobairitz*) and Marie de France provide two significant exceptions—I found myself coming back repeatedly to the fe-male characters in male-authored texts, looking for ways to read around the misogyny that structured their portraits.[2] I began attempting to reread those paradigmatically "feminine" bodies by listening to their speech, however constructed it may admittedly be, listening for something other than the dominant discourse that medieval heroines' bodies and voices were designed to convey. Something in the problematic positioning of these female characters acting within, as they also acted out, established conventions of femininity kept reminding me hauntingly of our own po-sition as female academics speaking and acting within an institution that officially constructs our thought and speech.[3] The analogy is of course not exact, but I find it to be more compelling than we might normally allow.

I feel at times that we, as female academics or even more pointedly as feminist medievalists, are characters in a text that we did not write. And yet to a significant degree the institutional narrative we are living is our text too.

It was initially this feeling of standing between ill-defined spheres of gendered activity in the academy that encouraged me to wonder if there were not some space within the highly misogynous medieval depictions of female bodies and voices that might enable us to read nonetheless "for the feminine" in such male-authored texts. Would it be possible to read the ambiguous status of the female speaking body in Old French texts as we might read our own ambiguous status as female speakers in the academy, respecting all the while the specifically medieval subjectivity of these problematic heroines?[4] How could we, as contemporary feminist readers, find a way to hear the medieval heroine's body talk?

As I pondered this question from various angles over the years and attempted to explain my position on the inscribed woman's body and voice to interested and sometimes skeptical colleagues, one image in particular, one possible model for reading the problematic position of female protagonists, proved especially useful: the unlikely and provocative example of Mae West.

Mae West in the Middle Ages?

Indeed this stereotypical Hollywood sex goddess provides a key point on the continuum I want to map out between the contemporary feminist reader and the wholly fictive female characters we confront in texts authored by men. Whereas the voices and bodies of inscribed medieval heroines have been fabricated most often by an anonymous or reputedly male author, Mae West offers the image of a "real woman" who speaks from a material body. As a stage performer in small-time vaudeville and later as a Hollywood starlet, this highly stereotyped and seemingly fabricated "woman" exercised at least some choice over the words that her female persona expressed. Mae West thus stands at the midpoint of the spectrum I want to explore, serving as a bridge between our existence as women who are necessarily "constructed" by and within the dominant discourses of Western culture and the more obviously constructed female protagonists who speak from the pages of Old French literature.

In a magazine interview Mae West once characterized the key role she played in forging her eroticized stage and film persona by insisting, "I am my own original creation."[5] The statement provides a perplexing echo of the phrase chosen by Hélène Cixous to represent the necessary estrangement that woman suffers as a result of having been labeled the "dark continent." Explaining how woman has not been able "to live in her own house, her very body," Cixous contends that woman "could never have exclaimed: 'The house I live in is my own, / I never copied anyone.'"[6] And yet isn't this precisely what the full-figured body of Mae West proclaims when announcing, "I am my own original creation"?

Taken at face value, Mae West's statement implies that the voluptuous heroine of the silver screen existed independently of the Western mythic traditions that so obviously formed her identity. She asserts that her voice and the curvy female body conditioning it derives only from the conscious choices of an empowered and individualized woman. To outside observers of the Mae West phenonemon and those sensitive to Cixous's observation about women and their bodily houses, Mae West's emphatic statement rings as false as it does true. The voice she created for herself was clearly hers and not hers at the same time. While Mae West's fictive voice could not be a culturally free woman's voice as she mockingly asserted, neither can her pat speech be taken as a straightforward enactment of Western stereotypes of femininity. The very fact that a woman actively speaks the stereotypes that are typically uttered by men about women allows for a different reading: one that would significantly change the terms of the standard hierarchical equation.[7] As Mae West herself put it in the closing tagline that became the trademark of her vaudeville act, "It isn't what you do, it's how you do it."[8] By simply embracing wholeheartedly her culture's patriarchal views of femaleness and femininity, Mae West invites us to overturn the predictable formulation of those views. In her mimicry we can hear difference, the difference created by a woman speaking "as a woman" while still speaking about women "as a man" might.

Christine Brooke-Rose has reminded us that Heidegger once posed the question of a speaker's ability to control language by stating that "Man acts as if he were the shaper and master of language, while it is language which remains the mistress of man. . . . In fact it is language that speaks" not man.[9] Mae West's cocky speech seems an apt illustration of the mistress having taken over what man thought to be his own linguistic territory. Using his language, the metaphors he had devised over centuries to type-cast and silence the female as a libidinous, nonthinking body, she turns them back against him by simply speaking the stereotype from her eroticized female mouth. To be constructed as the eager blonde that gentlemen are supposed to prefer is different from speaking the part. When Mae West says, for example, "I've been on more laps than a napkin," she allows us to reread the flagrantly sexist connotations that such a statement would carry if uttered by a man about a woman. When the predictable "She's been on more laps than a napkin," is transferred to the woman's voice, the very words used typically to reduce the female to a brainless lap-sitter can take on an altogether different valence, voicing an assertive challenge to the ideology they were designed initially to convey.

The staged and constructed persona of this bawdy and highly embodied female provides, then, a particularly apt point of reference for our discussion of female subjectivity because it reveals a woman's voice and body enacting cultural stereotypes of femininity while also simultaneously critiquing them. A passage from Mae West's memoirs reveals the extent to which she herself was conscious of playing the sex symbol while ironizing that role: "Behind the symbol I was becoming, there was much good material for drama, satire and some kind of ironic comment on the war of the sexes."[10]

As a speaker Mae West remains, to be sure, along with Heidegger's male example, subject to the range of meanings available in signifying practice at a particular historical moment. If the subject is not, as Catherine Belsey reminds us, "an origin of meaning,"[11] it is not so much a source as a reflection of received meanings. Or as Toril Moi has argued, the subject results from "a host of conflicting material, social, political, and ideological factors. . . . It is this highly complex network of conflicting structures . . . that produces the subject and its experiences, rather than the other way around."[12] The subject then, any subject, is itself a subjected being.

But the case of the female speaker further complicates the process. When the woman's body speaks, it does not simply reverse the terms of the standard equation, assuming the place of the rational male voice that stands traditionally in opposition to bodily female silence. The female speaker moves toward subjectivity in a way that necessarily destabilizes and redefines the notion of subjectivity itself. For women to speak is, in Belsey's terms, "to threaten the system of differences which gives meaning to patriarchy" (*The Subject of Tragedy*, 191). Indeed, the very status of Mae West's voice—at once so incontestably dominant and so utterly female—significantly unsettles the expected hierarchy of male subject and female object. It does so, to a certain extent at least, because that voice issues from a woman's body. The modern sex queen's words show us to what extent female anatomy matters in our reading of women characters while establishing at the same time that it does not matter in a single, predictable, or reductive way.[13] If her voice is contained within the dominant voice of male culture, it can also speak to us in registers generally foreign to that dominant voice.

If we dare to put the example of the sassy blonde bombshell's speech together with that of any number of medieval heroines, we are spurred to pose the question of female subjectivity in a new way. Recognizing in both Mae West and more thoroughly fictive female heroines examples of a textualized woman speaking simultaneously in her own voice and in the dominant voice that culture imposes on her speech, we can begin to search the Old French literary text for women's voices that are not wholly, characteristically, or symptomatically female. We will be listening instead for women's voices that are situated within but also apart from traditional images of femininity and femaleness.[14]

Let us begin with the words of another blonde beauty, this one from the thirteenth rather than the twentieth century, the stunningly gorgeous Old French Philomena.

Notes

1. My debt to Jane Gallop's wonderful *Thinking Through the Body* and Susan Suleiman's earlier *The Female Body in Western Culture: Contemporary Perspectives* will be obvious. What I hope to offer here is a partial historical contextualizing of some key issues that they and others have raised.

2. Like Elaine Marks, who confessed some years ago that she loved to read Proust, and Jane Gallop, who has admitted more recently the same "weakness" for Barthes (see *Thinking Through the Body*, 108–9), I am not willing to abandon works by male authors. Since I often find within their pages female characters who speak to me in significant and telling ways, I prefer to echo Nina Auerbach's project of "engorging the patriarchy" by tracing the resilient, mutable female voices couched in male texts ("Engorging the Patriarchy" and *Woman and the Demon: The Life of a Victorian Myth*).

3. See Nancy K. Miller, "Changing the Subject: Authorship, Writing, and the Reader," 112.

4. For an assessment of the problematic intersection between feminism and Old French Studies, see E. Jane Burns, Sarah Kay, Roberta L. Krueger, and Helen Solterer, "Feminism and the Discipline of Old French Studies: Une Bele Disjointure."

5. Jon Tuska, *The Films of Mae West*, 188.

6. Hélène Cixous and Catherine Clément, *The Newly Born Woman*, 68.

7. This is the point made so cogently in Irigaray's pure mimicry of Plotinus's *Enneads* (*Spéculum de l'autre femme*, 210–24). Because she repeats his words in her voice, inserting them into her book, the master's words take on a new valance.

8. For a fascinating account of Mae West's early stage performances, including a mention of two unproduced plays she wrote that feature women who use their sexual charms to dominate men and two others that were performed under the titles of "Sex" and "The Drag," see Robert C. Allen, *Horrible Prettiness: Burlesque and American Culture*, 274–81.

9. Christine Brooke-Rose, "Woman as a Semiotic Object."

10. Allen, *Horrible Prettiness*, 275. See in a similar vein, Susan Suleiman's reading of Erica Jong's *Fear of Flying* as a parodic, self-conscious reversal of female stereotypes through which the objectified woman usurps the male gaze on and language about the opposite sex (*The Female Body*, 9–10).

11. Catherine Belsey, *The Subject of Tragedy: Identity and Difference in Renaissance Drama*, x.

12. Toril Moi, *Sexual/Textual Politics: Feminist Literary Theory*, 10.

13. See in this regard, Diana Fuss, *Essentially Speaking: Feminism, Nature, and Difference*, 51; and Denise Riley, *Am I That Name? Feminism and the Category of "Women" in History*, 98–114. Mae West's ambiguous status as a speaking subject significantly erodes the rigid categories of essentialism and constructionism typically invoked to argue for or against an inherent female identity.

14. Nancy Miller has uncovered a similarly ambiguous female space in Charlotte Brontë's *Villette*, where she reads Lucy Snowe as a figure of the female writing subject, one who writes "as a woman" but does so within the necessary ambiguities and ironies of an enabling "feminine" fraternity. It is precisely in the ambiguities of this heroine's position that we find, according to Miller, the essential ingredients of a female writing subject ("Changing the Subject," 114–16).

Introduction: Listening to Bodies Talk

Philomena Asks the Question

In the Old French reworking of a tale from Ovid's *Metamorphoses*, the beautiful virgin Philomena confronts her authoritative brother-in-law Tereus with a question that speaks tellingly to the contemporary debate about female subjectivity:

"My speech, sir, in comparison to yours, what could it be worth?" ("Sire, ma parole / Anvers la vostre que vaudroit?")[1] Responding to Tereus's request that she use her speech persuasively on his behalf—to convince her father that he should allow her to accompany Tereus on a long-distance sea voyage to visit her sister Progne, Philomena appears, at first reading, to profess linguistic helplessness. Speaking as a beautiful body excluded from the realm of male-dominated discourse and cognition, Philomena here asks essentially how she could possibly replace Tereus in his role as speaking subject. How could her words convince her father, Pandions, to entrust her to Tereus's care if the influential speech of the more mature, powerful, and reputable Tereus has failed at the task? "In comparison to his speech, what could hers be worth?"

We have here a particularly striking version of what contemporary feminist thinkers have termed the paradox of the female speaking subject: a heroine who, even as she speaks, cannot, it seems, escape primary identification as an object. The attentive reader hears the ring of subservience in nearly every word of Philomena's reply, from the deferential "sire" and the formal "vostre" to the conditional proposition of "vaudroit." The verbal construction of her sentence itself suggests passivity. To ask what her words could *be worth* implies deference to another's evaluation of them, marking herself as a object to be scrutinized by a more authoritative subject.

This medieval heroine seems then to define herself as occupying the space that Luce Irigaray has designated as "off stage, outside representation, out of play (outside the game), beyond subjectivity and identity."[2]

Subjectivity having been denied her in the specular logic of Western philo-sophical thought that constructs man as *homo loquens* and woman as the objectified "other" of his discourse, Philomena here becomes, in Irigaray's terms, the necessary ground for, the complementary support for, a subjec-tivity that excludes her.[3] Or does she?

If we listen again to Philomena's rhetorical question, we can hear another more pointed query concealed within its unassuming veneer, a question of broader scope that suggests a different role and function for woman's speech in patriarchal culture. Read in a straightforward manner with no rhetorical twist, Philomena's words to Tereus can be understood to ask, "What precisely *is* the value of the woman's voice when set against the words of a man?" Asking Tereus, in this second register, whether he knows the actual force and value of her speech, Philomena seems also to ask, "How and under what circumstances could a woman accede to the position of the speaking subject? And to what effect?" What happens—or what can happen—when the typically objectified and properly silent woman's body speaks?[4]

Philomena's critically doubled question is significant for feminist readers of literary texts—both medieval and modern—because it raises the issue of female subjectivity that has been systematically problematized in Western philosophical and theological traditions, and raises it specifically in terms of the female body. Readers familiar with the Ovidian tale know the ancient Philomel to be the victim of one of the most violent sexual assaults in all of Western literature. In the Old French version, Philomena innocently follows Tereus to a secluded hideaway, where he asks her to become his secret lover. When the maiden refuses, Tereus brutally violates her, attacking the offending female mouth along with her resistant body. Deep in the forest where "no one can see or hear them,"[5] Tereus savagely rapes his wife's sister and, to keep the secret, cuts out her tongue. The story of the woman's dual voice recounted in the Old French *Philomena* is thus embedded in an account of sexual assault from which it cannot be dissociated. The gruesome rape that this heroine suffers establishes a crucial link between the sexual subjugation of women and female silence, positing them as necessary partners in the creation of male pleasure.

But Philomena's fictive body also becomes an important vehicle for conveying to the attentive reader that female subjectivity does not reside in speech alone. The contradictory "women's" voices encoded in Philo-mena's question are both conditioned, if in opposite ways, by the rhetori-cal female body that pronounces them. In the first instance we hear a woman's voice that underwrites the stereotypical privileging of male speech with its corollary imposition of female silence: Philomena locates her identity in a body that ostensibly does not need speech as she underwrites a female identity that exists as corporeality alone. In the second instance, where the woman's voice refuses to adopt the binary logic that pits subject against object, it is also the female anatomy, though in a very different way, that allows us to hear a nonstereotypical voice behind Philomena's question. It is because we as readers know Philomena to be a female character that we can reread her question as an interrogation of the power dynamic in male/female relations. The very female body that would traditionally incite a standardized gender-determined interpretation of Philomena's feminine voice can also provoke us to hear in that voice a forceful alternative response. If the known context of medieval love lyric and romance convention suggests that we understand Philomena's question as the capitulation of a powerless beauty, those conventions do not determine all the rhetorical possibilities that might be included in such a question. There are others.

In fact, if we pause for a moment to consider the conditions of text production and delivery in the High Middle Ages, it is likely that *Philomena*, along with most medieval romance narrative, was read aloud to a listening audience. Little is known about the actual features of that oral reading, but it is not unreasonable to imagine that a single reader might have "played" the characters of a given text, imparting individualized voices to each, or that the presentation might have resembled more closely a kind of reader's theater with several actors playing individual parts. In either case, the range of interpretation for a character's literary voice could have varied widely from one performance to the next, allowing for the very extremes of coloration in Philomena's words that we have been discussing. The space lying between these extremes is the space occupied by the rhetorical female body in this Old French tale. It is that rhetorical body and the way it provides for us the possibility of reading woman's speech differently from its more stereotypical formulations that will concern us in the pages to follow.

Philomena's legacy to the feminist reader of medieval texts is that she indicates, through her subtle questioning, a path to follow, a line of inquiry to pursue. Her doubled question, which hovers uncertainly between the opposite poles of specular logic, destabilizes the standard gender associations of subject/object, voyeur/object of the gaze, masculine/ feminine, speaking/silence. Speaking as a cognitive subject from a highly eroticized body, Philomena asks questions that call into question the very terms of male/female exchange, inquiring who *is* the subject of this sentence? Is there only one? Her rich query, "My speech, sir, in comparison to yours, what could it be worth?" asks in essence what are the possibilities for subject/object relations between us? What is at stake in our struggle for the subject position?

Following Philomena's lead, we can thus begin to recast the question overtly posed by a range of misogynous Old French narratives: How can the curving woman's body possibly have a voice? Reframing that question without its rhetorical twist, we can explore instead how—that is to say in what ways—*can* the fleshly woman's body speak? How can we hear her body talk?

Bodytalk

My thinking about women's bodies and voices in Old French literary texts has been informed by a range of contemporary feminist theorists, most notably among them Luce Irigaray and Teresa de Lauretis. I take as a point of departure for this book Irigaray's double contention that: (1) the woman's body—figured as absence, silence, and nonrepresentability in the phallocentric discourses of Western metaphysics—provides the groundwork for the construction of male subjectivity; and (2) the female body, as the site of patriarchy's construction of the feminine, also constitutes a locus of possible revision.[6] I am most interested in the second term of Irigaray's doubled critique of Western metaphysics because of its clear political implications. There the female body, as the direct empirical referent for all that has been theorized about femininity, can also become a place from which to dismantle the male imaginary and begin constructing a speaking female subject on different terms. Elizabeth Grosz has most succinctly explained Irigaray's project as follows:

> Irigaray does not aim to create a new women's language. Her project, rather, is to utilize already existing systems of meaning or signification, to exceed or overflow the oppositional structures and hierarchizing procedures of phallocentric texts. She stresses their possibilities of ambiguity, their material processes of production and renewal. She affirms the plurality and multiplicity dormant in dominant discourses, which cover over and rely on the inclusions and ex-

clusions of femininity and its associated attributes. She refuses the "either/or" logic of dichotomous models by presenting the feminine as a mode of occupying both alternatives, asserting a "both/and" logic of difference in its place. To speak *as woman* is already to defy the monologism of discursive domination under phallocentrism.[7]

This conception of the female speaking body does not equate biology with subjectivity, claiming that women are women naturally, from birth. Nor does it advance the opposite, purely constructionist position that anatomy plays no part in the social construction of gender.[8] I for one agree with Denise Riley that "there really is biology" and that we feminists must take it into account.[9] But if we want to acknowledge the significant difference of anatomical sex, biology must be theorized, as Diana Fuss has explained, so that our understanding of sex does not simply naturalize gender.[10] For many feminists this has meant devising a double strategy of deconstruction and construction: forging critical practices of doubling that allow one to insist on feminine difference—in counterpoint to many male theoreticians' calls for an end to difference—while also guarding against the danger of simply replacing the male phallocentric subject with a female one.[11]

The specificity of femaleness can thus be tied to the body not as a biological entity but as a biocultural construct. Naomi Schor has explained this point most cogently as follows: "Women occupy in modern Western culture a *specific liminal cultural position* which is through a tangled skein of mediations somehow connected to their anatomical difference, to their femaleness" ("Dreaming Dissymetry," 110).[12] From this perspective the body can be understood to make a difference in the articulation of female subjectivity because that body, the direct empirical referent on which Western culture has imposed all its theorizing about femininity, is our history (Braidotti, "Politics," 107). It is our "historical essence," whether we like it or not.

Our option as feminists seeking to forge a place for female subjectivity then becomes, to a large extent, one of acknowledging that constructed female body and "doing" or "redoing" the cultural construction in which we invariably find ourselves. We can, in Judith Butler's sense, make "gender trouble" as we perform the roles allotted to us and thus partially rewrite the cultural narratives we are living.[13] This does not mean that we can fully repudiate the stereotypes of voice and body that constitute our history, for such a task is literally impossible. But we can begin to embrace stereotypes of the female body that women in the seventies fought so hard to destroy in order to make them over, to make them ours.

From my position as a medievalist, a feminist, and an interpreter of texts, I can best carry out this project by developing a reading practice that will define the terms of another perspective on women's bodies and voices, offering one version of what Teresa de Lauretis has called a view from "elsewhere."[14] For her, "'elsewhere' is not some mythic distant past or some utopian future history: it is the elsewhere of discourse here and now, the blind spots, or the space-off, of its representations" (*Technologies*, 26). Although de Lauretis thinks of this "other place" as standing "outside the heterosexual social contract" (18), her definition of "elsewhere" can also prove useful, I think, in developing a strategy of reading "for the female" within the dominant discourses of heterosexist texts. De Lauretis's "else-where" is constituted by "spaces in the margins of hegemonic discourses, social spaces carved in the interstices of institutions and in the chinks and cracks of the power-knowledge apparati." And "it is there," she claims, "that the terms of a different construction of gender can be posed" (26).

I wish to argue in the following pages that Old French literary texts offer rich possibilities for the reader interested in constructing gender on different terms. If medieval texts appear to the modern reader somewhat distanced and inaccessible due to a language barrier that marks their specific historicity, these tales are not at all distanced from us in their theoretical concerns. Indeed we find in Old French narratives of love and romance an especially rich storehouse of heroines like Philomena who play out before our eyes the highly ambiguous and problematic status of the female speaking subject so widely contested in current feminist debate. In fact, even the most misogynous of medieval literary texts, where a long-standing tradition figures woman's body as the precondition for and guarantor of male intellectual, sexual, and chivalric prowess, can be seen to reveal repeatedly how women's bodies and the voices issuing from them can resist the constructions that contain and define them.

To say this is not to believe naively that the representations of female bodies and voices in Old French texts somehow transparently reflect bodies and voices of real-life women in the Middle Ages. Indeed female protagonists in varied genres of medieval literature bear little relation to actual historical women. But I do not wish to argue, conversely, that there are "no women at all" in these highly complex literary portraits of femininity, that all we can find there is a lady vanished, a textual feminine, an empty metaphorization of Woman.[15] Feminist medievalists have made a convincing case that many of the literary productions we study are more about men than about women, about textual relations between men, homosocial bonding, male desire and imagination.[16] I myself have argued the case for early troubadour lyric.[17] But I now want to take another tack without repudiating that earlier approach or work done by others in that vein.

My project here is to provide the feminist reader of medieval literary texts with a strategy for interpreting the female body as it has been encoded (stereotyped, fetishized, fantasized) within Old French literary texts, by listening to what it says. That is, I attempt to hear, within the dominant discourses that construct female nature in the French Middle Ages—the religiously-conditioned discourse of paraliturgical theater and the patristic commentaries that inform it, the idealizing discourse of courtly romancers in the twelfth century, and the more overtly misogynous discourse employed by writers of fabliau and farce in the thirteenth through the fifteenth centuries—other voices that speak against and dissent from the dominant tradition.[18]

I have chosen to call this resistant doubled discourse "bodytalk." And in proposing that we listen for it, I do not mean to imply that such bodytalk exists de facto in the literary text. It is not something that authors—consciously or not—make their characters do; rather bodytalk is something that we as feminist readers can choose to hear. I am thus not making a case for an inherent "female subjectivity" in Old French texts. Such a move would simply replicate, while inverting its terms, the existing ontological, theological model of male subjectivity. In listening for bodytalk, for the varied ways that female protagonists speak problematically "from the body" in a range of Old French literary texts, I want to record how medieval heroines can speak both within and against the social and rhetorical conventions used to construct them. This book explores then how female voices, fashioned by a male author to represent misogynous fantasies of female corporeality, can also be heard to rewrite the tales in which they appear.[19]

Reading The Body

A similarly perplexing paradox forms the core of the often misunderstood contemporary French theory of "writing the body," known commonly as *écriture féminine*.[20] Working from the perspective of writing rather than reading the body, the practitioners of *écriture féminine* ask, in different ways, whether it is possible to write from the female body without being reduced to bodily existence? Can we reclaim for women the female body and the speech issuing from it in such a way that would enable us to "write the body" instead of being the body? Hélène Cixous and Luce Irigaray have worked, in different ways, toward putting into play the conventionally repressed aspects of woman's sexuality, insisting that they be spoken, not hidden, and spoken by women, not men. Hence the criticism of essentialism that their theories have drawn.[21] Metaphors of female anatomy do abound in the works of both authors, making some readers feel that women here are reduced once again to pure biology. But if Irigaray makes female writing into the speech produced by the two lips of the vagina,[22] while Cixous compares her writing to the flow of menstrual blood, amniotic fluid, and lactation,[23] each does so in an attempt to reclaim and rename those body parts from a new perspective. Their project, in brief, is to redefine femaleness in its relation to representation. Stemming from a desire to undermine the binary oppositions of phallogocentric logic that privilege the speaking male subject over its female object, these proponents of *écriture féminine* forge a mythically powerful voice for women authors anchored inextricably in female biology, but in a biology redefined to subvert established hierarchies. Conceptualizing woman as a writing-effect rather than as an origin of representation, Cixous and Irigaray envision feminine writing as something *producing* the difference specified as femininty. Woman is here a *process* coming from the female body, but not a purely biological entity.[24]

Whatever its weaknesses—a tendency to look for woman at the expense of women, an avowed ahistoricity, an illogical desire to speak as the Other, a tendency to ascribe monolithic significance to the maternal metaphor—[25] the concept of *écriture féminine* can help us to understand something we too easily forget: femininity in literary texts and in life is not an essence opposed to masculinity. Different from the bedrock female nature derived solely from woman's physiology and bodily instincts that the radical French group of "neofeminists" called "Psych. et Po." claims to discern,[26] femininity for Cixous and Irigaray results from a structuring of the libido through patriarchal discourse. It is a female identity created in and through language. This approach helps to explain how male and female modes of imagination cannot ever really be separated because they are created, in Leslie Rabine's terms, by a spacing on a continuum.[27] The difference between masculinity and femininity results not from a unity that has fallen apart but from an originary play of difference through which each gender partakes of and depends on the other for its very definition. By putting the female body back into play, proponents of *écriture féminine* remind us that we cannot fully distinguish the cultural and ideological determinators of the feminine from the "real" woman. The female body here becomes something of a text, or a narrative—like Mae West's own original creation—while remaining all the while a biological entity. So who is speaking when the female body speaks?

Who's Speaking? And How Can She?

One of the most cogent early critiques of Irigaray's "theory of the subject" in *Speculum of the Other Woman* came from Shoshona Felman, who asked how we were to evaluate the speech of the woman theorist, Irigaray, whose voice was telling us that woman's speech had no value. Felman's pointed question, "Who is speaking here?"[28] formed the nexus of a subsequent and still ongoing dialogue about authorship and the status of the female signature staged between Nancy K. Miller and Peggy Kamuf.[29] Each critic asked, in her own way, to what extent we need to know "who's speaking" in order to determine the value of a literary protagonist's speech. How much does the author's voice condition the voices of his or her fictive characters? Miller's arguments in favor of knowing the sex of an author and Kamuf's reticence to place ultimate value on authorial gender together trace the outline of a larger question for feminist critics of varied critical stripes: How can we acknowledge a specifically female contribution to literary creation without essentializing women into the mythic category of Woman?[30] Or in Nancy Miller's more recent formulation, how can we get beyond the binary terms of the original debate that pits empiricism against theory, authorial identity against indifference to gender?[31] Recognizing that historical women never really write or speak purely "as women" anymore than they read "as women,"[32] can we look nonetheless for some kind of subjectivity in the female voices inscribed within literary texts?

Two principal responses to this question have emerged in the critical practice of scholars working on Old French texts: those that look for some telling indication of female presence in works authored by women and those that reveal the concerted absence of female subjectivity from texts composed by men. Critics pursuing the route of female authorship focus on the few women writers known to us—the Provençal trobairitz,

Marie de France and Christine de Pizan—attempt to establish a clearly feminine poetics within these works.[33] The most interesting of these efforts, to my mind, are those that reveal an ambiguous status for female authors who emerge from the pages of the literary text only to recede again before our eyes. Addressing the ways in which individual historic women make their voices heard within established male traditions of poetic composition, many recent studies ask how women can express their cultural experiences using the rhetorical tools of traditional male expression. They show us the trobairitz Na Castelloza defining her right to "make love and poetry" in spite of the established conventions of troubadour lyric,[34] Marie de France forging a feminine poetics grounded in silence or a consciously androgynous voice,[35] and Christine de Pizan boldly incorporating metaphors of the female body and reproductive capacity within an otherwise conservative literary idealism.[36] In these key instances the female emerges piecemeal, speaking in a voice that is at once her own and not her own,[37] reminding us that there is no totalizing woman's voice or coherent female subjectivity to be found in Old French works written by women. The value of these studies lies precisely in the way they demonstrate how women's speech is necessarily both inscribed within the dominant cultural mode that structures it and also marginalized from that culture's center. As the female author moves from the position of the object of discourse to become its speaking subject, she makes the shift only partially and incompletely. For her, as for Philomena, the subject position remains tentative and unstable as her speech moves subtly between the poles of describer and described.

If these observations ring true for female authors of diverse historical epochs, additional peculiarities of medieval text production complicate the study of female authorship in Old French texts. Not only do the works of the Provençal trobairitz, Marie de France, and Christine de Pizan represent an extremely small sampling of extant literary texts, the names of the earliest authors cannot be linked with certainty to known historical personages. Whereas Christine de Pizan's signature most certainly represents the hand of the widow who lived and wrote at the court of Charles V, Marie's name, which appears in only one manuscript, bears a generic ambiguity not uncommon in medieval French texts. Although Marie's twelfth-century male counterpart identifies himself simply, and perhaps jokingly, as Christian from the city of Troyes (Chrétien de Troyes),[38] she hails more generally from the area around Paris controlled by the French king. Her given name, Marie, tells us nothing more specific about her historical identity than does the humorous moniker of the thirteenth-century author Johnny Fox (Jean Renard) or the wholly bogus attribution of the thirteenth-century Arthurian Vulgate Cycle to Walter Map, a man who died five to ten years before the composition of the tales penned in his name.[39]

The tendency of medieval authorship generally to elude our grasp, hiding as it does behind imprecise or inaccurate signatures, is further complicated by the process of manuscript transmission that often fails to distinguish the invention of an original hand from contributions made by later redactors. Even if we could establish with certainty the actual sex of the historical author corresponding to an individual trobairitz or Marie de France, we would still be at a loss to know how much of their independent poetic creations, as we now have them, came to us from the original author and how much was contributed by scribes who copied and recopied the manuscripts containing their texts.[40] Having learned that we cannot reasonably rely on the medieval signature as a means of validating the authenticity or authority of Old French texts, we must be wary of looking to the female signature as an absolute indication of biological identity or ideological bent.

This does not mean that the signature is a matter of indifference, that we should abandon studies of the few medieval women authors we have, or that we as medievalists and feminists do not still want to know "who's speaking" in the texts we read. But our efforts to recover the woman behind the signature are necessarily more treacherous than those of scholars working in more recent literatures. To put too much store by the signature in medieval manuscripts is to forget, for example, that roughly two-thirds of extant Old French texts are anonymous.[41] What are we as feminist readers to do with those works that, like the Old French *Philomena*, bear no signature at all? If it is too rash to assume that fifty percent of them may have been authored by women, it is probably equally risky to suppose that they were all created by men. In either case the uncertainty of codicological evidence makes it impossible to speak of a distinctly male or female voice—at least one that is biologically conditioned—in the majority of Old French literary works.

These factors of medieval text production alert us to the particular limits and dangers of gynocritics practiced on Old French texts.[42] They also liberate us in a significant way from the modernist quest for a coherent subject. Feminist medievalists, especially those working in the early periods of Old French literature, have never had the illusion of a totalizing female subject. Our work with manuscript fragments, variants, and palimpsests reminds us constantly of the absent author whose subjectivity has been repeatedly constructed and reconstructed by a succession of medieval scribes and their later incarnations in modern editors, translators, and interpreters. As the latter practitioners dispute variant readings, champion particular versions, or add and subtract lines of text, they effectively create the literary work that has come down to us only in fragments.[43]

But if our training as medievalists helps us to avoid reifying the presence of "woman" in the text, encouraging us to avoid the assumption that writing necessarily communicates a gendered essence, that an unbroken continuity between life and text establishes a mimetic relation linking women's writing, reading, and culture,[44] must we necessarily embrace the opposite view—that women are nowhere to be found in the patriarchal discourse of medieval literature?[45]

Who's Listening When the Female Body Speaks?

To date, feminist studies of medieval heroines have often chosen to read women as a cipher for maleness in disguise. And justifiably so. Looking behind the literary woman to the man that she conceals, we have demonstrated in varied ways how the portrait of the woman in medieval literary works outlines the contours of a partially missing person.[46] The image of woman created and manipulated by the antifeminist sentiment governing much Old French farce, fabliau, and paraliturgical theater provides only a misogynous mask of femaleness. Beyond the limiting stereotypes of romance's damsel in distress or epic's powerless or absent lady, the diversity of roles available to women—as mothers, princesses, Amazons, prostitutes, and fairies, to name some of the best documented instances—offer other limiting constructions of the female. Even literary allusions to a *mécénat féminin*, influential women patrons who are credited in the dedications of many literary works with instigating and controlling the production of medieval love stories, may prove simply to be a rhetorical convention ungrounded in historical practice.[47] Images of the powerful courtly lady in troubadour lyric and romance clash disturbingly with the historical reduction of woman's power in the High Middle Ages,[48] suggesting that these literary accounts serve, at least to some extent, to obscure the oppression of medieval women behind a fiction of authority. Literary texts long extolled for elevating the courtly lady to a position of

power and influence have been shown similarly to promote male, not female subjectivity.[49] Psychosocial studies have demonstrated how the troubadour poet's *fin amors* expresses a narcissistic obsession with the male
self more than a passion for the adored lady,[50] while more sociocultural
readings reveal how the lady's portrait embodies not women as subjects
but medieval culture's ambivalent fear of and desire for women.[51] The
elaborate ideology of courtliness that conditions so many medieval texts
fashions an ideal of femininity that actually alienates female identity,
often using it as a foil to stage primary relationships of power between
men.[52] If the courtly lady is always present, always watching, waiting, listening, and thereby validating the existence of her courageous savior-
knight, she is also always marginalized—whether socially, psychologically,
or historically—standing beside, walking behind, or lying beneath the
principal male subject of the chivalric adventure story.

Postmodernist studies of medieval texts have tended problematically
to promulgate a further elision of female subjectivity in Old French literary texts by reading woman as a metaphor of literary creation. Whether
insisting that literary femininity is a purely textual phenomenon, existing
independently of the biological sex of the author,[53] or that the male author
becomes the mother of his own text, coming thereby to know the excess
of female desire that provides the generative force behind writing,[54] studies that read woman as a metaphor for male poetic invention effect a sur-
prising and subtle erasure of female subjectivity.[55] Advantageous to the
extent that they validate the feminine as a cultural construction apart from
restrictive considerations of biology, such approaches tend nonetheless to
metaphorize women out of existence. They claim, for example, that "discourse about women allows literature to talk about something else, notably about itself."[56] To establish woman in this way as a figure for the
process of literary invention in the Middle Ages is to blur the existence
and significance of real sexual difference. Taken to its logical conclusion,
this line of thinking will lead us to deduce along with R. Howard Bloch
that "If a woman [in misogynous discourse] is defined as verbal transgression, indiscretion, and contradiction, then Walter Map, indeed any
writer, can only be defined as a woman."[57] Such a deduction effectively
reads woman out of the literary equation.

Once we subsume the gender issue within the question of language,
woman—whether we envision her in historical, cultural, psychoanalytic,
or literary terms—tends to disappear. And we are led to make genderless
conclusions that excuse antifeminism of the worst sort as if it were a purely

rhetorical mode without historical consequence: "The discourse of misogyny then becomes," in Bloch's rhetorically deft analysis, "a plaint against the self or against writing itself" and women, whether in voice, body, name, spirit, fact, or fiction, are magically erased ("Medieval Misogyny," 19). The discourse of misogyny becomes a discourse having nothing really to do with women. Misogyny in this paradigm speaks only about "literature itself."[58]

We must ask to what extent such postmodernist moves to incorporate the feminine and address the gender issue are in fact counterproductive to our task. They follow the pattern of literary gynesis that Alice Jardine has so cogently traced, a process of putting woman into discourse that ends up reducing her to a sign for something else, in this case something larger, better, more patriarchal.[59] By embracing this semiosis of woman, do we not run the risk of erasing female subjectivity in yet another, unexpected way? To what extent is this theoretical strategy simply a new attempt to "escape the rising voices of women," as Jardine contends (*Gynesis*, 117)? When poststructuralist readings of medieval texts take woman as their subject and speak "about women" or "about the feminine," their gesture provides a haunting echo of medieval theologians' authoritative proclamations concerning the nature of woman. Although they do so in very different ways, both camps tend to efface the specificity of women as speaking subjects behind the creation of a mythic and silenced woman.

A different tack has been taken recently by feminist medievalists working on the genre of Old French romance in particular. While remaining wary of essentializing medieval women's experience, they attempt nonetheless to take women's bodies, actions, and historical specificity into account as they read, in varied ways, "for the feminine" in Old French texts. Kathryn Gravdal has read courtly fantasies of love and romance against the practices of rape and abduction in medieval society, showing how "medieval rape law patterns itself after medieval literature in the cultivation of textual practices that rationalize male violence against women."[60] Roberta L. Krueger attempts to recover the woman in the text by turning to the implied female reader who is simultaneously foregrounded and displaced by narratives that posit female agency only to undermine it. Here the "highly problematic presentation of women readers within romance fictions reflects the problem of historical women's reception of the genre."[61] Helen Solterer studies the relation between lay literate women and the clerical world of learning as it is figured in texts from the late Middle Ages. Tracking patterns of interaction between the medieval master and his female respondent, she shows how women challenge the textual monopoly of clerical knowledge, debating its lessons as they intervene in writing.[62] Each of these studies reads the woman inscribed in male-authored texts in relation to a hypothesized historical or cultural context, Gravdal suggesting that we read literary rape in line with its legal intertexts, Krueger arguing for the plausibility of the imagined woman reader of medieval romance, and Solterer charting the cultural pressures to create a written "female" response to authoritative male discourse.

My project joins those of the feminist readers mentioned here to the extent that we each map out, in different ways, a profile of the textualized medieval woman as both a construction of male discourse and a site of resistance to its conventions. My own "historicizing" gesture is less toward the past, however, than toward the present. I want to emphasize how the continuum of historical women reader/listeners and their inscribed literary counterparts stretches into the twentieth century to capture and also to represent—in a nonspecular reflection—the contemporary feminist medievalist. The bodytalk of heroines in the Old French texts I will analyze in the pages to follow records a fluctuating and unstable female subjectivity not dissimilar from our own complex, ambiguous, and uncertain identities as speakers in a culture not our own.

Knowing Women and Desiring Ladies

The chapters that follow investigate key moments in Old French literature where the words of fictive medieval "women" dissent from and significantly restructure conceptions of female sexuality, wifely obedience, courtly love, and adultery so often used to define and delimit femininity in the French Middle Ages. I have chosen to focus my remarks on the purportedly unattractive women of fabliau, farce, and the Old French play of Adam and Eve on the one hand and on the excessively beautiful ladies of courtly romance on the other. Both paradigms define women principally as bodies, though in very different ways. I want to begin with comic and often moralizing texts from the thirteenth through the fifteenth centuries, texts that claim to "know" female nature and teach it through misogynous stereotypes of the irrational, mindless, and wholly corporeal woman. We will then move back in time to twelfth-century romance texts where an ideology of courtly adoration and love, appearing to elevate women to a privileged position in social interaction, masks an alternate formulation of women as desired and desirable bodies. Beginning with the more overtly misogynous texts and moving to the more subtle obfuscation of female sexuality in courtly romance will enable us to see how the idealized portrait of the courtly lady proves much less ideal than many have supposed.

The book's first section, entitled "Knowing Women," will show both how men purport to "know" women, specifically in terms of female sexuality, in the Old French fabliau and farce and their predecessors in patristic writings that inform the antifeminist literary tradition of medieval France and how women "know differently." Looking closely at the speech of female protagonists whose bodies have been constructed to convey misogynous sentiments about female nature, we will listen to how the "bodytalk" of these protagonists restructures the antifeminist traditions that they both perpetuate and resist. The second section, "Desiring Ladies," outlines the Ovidian paradigm of men loving women as it emerges in the medieval French tradition where male suitors imagine and indeed create, Pygmalion-like, the feminine beauty that enthralls them. But what happens when these seemingly brainless beauties speak? "Desiring Ladies" in its second sense refers less to women's desire than to the varied ways in which romance heroines reposition themselves in the courtly love scenario so as to redefine the terms of heterosexual desire, passion, sexual indulgence, and adultery. This book will address then how female protagonists in a range of Old French literary texts refigure, through their speech, the terms of "knowing women" and "desiring ladies" that the dominant discourses of fabliau and romance respectively impose on the female body.

One can point of course to instances where the words of the Arthurian lady or the fabliau wife represent, as if in echo, the voice of the male author who fashioned the heroine's identity according to social convention and individual invention. But that voice remains nonetheless filtered through the female character's anatomy. And, as Ovid has taught us, the echo is not exact.[63] A man's words spoken through a woman's body, however fictive and fabricated, are not perceived or received by the reader as thoroughly male; their valence changes in accordance with the gender of the speaker articulating them. The point has been made most tellingly in recent years by Irigaray's practice of mimicry. When she quotes verbatim Plotinus's *Enneads*, placing his text squarely with her critique of Western metaphysics in *Speculum of the Other Woman*, the master's words are no longer his own. That is to say, Irigaray's literal repetition of Plotinus's text changes its meaning; we read his words differently when they come from a woman, as part of a feminist's text. Words that have historically constructed woman as matter can, in Irigaray's calculated repetition and repositioning of them, be used to critique the very system that they echo or mime.

Heroines in male-authored texts from the French Middle Ages do not, of course, share Irigaray's politically motivated feminist voice. Neither do they have real historical bodies from which to speak. But they do provide a particularly apt limit case for reading the problematic emergence of female subjectivity within a dominant discourse, for hearing a marginalized gendered speaker in a complex relational dynamic with a more central one. Fictive and constructed as the female protagonist's body is, we read that body as anatomically female, interpreting her voice and words in relation to a constellation of cultural codes that bear on female, not male, anatomy.[64] While often speaking a dominant discourse that figures woman's oppression, the Arthurian lady and fabliau wife can also be heard to speak against those dominant discourses, to resist and dissent, turning their borrowed speech into something else.[65] This, I think, is potentially a place where we can see a different construction of gender emerge. To read for this other view is to acknowledge along with Teresa de Lauretis that woman is both inside and outside gender, at once within and without representation (*Technologies*, 10–11), and to attempt to trace

> the movement back and forth between the representation of gender (in its male-centered frame of reference) and what that representation leaves out, or, more pointedly, makes unrepresentable. It is a movement between the (represented) discursive space of the positions made available by hegemonic discourses and the space-off, the elsewhere, of those discourses. . . . These two kinds of spaces are neither in opposition to one another nor strung along a chain of signification, but they coexist concurrently and in contradiction. (*Technologies*, 26)

I want to chart one version of this crucial contradiction, exploring how the female body often functions in a range of Old French literary texts both as a site for the construction of femininity according to a logic that bolsters male subjectivity and as a locus for developing an alternative reading of female subjectivity. Indeed, listening for bodytalk in Old French literary texts will mean listening for women's voices that neither fully underwrite the specular basis of male subjectivity nor thoroughly repudiate the culturally constructed female. It will mean listening for various kinds of doubled discourse that derive from the fundamental paradox of speaking from the female body.

Notes

1. Chrétien de Troyes, *Philomena*, vv. 276–77.
2. "Hors scène, hors représentation, hors jeu, hors je," Luce Irigaray, *Spéculum de l'autre femme*, 21; translation mine.
3. Irigaray argues:

> Subjectivity denied to woman: indisputably this provides the financial backing for every irreducible constitution as an object: of representation, of discourse, of desire. Once imagine that woman imagines and the object loses its fixed obsessional character.
> As a benchmark that is ultimately more crucial than the subject, for he can sustain himself only by bouncing back off some objectiveness, some objective. If there is no more "earth" to press down/repress, to work, to represent, but also and always to desire (for one's own), no opaque matter which in theory does not know herself, then what pedestal remains for the existence of the "subject"? If the earth turned and more especially turned upon herself, the erection of the subject might thereby be disconcerted and risk losing its elevation and penetration. For what would there be to rise up from and exercise his power over? And in?

(*Speculum of the Other Woman*, 22). For an extended discussion of modernity's struggle with subjectivity and an assessment of the problematic turn toward a fascination with otherness, see Alice Jardine, *Gynesis: Configurations of Women and Modernity*.
4. Or in Irigaray's formulation, "But what if the object started to speak? Which also means beginning to "see," etc. What disaggregation of the subject would that entail?" (*Speculum of the Other Woman*, 135).
5. Chrétien de Troyes, *Philomena*, "Que nus ne les voit ne ne ot" v. 743.
6. For a most lucid reading of the political implications of Irigaray's thought, see Margaret Whitford, "Rereading Irigaray" and *The Irigaray Reader*.
7. Elizabeth A. Grosz, *Jacques Lacan: A Feminist Introduction*, 176 and further 167–87. See also her "Luce Irigaray and the Ethics of Alterity" in *Sexual Subversions: Three French Feminists* and recent explanations of why Irigaray is not an essentialist by Naomi Schor, "This Essentialism Which Is Not One"; Diana Fuss, *Essentially Speaking*, 55–72; Jane Gallop, "Lip Service," in her *Thinking Through the Body*, 92–99.
8. For an incisive rethinking of the essentialism/constructionism debate that shows the binary pair to be a false dichotomy and demonstrates that in different ways most feminists are both essentialists and constructionists, see Diana Fuss, *Essentially Speaking*, 1–72.

9. Denise Riley, *War in the Nursery*, 2.

10. This is the fear of theorists like Christine Delphy and Monique Wittig, as Fuss explains (*Essentially Speaking*, 49–53).

11. See Rosi Braidotti's concise questioning of the politics of the female split subject in "The Politics of Ontological Difference," esp. 92; and Elizabeth Weed's description of the task undertaken by many feminists working both inside and outside the academy as "constructing a female subject in order to obtain for women a better, and in many cases less oppressive and literally safer place in the social field, while *at the same time* always displacing boundaries, always shifting positions to work against the erection of the same old phallocratic structures in the name of identity and the unifying subject" ("A Man's Place," 75). Naomi Schor cites, along with Irigaray, the following practitioners of a doubled critical discourse: Annette Kolodny, Laura Mulvey, Mary Ann Doane, Teresa de Lauretis, Sandra Gilbert, Susan Gubar, Sarah Kofman, Elizabeth Berg, Jane Gallop, and Biddy Martin ("Dreaming Dissymetry: Barthes, Foucault, and Sexual Difference," esp. n. 24).

12. As Rosi Braidotti explains, "One is both born and constructed as a woman, the fact of being a woman is neither merely biological nor solely historical and the polemical edge of the debate should not, in my opinion, go on being polarized in either of these ways" ("The Politics of Ontological Difference," 101).

13. Judith Butler, *Gender Trouble*, 31.

14. Teresa de Lauretis, *Technologies of Gender: Essays on Theory, Film, and Fiction*, 26.

15. This claim has been made most persuasively in a collection of essays entitled *Seeking the Woman in Late Medieval and Renaissance Writings: Essays in Feminist Contextual Criticism*, ed. Sheila Fisher and Janet E. Halley.

16. Early examples are Joan Ferrante's *Woman as Image in Medieval Literature* and "Male Fantasy and Female Reality in Courtly Literature."

17. E. Jane Burns, "The Man Behind the Lady in Troubadour Lyric."

18. This approach draws heavily on Nancy Miller's work on female authors, where she defines women's writing as a "feminist literature of dissent" and argues that "to read women's literature is to see and hear repeatedly a chafing against the unsatisfactory reality contained in the maxim" (*Subject to Change: Reading Feminist Writing*, 5, 44).

19. My use of the term "bodytalk" differs significantly from that of Kaja Silverman's chapter called "Body Talk" in *The Acoustic Mirror: The Female Voice in Psychoanalysis and Cinema*, which shows how classic Hollywood cinema conflates the female voice with the female body, obliging the female subject "to bear a double burden of lack—to absorb the male subject's castration as well as her own" (63). I want here to explore the possibility of bodytalk in another sense, examining how the stereotypical reduction of female voice to body in medieval literature also stages key moments of resistance to that stereotype.

20. Hélène Cixous and Catherine Clément, *The Newly Born Woman*; Hélène Cixous, "The Laugh of the Medusa"; and Luce Irigaray, "Ce Sexe qui n'en est pas un." On *écriture féminine* see also Ann Rosalind Jones, "Writing the Body: Toward an Understanding of *L'Ecriture féminine*."

21. For an answer to charges of essentialism in Irigaray, see note 7.

22. Irigaray, "Quand nos lèvres se parlent," in *Ce Sexe qui n'en est pas un*, 203–17.

23. Cixous, "The Laugh of the Medusa," 250–51.

24. See Mary Jacobus, *Reading Woman: Essays in Feminist Criticism*, 109; Leslie Rabine, "A Feminist Politics of Non-Identity"; Mary Poovey, "Feminism and Deconstruction."

25. See especially Toril Moi, *Sexual/Textual Politics*, 116; also Shoshana Felman, "Women and Madness: The Critical Phallacy"; and Domna Stanton, "Difference on Trial: A Critique of the Maternal Metaphor in Cixous, Irigaray, and Kristeva."

26. Alice Jardine, *Gynesis*, 41, n. 31.

27. Leslie Rabine, "A Feminist Politics of Non-Identity," 19–22.

28. Felman, "Women and Madness," 2–16. On another difficulty inherent in Irigaray's project, see Jane Gallop, "The Father's Seduction."

29. In *Diacritics* (Summer 1982), see Peggy Kamuf, "Replacing Feminist Criticism," 42–47; and Nancy K. Miller, "The Text's Heroine: A Feminist Critic and Her Fictions," 48–53. The dialogue is updated in a further exchange in "Parisian Letters: Between Feminism and Deconstruction." The question has been posed in various ways by feminist critics attempting to read for the feminine, either in texts written by women or in male-authored texts. See especially Nancy K. Miller, *Subject to Change*; Mary Jacobus, *Reading Woman*; Nina Auerbach, "Engorging the Patriarchy."

30. This tension is recorded in general terms in the rift between French and American feminist theorists. For an explanation of their basic differences, see Alice Jardine, "Gynesis"; and Toril Moi, *Sexual/Textual Politics*.

31. Miller, *Subject to Change*, 67.

32. On the phenomenon of women reading as men, see Judith Fetterly, *The Resisting Reader: A Feminist Approach to American Modern Fiction*; and Jonathan Culler, "Reading as a Woman."

33. For example, Peter Dronke, *Women Writers of the Middle Ages: A Critical Study of Texts from Perpetua to Marguerite Porete*; Charity Cannon Willard, *Christine de Pizan: Her Life and Works*; Katharina M. Wilson, ed., *Medieval Women Writers*; Meg Bogin, *The Women Troubadours*; John F. Plummer, ed., *Vox Feminae*. Arguing most recently, and I think problematically, for a clearly feminine poetics based, in this case, on a male model of thought, see Stephen G. Nichols, "Medieval Women Writers: Aisthesis and the Powers of Marginality."

34. Matilda T. Bruckner, "Na Castelloza, *Trobairitz*, and Troubadour Lyric"; and the most recent anthology of essays on the women troubadours, *The Voice of the Trobairitz: Perspectives on the Women Troubadours*, ed. William Paden. Some of these essays argue for a feminine poetics while others impute a more problematic status to the female speaking/singing subject.

35. Michelle Freeman, "Marie de France's Poetics of Silence: Implications for a Feminist *Translatio*" and "Dual Natures and Subverted Glosses: Marie de France's 'Bisclavret.'" For the extensive scholarship on Marie de France, see Glyn Burgess, *Marie de France: An Analytical Bibliography*. Most recently see articles by

R. Howard Bloch, "New Philosophy and Old French"; Diana M. Faust, "Women Narrators in the *Lais* of Marie de France"; and Stephen G. Nichols, "Working Late: Marie de France and the Value of Poetry."

36. See Sylvia Huot, "Seduction and Sublimation: Christine de Pisan, Jean de Meun, and Dante." For the scholarship on Christine de Pisan, see Angus Kennedy, *Christine de Pizan: A Bibliographical Guide*; and Edith Yenal, *Christine de Pisan: A Bibliography of Writings by Her and About Her*. For a more complete accounting of work on medieval women writers, see the Select Bibliography in *Romance Notes* 25, 3 (Spring 1985) and issues of the *Medieval Feminist Newsletter*, ed. E. Jane Burns, Thelma Fenster, Roberta L. Krueger, and Elizabeth Robertson.

37. See, in this regard, the problematic status of the lady's *Response* to the *Bestiaires d'Amours* by Richard de Fournival as analyzed by Helen Solterer, "Seeing, Hearing, Tasting Woman: The Senses of Medieval Reading"; Nancy Regalado, "Vos Paroles ont mains et pies"; and Alexandre Leupin, "Composing the Feminine: Richard de Fournival's *Bestiaires d'Amours*," in his *Barbarolexis: Medieval Writing and Sexuality*. See also Leupin's analysis of how the woman's voice resists and subverts the king's reputed "parole pleine" ("La Compromission: Sur *Le Voyage de Charlemagne à Jérusalem et à Constantinople*").

38. Roger Dragonetti, *La Vie de la lettre au Moyen Âge: Le conte du Graal*.

39. On the problem of authorship in the Vulgate Cycle, see E. Jane Burns, *Arthurian Fictions: Rereading the Vulgate Cycle*; and Alexandre Leupin, *Le Graal et la littérature: Étude sur la vulgate arthurienne en prose*. A most complex case is provided by the Old French *chansons de femme*, ostensible "women's songs" whose actual authorship remains subject to debate. See E. Jane Burns, Sarah Kay, Roberta L. Krueger, and Helen Solterer, "Feminism and the Discipline of Medieval Studies: *Une Bele Disjointure*."

40. Dragonetti, *La vie de la lettre*, 41–61.

41. Paul Zumthor, *Essai de poétique médiévale*, 64–75.

42. See Elaine Showalter's distinction between feminist critique and gynocritics, "Toward a Feminist Poetics," and her *A Literature of Their Own: British Women Novelists from Bronte to Lessing*, along with Sandra Gilbert and Susan Gubar, *The Madwoman in the Attic: The Woman Writer and the Nineteenth-century Imagination*.

43. Paul Zumthor, "Le Texte-fragment"; Bernard Cerquiglini, *Éloge de la variante: Histoire critique de la philologie*.

44. In listening to these textualized female voices, we must be careful not to reify or privilege them. It is not my goal to expose a true "woman's presence" in texts written by men, a presence detected by reading signs of "real female power" as does Adrienne Munich, "Notorious Signs, Feminist Criticism and Literary Tradition," 252. I do not believe that such a presence exists any more than I believe Molly Hite to have revealed a "pure corporeality" in the frankly erotic writings of contemporary women authors ("Writing—and Reading—the Body: Female Sexuality and Recent Feminist Fiction," 122). Certainly it makes a difference when women writers offer alternatives to standard male descriptions of female sexuality, but that does not amount to a pure woman's voice.

45. Though we can acknowledge along with Julia Kristeva the theoretical and political validity of insisting on woman's essential unrepresentability, asserting that

woman cannot be defined because that definition will necessarily be a social, not a natural construct, we need not stop there ("Woman Can Never Be Defined"). We can also appreciate Kristeva's rejection of the masculine/feminine dichotomy as a metaphysical construct that needs to be challenged without accepting her corollary proposition that this challenge to the very status of identity will require us to forfeit any notion of sexual identity ("Women's Time").

46. Sheila Fisher and Janet E. Halley, eds., *Seeking the Woman in Late Medieval and Renaissance Writings.*

47. See E. Jane Burns and Roberta L. Krueger, "Courtly Ideology and Woman's Place in Medieval French Literature," 205–219.

48. See Jo Ann McNamara and Suzanne Wemple, "Sanctity and Power: The Dual Pursuit of Medieval Women"; Shulamith Shahar, *The Fourth Estate: A History of Women in the Middle Ages.*

49. An extreme case is provided by the nonaristocratic shepherdess in the Old French *pastourelle*, whose encounters with propositioning knights have been tellingly revealed to camouflage rape; see Kathryn Gravdal, "Camouflaging Rape: The Rhetoric of Sexual Violence in the Medieval Pastourelle," and *Ravishing Maidens: Writing Rape in Medieval French Literature and Law.*

50. See Frederick Goldin, *The Mirror of Narcissus and the Courtly Love Lyric*; Henri Rey-Flaud, *La Nevrose courtoise.*

51. See Joan Ferrante, *Woman as Image in Medieval Literature* and "Male Fantasy and Female Reality in Courtly Literature"; and E. Jane Burns, "The Man Behind the Lady in Troubadour Lyric."

52. Leslie Rabine, "The Establishment of Patriarchy in Tristan and Isolde"; Roberta L. Krueger, "Love, Honor, and the Exchange of Women in *Yvain*"; Christiane Marchello-Nizia, "Amour courtois, société masculine et figures du pouvoir"; Jean Charles Huchet, *L'Amour discourtois: La "fin amours" chez les premiers troubadours.*

53. Jean-Charles Huchet, "La Voix d'Héloïse" and "Nom de femme et écriture féminine au Moyen Âge. Les *Lais* de Marie de France." For a discussion of the implications of such an approach for feminist theory, see Roberta L. Krueger, "Double Jeopardy: The Appropriation of Woman in Four Old French Romances of the 'Cycle de la Gageure,'" Alexandre Leupin, *Barbarolexis: Medieval Writing and Sexuality*, offers the most recent and most extensive example of reading woman out of the medieval text: "In the final analysis, sexual difference is a textual matter, and it is important to perceive it this way," 166.

54. Jean Charles Huchet, *Le Roman médiéval.*

55. A most extreme example is found in Michel Zink's contention that the Old French "women's songs" are false citations of women's voices designed to establish a homoerotic bond between the male poet and his male audience (*Les Chansons de toile*). For a feminist reading of woman's song more generally, see Ria Lemaire, *Passions et positions: Contribution à une sémiotique du sujet dans la poésie lyrique médiévale en langues romanes*; and for an analysis of subjectivity in troubadour lyric that addresses the issues of woman's voice, see Sarah Kay, *Subjectivity in Troubadour Poetry.* Other readings of the textual feminine include Kate Cooper, "Elle and

L: Sexualized Textuality in *Le Roman de Silence*"; Kevin Brownlee, "Discourse and *Proueces* in *Aucassin et Nicolette*."

56. "J'ai cepedant l'impression que le discours sur la femme permet à la littérature de parler d'autre chose, d'elle-même notamment," Jean Charles Huchet in "Un Entretien avec Georges Duby sur la littérature courtoise," 190. Charles Méla contends similarly that "Le roman c'est Elle" (*La Reine et le Graal: La conjointure dans les romans du Graal de Chrétien de Troyes au "Livre de Lancelot."*

57. R. Howard Bloch, "Medieval Misogyny,"; and subsequently *Medieval Misogyny and the Invention of Western Romantic Love*, 56.

58. For a range of feminist responses to Bloch's article, see *Medieval Feminist Newsletter* 6 (November, 1988) and Bloch's response in issue 7.

59. Alice Jardine, *Gynesis: Configurations of Women and Modernity*.

60. Gravdal, *Ravishing Maidens*, 20.

61. Roberta L. Krueger, *Women Readers and the Ideology of Gender in Old French Romance*, 44.

62. Helen Solterer, *The Master and Minerva: Disputing Women in Late Medieval French Culture*.

63. See especially Caren Greenberg, "Rereading Reading: Echo's Abduction of Language."

64. For a fascinating reversal of this phenomenon, demonstrating how we tend automatically to read the male body/author as a carrier of the patriarchal mode, see Meghan Morris's pointed reaction to Paul Smith's article in *Men in Feminism* ("Men in Feminism: Men in Feminist Theory"): "In any event. . . ."

65. Listening to these rhetorical female bodies speak opens up for the feminist reader an enormous store of literary works now only approachable as attestations of male hegemonic subjectivity. They provide a tangible, if fabricated, physicality and an indisputable, if attributed, sex. We do not need to worry that new archival evidence might one day prove that Philomena, Guenevere, or Iseut were actually men. If their words are filtered through the writing of a male author, the femaleness of these fictive women, both by design and by effect is, in the end, less debatable than the historical sex of Marie de France.

PART I

Knowing Women

Among the genres of Old French literature, the fabliau holds the distinction of focusing repeatedly, even obsessively, on the body. In stark contrast to Arthurian love stories, which so often conceal the sexual act behind the inexpressibility topos, claiming that what couples do in the bedchamber is too wonderful to be narrated, fabliau tales of conjugal unrest speak openly, often crudely, about human genitalia and their various functions in the sex act. Racy descriptions of body parts creep in and out of narratives centered on wifely disobedience, *gourmandise*, materialism, and hedonism in various guises. Although most of the 150 fabliaux, composed in the thirteenth and fourteenth centuries in France, are not essentially about women, the genre as a whole bears the marks of misogynous comedy.[1] Women in these tales are featured typically as lascivious, demanding, verbose, irrational, and not very smart. Yet of the entire corpus only a dozen or so fabliaux focus explicitly on female sexuality, giving us a view of the female body as it is defined and constructed by anonymous narrators who purport to "know" what women are like.[2]

What these narrators know, and what their comic tales teach through the moralizing statements often appended to them, is that female identity resides in one key body part: that stereotypically female orifice, the vagina. A well-known fabliau, "Les Quatre Souhaits de Saint Martin" ("The Four Wishes of St. Martin"), makes especially clear the link between what was perceived to be medieval female nature and the woman's genital orifice by exploiting the linguistic homophony between the Old French verb to know (*conoistre*) and the noun meaning vagina (*con*). When the browbeaten husband of this tale attempts to punish his shrewish and lascivious wife by wishing that her body be covered with cunts, the transformation occurs instantly and the narrator explains tellingly, "Adonc fut-elle bien connue."[3] The literal meaning of the sentence, "thus was she covered completely with cunts," contains a second sense emphasized in the husband's subsequent justification for having caused this anatomical change in his wife:

Bele suer, ne vous esmaiez
Que jamès ne vendroiz par rue
Que vous ne soiez bien *connue*
          (MR V, 206; N IV, 215, my emphasis)

(Honey, don't worry, because now you will never walk down
the street without being well known [recognized for what you
really are])

Men "know" women in these bawdy tales, not as lovers or mothers
or workers or wives, but stereotypically as a single sexual orifice. And that
orifice appears more specifically as a vaginal mouth, a mouth without teeth
or tongue, a mouth devoid of speech. Rather than a defining feature of
female anatomy per se, the vagina is "known," by the male observers who
have mythologized it, as a mindless and silent hole begging to be filled.
The anonymous narrator of "Le Dit de cons" exhorts his male audience to
indulge in sex because that is what "cunts" are known (here expressed by
the verb *savoir*) to want:

Seignor, qui les bons *cons savez*,
Qui *savez* que li *cons* est tels
Que il demande sa droiture,
Foutez assez tant comme il dure
          (MR II, 137, my emphasis)

(Noble men, who know cunts, who know that the cunt demands its
due, fuck as much as you can)

To "know" women in this standard fabliau paradigm is to define female nature as irrational, pleasure-seeking, and wholly corporeal in opposition to the rationally endowed, thinking male. The fabliau inherits this
gendered dichotomy that pits knowledge against pleasure from the Genesis narrative in which the fleshly Eve seduces the first man away from his
more rational bond with God. The Old French *Jeu d'Adam*, a twelfth-
century paraliturgical drama based on the biblical tale, stages the conflict
most succinctly when Eve responds to the devil's offer of complete knowledge (*savoir*) by inquiring, "what does it taste like?" (Quel savor a? v. 252).
The pun between *savoir* and *savor*, which resonates throughout the Old

French play, seems at first to underwrite the knowledge/pleasure dichotomy, locating Eve at its lesser pole as the libidinous, pleasure-seeking
woman who has neither interest in nor understanding of what knowledge
might be like. But as we reread Eve's wry comment, we can see how her
inquiry about what knowledge tastes like radically undermines the neat
opposition between knowledge and pleasure that the patristic writers and
medieval church authorities fervently upheld. The apparently innocuous
words of this vernacular Eve suggest, in essence, that knowledge can be
pleasurable, that one can taste with the mind or think from the body, that
the binary opposition does not hold.

That too is the gist of many comments articulated by the libidinous
fabliau women, whose speech often undercuts the very stereotypes of
femininity that their fictive bodies are designed to display. As we see
women in these tales reduced to headless, silenced bodies, talking vaginas,
and ungendered asses, we also hear within those same texts women's
voices that resist such pat formulations. In fact such extreme constructions
of femininity that reduce medieval woman to pure body are of interest to
the contemporary feminist reader because they play out, before our eyes,
the problematic implications of their own limiting definition of female
sexuality. However much the fabliaux and their paraliturgical predecessor
in the *Jeu d'Adam* reiterate a portrait of woman as a welcoming sexual
orifice without meaningful thought or speech, they also show us female
protagonists who talk and think and know. It is this paradox of the speaking and thinking female body, a paradox that contravenes standard medieval proscriptions of the speaking and thinking woman, that interests me
here. What happens when the very texts that purport to know women as
brainless bodies also reveal how those bodies know, know enough to
speak, and to explain, in different ways, what they know?

The purposefully ambiguous title of this section, "Knowing Women,"
is thus designed to encourage the reader to think of "knowing women" in
two distinct senses. Aside from the obvious sexual dimension of carnal
knowledge, in which men know the female body in the biblical sense
through direct physical contact, what do male protagonists in this dispa-
rate array of literary texts know about women? How do men in the purportedly bourgeois and racy theatrical pieces of the fifteenth and sixteenth
centuries and their equally ribald fabliau counterparts from the thirteenth
and fourteenth centuries depict and define what women are like?[4] How
do they perceive the sexual difference that makes women distinct from
men?[5] And how are their perceptions of female nature conditioned by the

Genesis story and Old French reworkings of it? But the phrase "knowing women" can also evoke a female subject, a category of women in farce, fabliau, and paraliturgical theater who possess knowledge. In this instance it is a knowledge about woman's sexuality and thought that female protagonists impart when speaking to a male listener.

The chapters in this section ask where the two phenomena of "knowing women" intersect. What is the relation between the knowledge generally reserved in Western philosophical and theological traditions for the thinking male head[6] on the one hand and the "Dark Continent" of female sexuality cast as the unknown and unknowable territory on the other?[7] What happens when the stereotypically silent, unknowing, unthinking female object of male desire begins to speak, and to speak knowledgeably about the very subject man knows least: the subject of woman?

Let us begin with the fabliau and farce and circle back in Chapter Two to the privileged intertext provided by the Old French *Jeu d'Adam* and earlier patristic commentaries on the Genesis narrative.

1. A Close Look at Female Orifices in Farce and Fabliau

HEAD OR ASS? REFOCUSING THE PENIS EYE

Consider the "Farce moralisée à quatre personnaiges," a dirty story, in theatrical form, about woman's body parts, sexual pleasure, and conjugal unrest that reflects the standard fare of many Old French fabliaux. In this farce two husbands deduce, from a conversation about their individual marital dilemmas, the following aphorism concerning women: "Icy concluons qu'il n'est femme / Qui n'ayt mal cul ou malle teste" (There is not a woman who doesn't have either a bad ass or a bad head).[8]

In defining woman as fundamentally problematic—as composed of bad or evil substantive parts—this male construction of female identity locates woman's difficult nature in two specific body parts, the head and the ass. But as we read on, it becomes clear that the subject under consideration is neither woman's head nor her ass. The husbands' objection to the female "head" alludes to problems posed by woman's speech, and the trouble with the woman's "ass" involves her sexual activity. The defining features of the female body invoked by these spouses—head and ass—are ciphers for the woman's mouth and vagina, female orifices that, within the antifeminist discourse of the French Middle Ages, typically make trouble for men.[9]

Despite the either/or construction of the husbands' speech, the female head and ass emerge in this definition not as two distinct and opposed features of woman's anatomy, but as equivalent and interchangeable body parts. The husbands' dialogue in the "Farce moralisée à quatre personnaiges" outlines a relentless struggle against two complementary sets of female lips. The first man claims to be the victim of a verbose and spiteful wife, one who thunders orders at her henpecked spouse from the lips of her mouth while refusing to grant him sexual congress. This man's fear of his domineering wife is focused significantly on "her head" because, as he explains to his comrade, "je n'ay que bruyt et tempeste / En la maison, dont que je vienne" (I have nothing but noise and thundering in the house I

come from, vv. 104–5). Reference to the head of the first wife thus connotes a disorder of excessive speech paired with the absence of sexual gratification. The second husband by contrast receives the ample sexual favors
of an accommodating wife who speaks in a sweet, seductive voice. "Tout
mon plaisir accorde," he explains (She grants me every pleasure, v. 27),
elaborating further:

> Impossible t'est de penser
> Le plaisir qu'ay avec la mienne,
> Car de quelque part que je viengne,
> Je luy porteray ce regnom,
> Jamais ne me dira sinon:
> 'Mon amy, bien soyez venu.'
> Et puis je sui entretenu,
> Scez tu comment? Impossible est
> De le sçavoir dire, car c'est
> Ung vray paradis que d'y estre.
> (vv. 48–57)

(It is impossible to conceive of the pleasure I have with mine [my
wife]. Wherever I might return from, I'll credit her with this, she
will always say to me, "sweetheart, welcome." And then I am
entertained. Do you know how? It would be impossible to describe
because it is truly paradise.)

But this man fears his wife's "ass"—"Et je crains le cul de la mienne"
(v. 106)—because she is known to spread her favors widely, pleasing other
men as well as her spouse. The "ass" of the second wife thus represents
her vagina, the orifice whose sexual "lips" offer pleasure to all comers.

Problems of speech attributed to each wife are here defined in relation
to problems of sexual activity through a pairing of stereotypical female
body parts. The sweet-voiced woman has a sweet, alluring, "tender ass"
("elle a le cul tendre," v. 108), whereas the wife with a harsh voice has a
more "closed cunt." The perceived equivalence between the sexualized female body and the woman's voice in these examples allows husband number one to establish what appears to be a biological identity between the
female head and ass. But his remark, "Que test et teste de la mienne/
Ressemblast le cul de la tienne!" (The skull and head of mine resemble the

ass of yours! vv. III–12) refers less to a physiological likeness than to a functional one. The ass of the second wife poses as great a problem as the head of the first because neither gives satisfactory pleasure to her mate.

Yet if the subject under discussion in the "Farce moralisée" is female orifices and their ability to please or displease men, why do the husbands in this play not simply call a mouth a mouth or a vagina a "cunt" as in so many fabliaux? Why the mystery and metaphorization in this purportedly anatomical lesson about women and their bodies? Why the references to head and ass?

How Men Know Women: The Logic of the Same

Could it be that this medieval biology lesson has more to do with the male body politic than with female body parts? Indeed it seems that what the husbands of the "Farce moralisée" profess to know about women derives principally from a knowledge about men. Proclaiming authoritatively how female speech and sexuality should be, the men in this theatrical piece decry their individual wives' failure to measure up to a preconceived notion of femininity that reflects a male model. If the husbands had the power of Pygmalion to sculpt female anatomy and behavior according to the recipe they outline, the resultant woman would resemble the ideally silent and sexually submissive female represented in Luce Irigaray's analysis of the logic of the same (*Spéculum*, 9–162). In her critique of Freud's essays on femininity, Irigaray shows how the specular logic governing Western thought about female sexuality leads men to imagine that women exist as a reflection, though reduced and wanting, of themselves. Casting woman as the negative counterpart of male sexuality, this process of defining woman as not-man effectively obscures the sexual difference represented by female genitalia.[10] She who lacks the penis becomes the negative pole of a series of binary oppositions that pit phallic against nonphallic, the clearly representable against the mysterious dark continent, and logos against silence (20).

The "Farce moralisée" offers a particularly medieval version of this specular logic, adding to Irigaray's series of uneven pairs the terms of head/not head and ass/not ass. By calling the first wife a thunderer and the second a sweet-talker, the husbands discredit female speech, decapitating their wives metaphorically to ensure the dominance of the rational male head over woman's idle chatter. Fabliau women appear typically as babblers or complainers, who harp and harass to no effect. They talk without speaking, in line with Hélène Cixous's formulation that women "do utter a little, but they don't speak. Always keep in mind the distinction between speaking and talking. It is said in philosophical texts that women's weapon is the word because they talk, talk endlessly, chatter, overflow with sound, mouthsound: but they don't actually speak, they have nothing to say" ("Castration," 49). In the "Farce moralisée" the hostile harassment of wife number one is as devoid of content as the seductive sweet nothings of wife number two. This is what Irigaray has called the view from the penis-eye, where woman, who lacks the signifying phallus, also lacks access to meaningful speech. She is in essence "châtrée notamment et surtout de paroles" (castrated and especially in speech, 176). In this formulation, as in the Old French farce we have been discussing, woman's empty head will always be bad or wanting in comparison to the man's rational, logos-endowed mind.[11]

But in evoking the asshole as a second point of comparison, the "Farce moralisée" departs from the strictly Freudian schema that devalues woman's speech and obscures the existence of female sexuality by calling the vagina a lack, a failed penis. This medieval construction of femininity instead masks the specificity of female genitalia by replacing the vagina with a roughly analogous male orifice. To call a vagina an asshole is to characterize woman's lower orifice in terms of man's own singular hole, obscuring the fact that women have two distinct openings in the lower body. Indeed the confusion of female *con* and *cul* is standard fare in Old French fabliaux, where terms such as *jouer du cul* routinely accompany the more traditional *foutre* to signify sexual intercourse.[12] Penitentials from the sixth through the twelfth centuries often confuse anal and dorsal sex; both positions were considered bestial by the medieval church.[13] Penetration from the rear ("dogstyle" or *more canino*—whether vaginal or anal—was censured as unnatural by theological, canonical, and legal authorities from the sixth through the thirteenth centuries. The nonstandard positions—anything but the missionary pose—were thought to be both contraceptive and more pleasurable.[14] But it is the perceived identity between female *cul* and *con,* whether by authors of farce and fabliau or their theological con-freres, that interests me here. It attests to a failure to understand fully the details of female anatomy, a tendency to view female sexuality as obscure, mysterious, and not quite male.

The result of the misprision in the "Farce moralisée" bears conse-quences that extend far beyond the biological. As man's negative counterpart in mind and body, woman becomes incapable of fully occupying the position of the speaking subject that binary logic reserves for him alone. Woman then provides the essential groundwork or foundation for the construction of male subjectivity, as Irigaray explains for female subjects of later historical periods, serving to erect an identity, authority, and power from which she remains excluded. Whether she talks or not, the female body in this Old French text stands in that marginal space "Off-stage, off-side, beyond representation, beyond selfhood."[15] Not allowed to possess the male's rationally endowed head, and stripped of the vagina around which her own subjectivity might have been formed, woman disappears into that indeterminate space between opposites.

Knowledge or Power?

At stake in the husbands' reductive definition of female anatomy in the "Farce moralisée" is then not so much knowledge of women's bodies as control over them. The husbands' professed mastery of a subject of conversation—in this instance, women—extends to mastering the referent of their discourse as well: their wives. The husbands' rhetoric makes the terms of the debate clear. They charge the woman's "pleasurable" body—and the wives possessing it—with insubordination. The first wife, who is said to be "mal plaisante" (v. 426) because she refuses to confer pleasure from mouth and vagina alike, also bears the reputation of being "disobedient" ("rebelle," v. 425). Her husband complains, "Helas! tu me deusses obeyr, /et je t'obeys; c'est au contraire" (Alas! You should obey me but I am obeying you. That's backwards, vv. 389–90). The second husband, who receives lavish pleasure from both of his wife's orifices, is deemed by his comrade to be "le maistre en ta maison" (vv. 58–59). But mastery over this pliant and accommodating wife remains problematic because it is incomplete. Although he may be the "master of his house," the second husband cannot control his wife's secret liaisons *outside the home* with other men. If the first man fails to dominate his wife both verbally and sexually and husband number two complains only of sexual infidelity, both men lament their lack of control over their wive's uncooperative bodies.

The medical remedies they propose for this social dilemma prove hilariously ineffectual, as they reveal the false logic underpinning the husbands' specular thought. Imagining cures that echo Aristotelian notions of the humors,[16] the first spouse contemplates administering a laxative in order to relieve the pressure from his wife's head by letting the steam escape from below: "Il luy fault prendre ung bon clystére / Pour luy alleger le cerveau" (She should take a nice laxative to ease her brain, vv. 120–21). The second husband considers a *restrainctif* to close up his wife's welcoming "ass" (v. 142). But once this lower orifice is restricted, the men reason, heat will rise to her head and make her shout and bray just as the first wife does, "Ung restrainctif; tu dois entendre / Que la fumée retournera / Au cerveau, qui la te fera / Incessamment crier et braire," (A constrictor, you understand, so that the smoke will return to the brain and make her shout and bray at you incessantly, vv. 142–45). Failing to inaugurate substantial change, the cures imagined by these "knowledgeable" men merely reiterate the perception of women in terms of indomitable orifices through an either/or logic we have heard before: "Ici nous disons qu'il n'est femme / Qui ne crie, tempeste ou blasme, / Ou a quelcun le bas ne preste" (We state here that there is no woman who doesn't either shout, thunder, and castigate or [on the other hand] give her backside to someone, vv. 151–53).

But this time we get a clearer indication of what the husband's specular logic is designed to protect. Whereas their first either/or statement proclaims authoritatively what women are really like—they either have a bad ass or a bad head—and thus shores up the male position of speaking subject against its female object of discussion, the second formulation reveals the possibility of female agency in speech and action. Woman here takes an active role by shouting or giving her backside to someone. More than ensuring sexual gratification or policing household politics, the husbands' doctrinaire claims that they know women serve to protect the privileged position of subjectivity itself and the dominance it guarantees.

That the head/ass binary is a false one, designed to keep women in their proper place—on the underside of a socially conditioned gender hierarchy—becomes apparent when we apply the husbands' logic to the situation at hand. It would be difficult to say with certainty which woman in the farce has the bad head and which suffers from the bad ass. If the denunciation of woman's evil head is directed most obviously at the wife who thunders orders at her husband, it applies equally well to the sweet-talking deceiver. And if the philandering wife's ass appears "bad" to her spouse, the thunderer's refusal to have sex puts her rear end in the same category. The supposed choice presented between women who harass and those who fornicate proves to be no choice at all. Neither the woman's head nor her ass can be valorized by the husbands no matter what function they fulfill. If woman's speech resists the designs men have on it through outright refusal, it also resists through straightforward agreement based ultimately on cajoling and deception. Her ass similarly quashes man's desire to possess it fully whether through direct defiance or apparent compliance.

Unanswered Questions

Female speech and sexuality emerge then in the "Farce moralisée," despite the husbands' normative definition of them, as something other than what is expected by patriarchal standards, something mysteriously elusive and unknown to man. Although the misogynous dialogue of the "Farce moralisée à quatre personnaiges" bolsters male subjective hegemony with facile either/or propositions, it also charts the female protagonists' resistance to the arbitrary imposition of binary patterning. Woman appears problematic in this portrait precisely because she refuses to be reduced to a failed imitation of the male head and ass, precisely because she has a head, a mouth, and a working mind, or because her "ass" dares to have a mind of its own. The authoritative words of the farce's distraught husbands provoke a series of unstated questions that raise alternate possibilities for defining the female mouth and body. The husbands' categorical statements lead us indirectly to wonder what would happen if women were speaking subjects? What if women were not castrated, if the vagina were not in fact a lack? What if female sexuality was distinct from the male model? Or as Irigaray has put it:

> Once imagine that woman imagines and the object loses its fixed obsessional character. As a benchmark that is ultimately more crucial than the subject, for he can sustain himself only by bouncing back off some objectiveness, some objective. If there is no more "earth" to press down/repress, to work, to represent, but also and always to desire (for one's own) no opaque matter which in theory does not know herself, then what pedestal remains for the ex-sistence of the "subject"? . . . (133). What if the "object" started to speak? Which also means beginning to "see," etc.? What disaggregation of the subject would that entail? (135)

These are the very questions that the husbands' comments in the "Farce moralisée" can raise for the feminist reader. The authoritative declarations of these stereotyped male protagonists provide no ready answers because the husbands cannot conceive of or outline an alternate model of female speech and sexuality. But we as modern readers can turn to other voices in fabliau narrative, listening specifically to the words of "knowing women" who talk, in a very different way, about female anatomy. When the erotic bodies of female protagonists speak and know and even speak about knowing, the pat dichotomy between knowledge and pleasure becomes infinitely more complex.

What Women Know

Moving from the discourse of the male anatomy lesson to the speech of female protagonists often inscribed within that very lesson necessarily raises the thorny issue of who is speaking in fabliau narrative. What status can we reasonably assign to the different voices found in these texts? Must we assume that all the voices issuing from Old French fabliaux represent the authoritative speech of the text's author/narrator, filtered through individual characters but constructed essentially by the logic of the penis-eye? Or can we hear within the woman's voice, which often articulates a different lesson in female anatomy, a more complex dynamic between the subject's speech and its objectified other? Is there a way that as the anonymous fabliau narrator makes a female character speak, that character can also talk back at her author? Do her words, however fabricated and fictive, ever suggest the possible existence of another logic lying beyond the limits of the specular logic that traditionally structures male/female relations in the fabliau?

Although we cannot read the speech of female protagonists as an unproblematic expression of female desire—mediated as it is through the author's voice, literary conventions, and social constructions of gender— we might nonetheless take the speech of certain fabliau women as an articulation of that imagined and imaginary realm that Irigaray describes.[17] Fabliau narrative in this sense would provide a forum for playing out different ways that the female object of desire *might* speak. It would allow the reader/listener to imagine the female speaking subject not as a fully endowed independent or real voice, but as a potential and partial one, a constructed voice that, while colonized, resists thorough appropriation.[18]

The significant difference, for our purposes, between the structure of the "Farce moralisée" and the fabliaux we will be discussing is the speaking role allotted to the female protagonist whose sexuality is in question. To be sure, the pronouncements that fabliau women make about female anatomy serve in certain instances to promote the specular logic that casts woman as man's negative counterpart both sexually and socially. But at other times these women's words can expose the fraud of male knowledge and mock mastery that the tales containing them set up. In many key instances fabliau women's speech reveals the extent to which male protagonists' claims to absolute knowledge are based on an anxiety about sexual difference, calling into question the authority of the fabliau narrator's pretense of knowing women. Those select fabliaux in which women speak about female sexuality present to the reader/listener the impossible conundrum that the texts' construction of femininity disallows: the conundrum of a purportedly headless female body that talks. How can that body speak? What could it say? And if it did speak, how might the female voice issuing from it refocus the phallic look of the penis eye?

The Male Gaze on the Long-Assed Woman

The fabliau entitled "Berangier au long cul" features a female protagonist who speaks specifically about heads and asses. In this tale a peasant masquerading as a knight is challenged to a duel by his wife, who has disguised herself in armor to test her husband's chivalric talents. When the cowardly and inept husband hesitates, the disguised wife offers an alternative to the duel: the fearful husband can, if he prefers, agree to kiss the "rival knight's" ass. As his wife bares her backside for the kiss, the unsuspecting husband:

> regarde la crevace;
> du cul et du con li resanble
> que trestot li tenist ensanble.
> A lui meisme pense et dit
> que onques si lonc cul ne vit.
>   (MR III, 260; N IV, 276)

gazed upon her *derrière*; from ass to cunt and all between / Appeared to him one great ravine, / And thinking to himself he swore / He'd seen no ass that long before (*Gallic Salt*, 57).

Not only does he not recognize his wife's ass when he sees it, he seems unaware of the most fundamental anatomical difference between women and men.

There could be no more tangible demonstration of the fabliau's tendency to erase female genitalia by imposing the model of a male asshole. In making the befuddled husband in "Berangier" assume that his opponent is a man whose anatomy should match his own, this fabliau reveals how the husband believes unknowingly that his wife's anatomy should reflect his exactly. If this meek husband appears at first to play a role opposite to that of the authoritative husbands in the "Farce moralisée," the perceptions of all three men concerning female anatomy are in fact identical, and equally faulty. By misperceiving the vagina as an exaggerated version of the male anus, this false knight casts a phallic look that mirrors the penis-eye view of his more haughty male counterparts in the farce. All assume, whether through ignorance or arrogance, that one can know a woman's body simply by knowing a man's. Their collective knowledge of female anatomy derives from a perception of absence: female genitalia have nothing to present to the viewer, nothing to be seen, nothing that can be substituted for the penis. Or as Irigaray puts it, "rien à voir équivaut à n'avoir rien" (having nothing to see is equivalent to having nothing at all, 54). This omnipotent gaze over the female body constructs man's presumed mastery and unassailable savoir.[19]

Women Talk Back

But in addition to articulating this predictable scenario, "Berangier" shows how the mastery of male knowledge can be complicated and questioned by the female character's voice. Listening to his wife speak, the male viewer in "Berangier" relinquishes, however temporarily, the omnipotence of the gaze, exchanging the presumed authority of sight for the uncertainty of hearing. The woman, no longer just a body to be seen and known, becomes a voice that can question man's authority in sex and in speech.

In "Berangier" it is the wife's praise of her family's chivalric successes that spurs her lazy husband into action. Her words are directed pointedly at him, "As armes sont hardiz et fiers. / A sejorner n'amoient rien. / Li chevalier entendi bien / Qu'ele nel dit se pour lui non" (MR III, 254; N, IV, 271) (They're bold and resolute in fights, / and never love to loll about. / The knight now entertained no doubt / her words were meant for him alone, *Gallic Salt*, 47). When the husband confronts his disguised wife in the forest, it is her voice again that sets the terms of their encounter, proposing two possible courses of action:

Quar ge vos partirai .I. geu:
Comment que vos jostez à moi,
Et ge vos creant et octroi,
Se vos cheez, ja n'i faudrez,
Maintenant la teste perdrez
que ja de vos n'aurai pitié.
Ou ge descendrai jus à pié,
Si me prenrai à abaissier,
Vos me venroiz el cul baisier,
Trés el milieu, se vos volez.
Prenez ce que mielz amerez;
De ce gieu ice vos commant
        (MR III, 259; N IV, 275)[20]

(I aim / to offer you a little game, / Whereby you'll wither joust with me. / I warn you though, I guarantee / If you should fall, you needn't worry; / You'll lose your head, and in a hurry, / For I shall show you no remorse / or else I'll get down off my horse / And bending over, let you come / And kiss me squarely on the bum, / Dead center, if it's all the same to you. / Now pick whichever game you wish: / I hereby order you *Gallic Salt*, 57).

If the tale of "Berangier" reiterates to a degree the danger of the kind of conjugal imbalance where the wife who wears the pants and speaks with authority is revealed as a threat, it also shows the potential of women's speech to restructure the traditional terms of male / female relations. By listening to his wife's voice, this man has come to play the fool, as she accurately observes (54). In simply speaking to him, she can reverse the terms of the standard equation that would typically endow him with knowledge and control.

And she does this by reformulating the very head / ass scenario invoked by the husbands in the "Farce moralisée" to typecast their wives' problematic sexuality. The husband in "Berangier" must choose between losing his head literally, in a pitched battled with his wife, or metaphorically, by foolishly kissing her ass. The latter gesture of subservience connotes, along with the knight's proven cowardice, the fact that his wife now rules the roost. The tale ends with the wife inviting her lover to bed at home *in the sight of* her weakened spouse. Sleeping with her lover in front of her husband is another way of putting her vagina in his face, as she did literally earlier in the tale. When Berangier's husband objects to the insult of watching his wife and her lover together, the wife responds in a resoundingly forceful voice:

> —Taisiez vos en, fait el, mauvais!
> Or gardez que n'en parlez mais,
> Quar, se vos m'aviez desdite,
> Foi que ge doi seint Esperite,
> Tantost de vos me clameroie
> Por le despit que g'en auroie;
> Si serez vos cous et jalous.
> —A qui vos clameriez vous
> De moi, par la vostre proiere?
> —A qui? A vostre chier compere,
> Qui vos tint ja en son dangier,
> Et c'est mesire Berangier
> Au lonc cul, qui vos fera honte.
> 　　MR III, 261–62; N IV, 277[21]

("Shut up," she says, "you surd! / Watch out—don't say another word / —For if you carry out that boast, / By the faith I owe the Holy Ghost / I promise I'll complain of you / And the malice you subject me to. / You'll prove a jealous cuckoo-bird." / "To whom then will you carry word / Of me, if I may beg your leave?" / "To whom? Your old pal—I believe / He had you lately in his sway / — I mean Sir Long-assed Berenger [sic], / Who'll put you in your proper place." *Gallic Salt*, 59–61).

With this one sentence the wife displaces her husband from his potential role as speaking subject, relegating him to the status of a meek and silenced observer. His gaze, now powerless to define the woman's sexuality as an inferior copy of his own, can only listen to words issuing from her newly authoritative head. He has lost the empowered male subject's ability to cast a castrating look upon the female body and has lost it through the effect of the woman's voice. In the future Berangier's husband will not dare to harangue her, we are told, and she will do as she pleases ("Onques puis ne l'osa desdire, / . . . Et cele fait sa volenté," MR III, 262; N IV, 277). The woman's voice has here reduced the powerful penis-eye to just a penis, a frankly sexual organ devoid of its exclusionary claims to superior knowledge. She reflects him, not as the Freudian mirror would have it, but more in line with Irigaray's speculum, a mirror that changes the standard hierarchical relation between the sexes by bringing man's superior head down low. This woman turns her husband metaphorically upside down, "la tête en bas" (*Spéculum*, 186), insisting that he look closely at the vagina he so blatantly misunderstands. "Just put your face right there" *Gallic Salt*, 57 ("Sire, metez ça vostre face,"), she says, pointing to the crevice he abhors. By forcing him to bring his head down to the level of her body, this wife literally throws female sexuality in her husband's face, insisting to his blind eye that there is more there than a simple asshole. "This is not a lack, it's a vagina," she seems to say. Her words and gestures reveal how his male-centered knowledge has overlooked the obvious. The fact that he doesn't see means that he doesn't know, as the young girl reacting to the castration complex in Irigaray's imagined scenario points out: "You men can see nothing, can know nothing of this; can neither discover nor recognize yourselves in this" (*Speculum*, 50). Speaking in this same register hundreds of years earlier, the voice of Berangier seems to say emphatically to her sex-blind spouse, "your penis-head is in the wrong place, bring it down to body level and you'll be able to see more clearly." As his voice "shuts up" in response to her command and he unwillingly observes his wife's sexual encounter with another man, this husband is led to recognize the sexual difference that Old French farce and fabliau try so hard to cover up.

What the Unknowing Knight Lacks

The lesson is taught even more directly to the protagonist in "Du Sot chevalier" (MR I, 220; N V, 328), who, after being married for a year, still does not *know* what "cunt" is or why it is praised: "Ne savoit que cons estoit / Ne porquant loé li estoit" (MR I, 221).[22] Repeated use of the verb *savoir* in the description of this knight suggests that his story is more than a tale of male virginity. Besides lacking sexual experience, the husband lacks knowledge of female sexuality and its difference. He is said specifically not to know how to please his wife. Because like the husband in "Berangier," this befuddled spouse cannot distinguish the large hole from the smaller one, "It weighed heavily on the young lady who wanted to have her pleasure. But this man did not know enough [n'avoit tant de savoir] to know how to approach her cunt:

> Moult en pesa la damoisele,
> Qui vausist ses deduis avoir;
> Mès cil n'avoit tant de *savoir*
> *Qu'il séust* au con adrecier
>   (MR I, 221; N V, 328, my emphasis)

The knight learns the appropriate behavior from his wife's mother, who is called in to solve the marital dilemma. Lifting high her skirts and exposing her genitals to view, she reveals her two holes as a model, explaining to the attentive son-in-law what Berangier left unsaid: when approaching his wife he should "Foutez le plus lonc anquenuit . . . le plus cort en batez / Quant vous au lonc vous combatez" MR I, 223, N V, 329 ("Each night go screw the longer one . . . Just thump the short one with it . . . while with the longer you contend," *Gallic Salt*, 329). Through this direct instruction, the hapless knight in "Du Sot chevalier" "learns to fuck," as the closing lines relate: "li sos ot apris à foutre" (MR I, 230; N V, 335). But he learns much more as well.

It is significant that the unknowing knight's instruction comes from one woman speaking to ensure another woman's pleasure. The mother intercedes so that her daughter's sexual desires will be fulfilled, we are told. Just what those desires are, however, is not revealed to us. One could read this fabliau, to be sure, as a standard misogynous portrait of the libidinous woman, set up so as to ridicule those men who fail to understand the obvious: women want men. In that case the mother's voice would be thoroughly co-opted into articulating an image of what men think women are like.

But we can also hear in this mother's words the possibility that women might want to be pleased in a way unknown to men, that women might in fact conceive of pleasure based on the specificity of female genitalia that the phallic look fails to perceive. Through the very act of giving her own anatomy lesson, the bride's mother in this fabliau expands the limits of male knowledge about the female body in a direction not typically reflected in the dominant voices of fabliau narrative. The very terms of male/female relations are here significantly redefined as women impart to men the knowledge of the female mysteries so often feared and mistrusted. In teaching this knight to know how to please, the female voice here challenges the logic of either/or propositions that pit *savoir* against *plaisir*, offering instead an alternative logic that suggests female pleasure might be a knowable phenomenon.

The Knowledge of Hot Bottoms

This is what the two raunchy females in the farce "Des femmes qui font renbourer leur bas" also tell us indirectly.[23] In an extended metaphorical pun, these women, seeking to have their saddles stuffed because they are uncomfortably hot, encounter two men who accept the straightforward terms of the search without debate. To the women's declaration, "Nous allons serché ung sellier / Pour embourer nos bas devant" ("We're looking for a saddler to stuff our saddles," 284) the men reply, "O n'alés plus nully serchant, / Car nous sommes ce qu'il vous fault" ("Don't look any further; we're just what you need," 284). And indeed they are. For in a mode atypical of farce and fabliau, which often focus on disputes and difficulties between the sexes, the partners of this chance encounter emerge well satisfied. The women have successfully sated their desire, expressed in an earlier scene: to find men whose knowledge includes an understanding of female pleasure. They have been searching for men who will *savoir fourrer le bas* (283), men who, in the colorful language of this ribald tale, know how to stuff a bottom. That is to say, men who know what the male protagonists of the "Farce moralisée à quatre personnaiges" and "Berangier" do not know: one might learn how to please women sexually, to conceive of woman as a desiring subject.

On one level, of course, the female protagonists in this farce, not unlike the daughter in "Du Sot chevalier," represent the stereotypically oversexed fabliau woman who can never be satisfied. Indeed it seems curious at first that the language used by the female protagonists in "Des femmes" echoes hauntingly the husbands' overly generalized reference to the female "ass" in the "Farce moralisée." In describing their sexualized "underside," these female voices make no anatomical distinction between *con* and *cul*, thus seeming to reiterate the dominant logic of the fabliau that promotes male *savoir*. But if these women borrow the antifeminist vocabulary so often used by their male counterparts, their words carry the possibility of a second meaning that cuts against the grain of male-defined knowledge. For like the fabliau's female characters, they stand in a different relation to knowledge than do male protagonists.

The question of knowledge provides the focus for many Old French fabliaux where the topic, couched within racy discussions of male and female sexuality, typically breaks down along gender lines. *Savoir*, extolled as a cardinal virtue possessed by men, connotes wisdom, intelligence, *maîtrise de soi*. Whereas male protagonists are encouraged to possess this knowledge and the wit (*engeing*) that accompanies it, female characters generally draw criticism for displaying the same traits.[24] And indeed many fabliau women termed "sage" do not seem to fit the paradigm. Their *sagesse* is mingled with problematic traces of wisdom's opposite, *folie*, as it emerges in the form of disloyalty, mendacity, quarrelsomeness. If male knowledge in this scenario resides appropriately in the rational male mind, female *sagesse* appears contaminated by the irrationality and disorder of the woman's pleasure-seeking body.[25]

Yet the savoir described by the women in "Des femmes" does not exist in opposition either to the irrationality of madness or its erotic counterpart: pleasure. In this version of *savoir*, mind and body merge in a way that the fabliau's standard specular logic does not allow. *Savoir* as evoked by the women's voices in "Des femmes" is inextricably linked to the act of pleasing, rather than being held disdainfully separate from it. These women's voices do not tell us what female pleasure is or how precisely men must proceed in order to please their female mates. But they do suggest that female pleasure exists and can be known. Savoir in the vocabulary of these women (*savoir fourrer*) connotes an acceptance of the difference of female genitalia and an acknowledgment that pleasure might exist on the woman's terms.

The Critical Lack

Old French farce and fabliau present a wide spectrum of female pronouncements on the issue of woman's sexuality, ranging even in the few examples we have seen from the clever demands of a properly suspicious wife in "Berangier" to the anatomical instruction of a mother to her son-in-law in "Du Sot chevalier" to the humorous request of women seeking lovers in "Des femmes." As diverse as these female voices may be, when taken together they provide a kind of collective choral response to the dominant antifeminist stance of the texts they inhabit. Even in the most rigorously conservative works, the remarks of female protagonists consistently help to reveal the limits of the misogynist logic that reduces woman to an irrational, unknowing body, a creature whose untutored mouth is desperately in need of a governing male head or whose vagina is considered to be a bad ass.

These female voices go unheard in strictly Freudian readings of the fabliaux, which, like R. Howard Bloch's *Scandal of the Fabliaux*, take the vagina as a quintessential image of absence. Reading the fabliaux as highly sophisticated commentary on the problematics of literary representation, Bloch sees the vagina as a cipher for literature's fundamental lack, "The fabliaux inscribe their own origin in such a way as to render absurd the question of source, authorial identity, and destination; this origin is marked by an absence that is particularly poignant in tales involving vaginal speech; this absence is synonymous with a castration—both a bodily dismemberment and a dismemberment of language; and finally this castration is assimilable to the contingent, partial, fragmentary nature of narrative itself."[26] If this analysis aptly shows on the one hand how the fabliaux reveal the pretense of representation, using dismembered body parts to talk about the dismemberment of meaning and the absence of literary origins, it says little on the other hand about the pretense of Freudian discourse to gender neutrality. Many feminist readers will wonder how much is gained ultimately when a deft deconstruction of the critical assumptions concerning the naturalistic representation of the fabliau ushers in, instead and without question, the phallogocentric logic of another set of critical assumptions—those concerning the realistic representation of Freud's theories of sexuality.

What does it mean ultimately that Freud and the fabliau form parallel, complementary discourses? What is the place of female protagonists who are "represented" within these tales figuring the lack of literary origins? What happens when we add gender to both equations, asking first of all, what are the gender biases that condition Freudian analysis—as Irigaray and others have done—and where is the blindspot of fabliau logic? Feminist readers will want to know whether there are not other voices within fabliau narrative that speak against the dominant Freudian strain, voices which deconstruct the logical paradigms that inform the tales containing them.

I think we can hear these voices couched within some of the most misogynous portraits of wives, mothers, and sweethearts in the Old French farce and fabliau. If we, as feminist readers, choose to decipher female "talk" in Old French texts as more than "mouthsound," or more than a thorough ventriloquizing of the male author's hegemonic control, we can begin to hear how the voices of female protagonists emit, however faintly or intermittently, a resistance to the pat medieval distinction between knowledge and pleasure. If fabliau women do not speak the language of the masterful, knowledgeable male subject, neither do they just babble, chatter, and talk mindlessly. These fictive female voices issue from a position lodged in between the stereotypical oppositions of phallic/nonphallic, logos/silence, rational head/irrational head, asshole/vaginal hole, thereby calling into question the very logic used to structure portraits of femininity in the texts they inhabit. Simply by speaking, these female protagonists suggest what might happen if women had thinking heads. In making visible and knowable the supposed secrets of the mysterious female body, a variety of women's voices in Old French farce and fabliau begin to restructure the entrenched medieval scenario of female lack, which their very bodies are used to depict.

When female voices in these medieval French texts assert with their mouths that woman's lower body contains two openings—vagina and anus—as opposed to the male's single asshole, they refocus the penis-eye of specular logic, suggesting that it might see differently, that it might know otherwise. Speaking from the female body, these voices reveal the problems inherent in speaking doctrinairely from the male mind. Offering lessons of difference in response to the texts' predominant logic of the same, women's voices here show how the essential lack of Old French farce and fabliau is not the woman's lack of a phallus, but man's lack of knowledge about women. As if answering to the male protagonists whose remarks about female sexuality often sound a tone of negative discovery as if to say in anger or astonishment, "why, women aren't men!" we can hear the voices of knowing women who explain sexual difference affirmatively, telling in varied ways simply "why women aren't men."

Lips or Labia? How Headless Women Speak

If the fabliaux we have been discussing provide intriguing glimpses of a doubled female speech, "The Four Wishes of St. Martin," with which we began, offers a more extended and more stunningly graphic exposition of the dangers inherent in allowing women's sexualized bodies to speak. The tale describes the activity of a woman who "wears the pants" in the family, a wife "qui chauce les braies" (MR V, 201) in a way that conforms to the stereotype of the domineering nag still current today. The characterization suggests that this nameless wife has obtained her power without merit; she doesn't know what she is doing. Her incompetence is registered through various demeaning depictions of her speech. Issuing constant threats to her henpecked spouse, this wife complains especially of her mate's laziness, excoriating his inability to earn money or provide for his family. "You've never liked to work," she says. "You love to party. May bad luck befall you since you're not doing your job!" ("Vous fetes molt volentiers feste! / A mal eür aiez vous beste, / Quant vous n'en fetes vostre esploit!" MR V, 202; N V, 212). We hear in these words the standard voice of the medieval scold. Annoying and valueless, it harasses and harps to no avail.

But as the tale unfolds we learn that the wife's dissatisfaction with her husband's meager economic production veils a more specific and devastating complaint. Just before the couple's spat, St. Martin had arrived fortuitously to grant the husband four wishes. When the hopeful man finally recounts this good fortune to his money-conscious wife, her speech turns immediately humble and honeyed as if she had exchanged her domineering pants for a more conventionally feminine dress. The wife now coyly persuades her pliable spouse to give one of the wishes to her: "When she heard this (news) she hugged him and spoke with humble words. . . . 'Sweet one,' she said, 'I have always loved you and served you with all my heart. Now you should repay me. I ask you to please give me one wish'" ("Quant cele l'oï, si l'acole, / si s'umelie de parole: 'Ahi,' fet ele, 'douz amis, / ja ai je en vous tout mon cuer mis / de vous amer, de vous servir / or le me devez bien merir: / Je vous demant, se il vous plaist, / que vous me donez .I. souhait," MR V, 203; N IV, 212).[27] This female voice, no less stereotypical than the first, cajoles and seduces. It is the sweet-talking voice that speaks of deference, subservience, and pleasing men.

When the husband reluctantly gives in to his wife's insistent pleas and grants her one of his precious wishes, she asks not for money, as her first harshly critical voice might have led us to expect, nor for an opportunity to please her husband sexually, as her second honeyed voice might imply. The unnamed wife here speaks in a third register lying somewhere between the standard stereotypes of demanding nag and caressing beguiler. She now speaks authoritatively and erotically at the same time, alluding to what is figured here as her pleasure, not his. Drawing out the sexual implications already latent in the scold's denunciation of her husband's failure to "do his job" ("fetes vostre esploit")—*esploit* in Old French can mean both work and performance—[28] the wife now explains that her husband's failure to perform fully as a laborer parallels his failure to satisfy her in bed. And in typical fabliau fashion, the terms that this woman uses to express her putative desire are utterly unladylike. She asks that her husband's body be covered with "pricks" (*vits*), that they appear on his eyes, face, head, arms, feet, and sides, that they be planted everywhere, and that all of them be erect and hard. "Je demant," dist ele, "en non Dieu, / que vous soiez chargiez de vis, / Ne vous remaingnent oiel ne vis, / Teste, ne braz, ne piez, ne coste / Où partout ne soit vit plante. / Si ne soient ne mol ne doille, / Ainz ait à chascun vit sa coille; / Toz dis soient li vit tendu, / Si samblerez vilain cornu" ("I ask," she said, "in the name of God that you be covered with pricks. Let not your eyes and face, head, arms, feet, and sides be without pricks planted all over them. And let them not be soft or pliable. Rather let each prick have its own [soft] balls. May the pricks always be stiff so you will appear to be a horned / horny guy," MR V, 204; N IV, 213).[29]

When the fabliau wife's wish comes true and her husband's body literally breaks out in penises, the extra members are long, square, fat, short, puffy, curved, and pointed: "Si ot vit lonc et vit quarré, / vit gros, vit cort, vit reboulé, / vit corbe, vit agu, vit gros" (MR V, 204–5; N IV, 214).[30] It is at this point that the humiliated husband responds by wishing that the wife's body be covered with cunts (*cons*) in number equal to his pricks. And soon she has vaginas everywhere, making her physical state reflect the exaggerated libido that her body is supposed to have contained and concealed:

> Adonc fu ele bien connue
> qu'ele ot .II. cons en la veue,
> .IIII. en ot ou front coste à coste,
> et con devant et con d'encoste;
> Si ot con de mainte maniere
> et con devant et con derriere
>   (MR V, 206; N IV, 215)

(Thus was she well-known/well-cunted, such that she had two cunts on her eyes, four on her forehead, next to each other, cunts in front and cunts on her sides. Thus did she have cunts in many places, cunts in front and cunts behind)

Eventually the couple regret their impulsive choices and decide to request an end to the mad proliferation of genitalia. They plan to use their one remaining wish wisely, asking only for money—the husband's original intent. But in a fatal lapse of reasoning the partners forget to stipulate that their original sex organs should remain intact. With the hasty formulation of the third wish, their genitals disappear altogether. They are forced to use their last wish to regain the normal sex organs with which they began.[31] Because of the woman, her unreasonable demands, her cajoling, her wild erotic desires, her uncontrollable speech, we are led to believe, this couple has lost all promise of profit or improvement.

Who Knows What?

In narrating its tale of conjugal unrest and the struggle over mastery in the bourgeois household, this fabliau addresses issues of money and who controls it, male prowess and who evaluates it, and female sexuality and who describes it. When the female protagonist in the "Four Wishes" asks for an abundance of penises to appear on her husband's body, readers familiar with Old French literature will hear in her brash statement a typical medieval characterization of the libidinous woman. Impossible to satisfy, always demanding more sex as she also often seeks more money or more food, this woman simply cannot ever get enough of her "man." We find her in such tales as "Du Vallet aus XII fames" (MR III, 186; N IV, 146)[32], as the lustful female used to illustrate the standard medieval contention that women are more sexually demanding than men. In this instance a husband, overcome by "too much" of his oversexed wife, gives her to a criminal as a punishment worse than death. Female desire, which is otherwise welcomed as an avenue to male pleasure, is here denounced as excessive. Extending beyond reasonable limits, beyond the limits imposed by his rational head, this female libido, like that of the wife in the "Four Wishes," has surpassed the male's ability to control and dominate it.

And yet it is significant that the competing forces portrayed in the "Four Wishes" are circumscribed in its closing moral statement in terms of a struggle between female pleasure and male knowledge. The moral of the tale warns predictably that "He who listens to his wife instead of himself is not wise [il n'a pas savoir]; shame and trouble often result."[33] The "Four Wishes" here shows us how the standard struggle between the fabliau's male and female protagonists over sexual prowess and erotic desire masks a more crucial dichotomy that erects male knowledge as an authoritative control over what is perceived to be the voicing of female pleasure. Whereas the man in this tale knows and thinks, his wife merely wants. Or at least that is how the husband in "The Four Wishes" sees it and how the narrator tells it.

What the husband of the "Four Wishes," along with the anonymous author/narrator of this cautionary tale, purports to know then about female sexuality boils down to an extreme, even parodic, rendition of Luce Irigaray's logic of the same. At first reading at least, the "Four Wishes" seems to illustrate in a most tangible way how the expression of female desire in the Western literary tradition often amounts only to a sham, a mimicry, as Irigaray says, of male speech and imagining about women (*Spéculum* 9–162). Indeed, the wife in this tale is shown to want men, and more of them, more pricks, as she herself candidly explains, because "One prick alone was never worth much to me" ("Sire," dist el, "je vous di bien / C'un seul vit ne me valoit rien," MR V, 205; N IV, 214). The phallus, ultimate guarantor of meaning in a system that privileges the male head over the female's lack of rational ability (49), is here enshrined as what women really want. As the unnamed wife of this fabliau is essentialized into erotic body parts, reduced to an amorphous heap of cunts crying out for male penetration, she seems to speak more as a body than a mind. Or does she? Who is speaking in the different voices that the wife articulates in this tale?

And what does her husband know? The value of money, and how to choose wisely and make his wishes count. Yet this knowledge proves ineffectual when it comes up against the unpredictability of female desire. That is the very thing that the husband of the "Four Wishes" does not in fact "know." By his own admission he remains thoroughly ignorant of his wife's deepest wishes. "Ne connois pas bien vos amors" (I don't know your longings), he says before she makes her wish, warning that her very words could turn him into a bear, a mare, a goat, or an ass. "Se deïssiez que fusse uns ours, / Ou asnes, ou chievre, ou jument, / Jel seroie tout esraument" (If you said I should be a bear, an ass, a goat or a mare, I would be one immediately, MR V, 204; N IV, 213). Would she want to do that? he wonders in an echo of Freud's later query about what women want. She contends not. What then would she want? Sewing supplies of hemp or wool or linen thread he guesses.[34] Like Freud, he does not know, he hasn't a clue. Hence the need for male-defined *savoir* that this fabliau promotes. It will help keep the unknown terrain of female desire in check.

Castration Anxiety?

That the "Four Wishes" records, on some level at least, a fundamental male fear of castration needs no explanation. When the wife articulates her "wish," she asks for too much of her man, challenging his manhood by putting his sexual prowess to an embarrassing public test. But what interests me most in this scenario of sexual competition is how male castration anxiety is registered—here and in many Old French comic texts of the thirteenth through the fifteenth centuries—specifically in terms of strategies to control woman's speech.

The implication played out in both initial depictions of female speech in the "Four Wishes"—that women are babblers and cajolers—is that woman cannot speak properly or effectively because indeed she has nothing significant to say.[35] Standing outside the privileged ranks of male cognition, she does not know enough to accede to the dominant position of speaking subject who, by definition, knows its object.[36] Woman in this fabliau, as in so many others, is denied meaningful speech because she lacks the rational male head necessary for thought. As Cixous reminds us further in "Castration and Decapitation," efforts to decapitate and silence women in Western narratives, especially those that stage a battle between the sexes, represent the castration complex at its most effective: "If man operates under the threat of castration, if masculinity is culturally ordered by the castration complex, it might be said that the backlash, the return, on women of this castration anxiety is its displacement as decapitation, execution, of women, as loss of her head" (43).

Old French fabliaux construct female protagonists as headless and unknowing in very specific, bodily ways. Elaborate strategies of female decapitation focus typically on one particular aspect of the head, the mouth—which in males serves as the organ that articulates thoughts from the brain. In female protagonists, association with the rational mind is denied as the female mouth is reduced—by association with the eroticized female body—to a wholly sexual orifice. The women of fabliau narrative lose their heads metaphorically to the extent that their mouths are shown to function as vaginas. Instead of bearing two distinctly different mouths—one facial and one vaginal, with independent functions—the sexualized female is shown to have only one kind of orifice. Whether it appears on her face or between her legs, the female mouth is erotic and wholly corporeal.[37] In the pages to follow we will look first at the fabliau's reduction of

female identity to sexualized orifices and then listen to how the voices of
female characters used to illustrate this view redefine its terms.

Headless Women

The image of the vaginalized mouth derives, in fabliau narrative, from the
sensual similarity between the eroticized lips of the mouth and the genital
labia. In "Le Fabliau du moigne," for example, a monk who dreams of
purchasing the ideal "cunt" from a salesman rejects one prospect because
it is not sufficiently mouthlike to satisfy his desire. Its *lips*, as he explains,
are too thin and blackened to please adequately: "Il avoit les levres ans-
deus / Maigres et plus noires que fer" ("Both its lips were thin and blacker
than iron").[38]

Such a favorable "cunt" that talks in silence wins the contest among
three sisters vying for the same mate in "Le Jugement des cons" ("The
Cunt Conundrum"). After testing the women by asking each to answer the
question "Which is older, you or your cunt?" the uncle judging the contest
awards the desired knight to the sister who boasts a welcoming orifice that
sucks like a mouth: "Mes cons a la goule baee / Jones est, si veut aletier"
(My cunt has a wide-open mouth. It is young and thus wants to suckle,
MR V, 114; N IV, 32—33). That the vagina is an orifice to be nourished
by male sperm is attested in the tale of "Connebert," where a *con* willingly
receives the sexual "food" of a priest: "Qant li orlages fu cheüz / Et Con-
neberz fu repeüz . . ." (When the storm / passion had subsided and Connebert was sated, MR V, 165). In "De Porcelet" a woman whose vagina is
called "piggy" devours all the "food" provided by her husband's "little
nothing" until his wheat is completely depleted. This tale links the wife's
voracious vagina specifically to her devouring mouth, stating that "the more
her cunt eats, the hungrier it is" (Quant plus manjue, plus fain a, MR IV,
146; N VI, 191). An equally rapacious and equally silent set of lips appears
in "Le Debat du cons et du cus," where the mouthlike *cons* is said to eat a
sausage: "Ersoir menjas tu une andoille." (Last night you ate a sausage,
MR II, 134). The vagina that eats, sucks, swallows, opens and closes its
mouth appears routinely as a *goule*, or gaping mouth ("Le Dit des cons,"
"Du Chevalier qui fist les cons parler"), even in one instance a "goulu
Goliath," or giant gaping mouth ("La Veuve," ed. Livingston, V. 382).[39]

But different from the visible, public mouth, the vagina bears no necessary connection to the brain. Rather than emitting words or sound, it takes in the penis in a wholly corporeal gesture that could not be more mindless. "Le Dit des cons" defines the problem most succinctly, stating that "li cons est .I. nice douaire" (The cunt is an innocent dowry MR II, 139). As a dowry, or marriage gift from wife to husband, this female orifice is by definition the husband's rightful property—his to have and to hold as he pleases, when it pleases him. But even more telling is the adjective *nice*, which characterizes the quintessential female orifice as wanting, stupid, or without value, and most significantly for our purposes: *niais* or *sot*: naive in the sense of *unknowing*. Positioned physically as far from the head as possible, the female orifice designated to represent woman's identity signals a brainless pleasure-giving body. One fabliau in particular reiterates the standard Old French portrait of women that proceeds from the head down toward the mouth, face, breasts, and finally the *con* ("Du Chevalier qui fist les cons parler" MR VI, 82; N III, 168).

The erotic joy of lips that do not speak, lips that please sensually without threatening to displease verbally, appears in "Du Chevalier qui fist les cons parler," where the young knight about to be seduced by a maiden's sensuously talkative labia questions her motive. Guarding against the potentially deceitful speech of the woman's mouth, the knight asks specifically that her other lips provide a truthful reply. The sensuous labia explain predictably that the maiden has come to please the knight, to offer "solaz et joie" (MR VI, 82; N III, 168). The Old French homophony between *con* (cunt) and *conter* (to tell a tale) reinforces linguistically the bond between the woman's lips and labia when the maiden later explains to her lady how her vaginal lips had been made literally to speak to the knight: "mes cons li conta" (my cunt spoke to him [my cunt told him a good story], MR VI, 83; N III, 169).

The flip side of this paradigm makes the female mouth into a vagina. Sarah White has shown how many of the fabliaux addressing female sexuality link woman's garrulousness to a rampant libido, the constant movement of the female mouth signaling the equally intense activity of its companion orifice.[40] The body here speaks in spite of the brain, even without the use of words. One of the few female figures in fabliaux to voluntarily repress her speech, the wife in "Li Sohaiz desvez" foregoes the opportunity to express her dissatisfaction with her husband's sexual performance only to have that desire reemerge in an erotic dream;[41] she shops for penises in a market filled with pricks of all sizes and shapes:

Plaines estoeynt les maisons
Et les chanbres et li solier
Et tot jorz venoient coler
Chargiez de viz de totes parz
Et à charretes et à charz.
(MR V, 187; N VI, 269)

(The houses, rooms, and attics were full of them, and every day cartpullers arrived with pricks everywhere in carts and wagons.)

Although this wife makes no comment about sex, the narrator describes an enormous and enormously desirable penis that underscores by contrast the limits of the woman's less fully endowed mate. In this case the excessive bodily desire that so often conditions the woman's voice in fabliau narrative is displaced temporarily into the narrator's visual representation of erotic indulgence. When the wife finally expresses her true feelings, explaining to her husband how she bought the biggest and fullest penis at the market, "lo plus gros et lo plus plenier" (MR V, 189; N VI, 271), it is as if her mouth has been conditioned by the uncontrollable urges of her body. The wife here speaks erotically, irrationally, as if talking from the vagina, not the head.

Whether the fabliau woman demands more and better sex or refuses insistently to grant sexual favors, her voice is condemned typically as suffering from bodily—and specifically vaginal—contamination. In the tale of "Black Balls," female speech figures literally as a guilty partner in woman's refusal of sexual activity.[42] This fabliau recounts the legal trial of a woman who commits two related offenses: she refuses to sleep with her husband after discovering that he has "black balls" and she dares further to accuse him publicly of this deviation, "oiant toute la cort" (MR VI, 93; N V, 188). The trial concludes with an overt denunciation of female genitalia for anatomical reasons. The proximity between anus and urethra is deemed to be unhealthy, as it is in "Le Debat du cons et du cus," where the vagina itself conveys the patriarchal view that "He who put you so near to me did a bad job. . . . If you were a little further away everyone would incline toward me. But in you I have such a disgusting neighbor, something you don't even realize or know. To all those who love you may God give bad luck, because they do so against Nature" ("Mauvesement en esploita / Qui si près moi te herbérga. . . . Se tu fusses .I. poi plus loins, / Toz li mons fust à moi aclin; / Mès j'ai en toi si ort voisin / Que tu ne vaus ne tu ne sez. / A toz cels dont tu es amez / Doinst Dame Diex male aventure, / Quar il le font contre nature," MR II, 135).

The tale of "Black Balls" links this commonplace denunciation of the dangerously ambiguous female genitalia with a concomitant devaluation of woman's speech. When pleading her case in the courtroom, the wife in this tale is cut short by her husband's protestations; he overrides her explanation with accusations of his own, literally cutting off her voice: "Sa parole li tranche" (MR VI, 93; N V, 188). The court then deems the woman insane, dismissing her defense because of the disruptive speech used to articulate it, "And the woman was held to be crazy because of all the noise she made." (Et la dame se tint por fole / De la clamor qu'ele a fait MR VI 94; N V, 188–89). This woman's voice is degraded and dismissed because of a metaphorical association with her unseemly genitalia. In this instance an unclean body is shown to have contaminated the female mouth and head, suggesting that the brain which makes the mouth speak has been replaced by another governing organ less capable of the task. This head talks like a cunt, and like a cunt it should keep quiet.

Such is the case with the wife in "The Little Rag Mouse," whose cunning speech successfully enables escape from her conjugal duty in sex.[43] This wily and sexually experienced wife convinces her peasant spouse on their wedding night that she has left her genitals in the neighboring town, at her mother's house. The unassuming man obtains from his mother-in-law a basket of rags containing a mouse with which he tries unsuccessfully to have intercourse.[44] It is the woman's verbal trickery in this case that enables her to withold sexual gratification, a move that the legal judgment in the tale "Black Balls" is designed to curtail.

The problem with the female voices attached to these "cunts" is that they attack and bite as if armed with teeth.[45] Different from the subdued and properly sensual voice of the vaginal mouth defined by lips alone, these mouths resemble more closely the male speaking mouth equipped with teeth and tongue. The "Jugement des cons" reveals the model for both types of female speech—accommodating and hostile—in terms of contrasting functions of the woman's vagina. The first image, as we have seen before, emerges in the reply of contestant number three, who boasts of an accommodating orifice that provides the pleasure of a mouth. But the second sister suggests the potential danger of a vagina that might truly resemble a mouth, possessing menacing teeth as well as inviting lips, "I have large, long teeth, and my cunt has none."[46] Her statement implies that some vaginas can literally bite.

This fabliau more than any other draws attention to the rich mythical heritage behind the medieval association of mouth and vagina, alluding most directly to the Indo-European tradition of the *vagina dentata*.[47] A woman whose vagina contains a tooth, a poisonous snake, or a penis in Indo-European myth is always an alluringly erotic woman, but one whose eroticism mimics that of the male. As Wendy O'Flaherty describes her, this mythic woman, luxuriating in her libido, experiences pleasure in sex in a way that usurps a long-standing male prerogative. When the male mythmaker identifies these women as evil and dangerous, it is because the woman's sexuality, her desire to have sex on her own terms, makes her a dangerous rival of man.

But if the emphasis in Hindu myth falls most heavily on the sexual aspect of the *vagina dentata*, recording a perceived threat to male sexual hegemony, the medieval fabliaux emphasize men's corollary fear of losing their heads. The desiring male subject in Old French fabliaux, who reluctantly allows himself to be engulfed by the woman's dangerously erotic lips during the sex act, reserves the right to dominate her through the companion orifice: through speech from the mouth. "The Knight Who Made Cunts Talk" provides a particularly apt case in point (MR VI, 68; N III, 158). The chivalric protagonist in this tale succeeds in keeping both his sexual prerogative and his head intact with the aid of several fairies who grant him three boons. The first and most practical gift, that he will never be penniless, is accompanied by two talents of less obvious use: he will have the power to make cunts talk and failing that, to make assholes speak. The knight puts these skills to use at a nearby castle when a countess dares him to make her cunt talk. Hoping to win the bet, she stuffs her vagina with cotton until its "whole mouth is full" ("la geule tote plaine" MR VI, 87; N III, 172).[48] The trick works, but the knight, drawing on his third boon, makes the woman's asshole speak instead, and because of the common confusion between the woman's ass and vagina that we discussed earlier in this chapter, the knight wins the bet. Having lost in this struggle for power against her male opponent, the female protagonist forfeits the independence of her speech. She is told by witnesses to the contest that her losing means she must now be silent, "Qu'el a perdu; ne parolt mais" (Once she had lost, she spoke no more, MR VI, 88; N III, 173). The knight who did not successfully appropriate the pleasure of woman's sexual lips manages instead to impose silence on her speaking lips.

Women Talk Back

Despite the fabliau's elaborate efforts to circumscribe its female protagon-ists' voices, the fact remains that these women are not literally headless. They do speak. If as fictive characters fabliau wives remain the literary fabrications of an anonymous author/narrator who constructs their voices along with their bodies, these women's words often reveal at the same time the unresolved paradox of the headless speaking female. Showing, on the one hand, how to make woman headless despite her ability to speak—how to reduce woman's speech to inconsequential bodysound—Old French fabliaux also reveal how woman, despite the imposition of her headless status, does "utter a little." Indeed, the voice of the nag, though dismissed, suggests the possible threat of female dominance in speech. The voice of the beguiler, though avowedly subservient, threatens to get what it wants through cajoling.

Whereas these voices do not represent what women might say or how they might express their desire, they do show that women could have a say, could have a head and a mouth and use them. At stake in the fabliau narratives we have been discussing is then not just female desire and how it might be articulated. Nor is the central issue male castration anxiety. Rather, the fabliau husband's fear of being swallowed up by his wife's desiring and devouring vaginal lips expresses a struggle over the status of the gendered subject. In other words, who has access to subjectivity and the authority that accompanies it?[49] Who should speak knowledgeably about money, power, conjugal relations, and sexual desire, men or women? The battle is staged typically in terms of an either/or proposition. If men give up their subjective stronghold, they will fall into the dreaded category of object: object of the cajoler's unpredictable desire, of the nag's threat-ening speech, an object without power or purchase on the world.

Yet it is these very terms of the subject/object dichotomy that are disrupted by the female protagonist's voice in the fabliaux we have been discussing. As they move from the position of object of desire (or disdain or jest) to that of the desiring subject, these fabliau women begin to erode, through their speech, the mind/body dichotomy that the tales they inhabit work so hard to assert.

In "Li Sohaiz desvez," where the female protagonist, not unlike the wife in the "Four Wishes," wants "viz de totes parz" (pricks everywhere), the woman's dream is not only about enjoying a larger, stiffer penis. Her dream world allows her to have sex on her own terms, specifically when she wants it, rather than according to her husband's whim, and with a partner of her own choosing. Her imagined wanderings through the "prick" market constitute a dream of selection, of locating a penis that will, as she explains to the merchant, satisfy her, "Que Deus m'an doint joie certaine" (May God give me certain joy, MR V, 188; N VI, 270). If she wants more pricks, indeed cartloads of them, it is not necessarily because she wants more men, more of man. Having more pricks can also mean having more pricks to choose from, having more options.

The countess in "Du Chevalier qui fist les cons parler" responds similarly to the knight's tactic of controlling what vaginal lips say. She proposes her challenge to rectify the experience of the maiden who went to seduce the knight only to have him end up controlling her, as the maiden now explains, "Il prist mon con à apeler / Assez l'a fait à lui paller" (He called to my cunt and thus made it talk to him, MR VI, 83; N III, 169). The knight's takeover of the maiden's vaginal lips is staged, tellingly, as a conversation between two men; as "Sire cons" addresses the knight as "sire," the woman and her putative voice are completely displaced.[50] This appropriation of female speech and desire is what the countess tries, albeit unsuccessfully, to rectify by stuffing her vagina with cotton. Her challenge indicates that the vagina should speak for women, not men: "James cons n'ert si fous ne yvres, / Qui por vos parolt un seul mot" (Never will a cunt be so foolish or drunk as to say a single word for you, MR VI, 85; N III, 170). Women's mouths, both private and public, should tell their story not someone else's.

The battle lines are drawn in "Black Balls" more specifically around the issue of knowledge. After five years of marriage, this wife has just learned of her husband's blackened genitals, to which she attributes his abstinence from sexual activity: "Que cinc ans m'a bien meintenue / Mes barons; ains mès nel connui: / Ersoir or primes aperçui / L'ochoison por coi il remaint" (For five years he fooled me, sirs; I never knew. Last night for the first time I understood the reason for his abstinence, MR VI, 92; N V, 187). The moral of the tale calls women who chastize their husbands for having black genitals "unwise," "Fame ne fait pas savoir" (MR VI, 94; N V, 189). The wife's professed knowledge of her husband's ailment is thus discredited, as it is earlier in the tale by verbal sparring that suggests that the woman knows less than her spouse. He claims she is to blame for their not having sex: she was so busy soliciting sex from others. The wife denies having engaged in any such activity (93). Then the husband triumphantly wins the debate with a comic twist of logic that asserts his superior knowledge, "Jel *savoie* bien: / Por c'est ma coille si noircie" (I knew it; this is why my balls were so black, MR VI, 93; N V, 188). This marital battle has been fought over who knows more and how each player in the marriage duo can assert that superior knowledge through speech.

The wife in the "Rag Mouse" is married to a man who knows nothing about pleasing women: "Qui fame prist, et rien ne sot / De nul deduit q'apartenist / A fame, se il la tenist" (He took a wife and knew nothing about women's pleasures; and he held her in that way, MR IV, 158; N VI, 178). He cannot even find her "cunt": "Je voil, fait il, vit avant traire / Si vos fotrai se j'onques puis, / Se vostre con delivre truis . . . O est il donc? Nel me celez" (I want, he said, to pull my prick out and fuck you if I can, if I find your cunt free. Where is it anyway? Don't hide it from me, MR IV, 159; N VI, 179). She offers knowledge of female genitalia: "Sire, qant savoir lo volez / Jel vos dirai o est, par m'ame" (Sir, since you want to know, I will tell you, by my soul, MR IV, 159; N VI, 179). If her first directives send him on a wild goose chase, subsequent explanation teaches what he doesn't know: "Sire, il est ja entre mes jambes" (Sir, it's still between my legs, MR IV, 164; N VI, 182). Here the moral warns against female deceit through speech: "Qant el viaut ome decevoir / Plus l'an decoit et plus l'afole / tot solemant par sa parole" (When she wants to deceive a man, she deceives him most and makes him craziest simply by using her voice, MR IV, 165; N VI, 183). But the moral also attests to women's knowledge: "Enseignier voil por ceste fable / Que fame set plus que deiable" (I want to teach through this story that woman knows more than the devil, MR IV, 165; N VI, 183).

The fabliau women we have been discussing thus redefine, in different ways, the knowledge/pleasure dichotomy used typically in these narratives to structure their identity as gaping, hungry holes. When they ask for more sex, or for more "pricks" in echo of the wife in the "Four Wishes," their words do not, as it might first appear, simply reenshrine the phallus as ultimate guarantor of meaning in a system that privileges the male head over the female's lack of rational ability. As these unnamed wives speak from the impossible position of the headless woman, their very activity as speaking subjects defies the gendered hierarchies of mind and body, knowledge and pleasure, head and ass that Old French farce and fabliau so often promote. These fabliau women speak rather as both subject and object, knowledgeable and pleasure-seeking, as the active and empowered recipient of sexual relations that they not only want but want also to define. Each of these female protagonists suggests alternatives to the stereotype of the indiscriminately avid female who simply wants men and more of them by arguing instead for having more choices, more of a voice, more say about the roles imputed to them in sex and marriage. Like the outspoken wife in the "Four Wishes," these protagonists' claims for more sex upset the very hierarchy of the speaking male head and silent female body that their fictive anatomy is designed to underwrite.

The Wife's Wish

If the wife in the "Four Wishes" speaks from the body, it is certainly not a body constructed as the subservient opposite of her husband's dominant head. Rather she occupies a space in between the mind/body extremes as her voice situates itself, uncomfortably, impossibly, at the nexus of subject and object positions, conflating reason and irrationality as she redefines the relation between knowledge and pleasure. Speaking of sex and desire, this fictive female says on the one hand that she wants her male mate, wants to be the object of his desire, wants to receive him, to have more of him. But in demanding more, more than he can give, she puts him in the position of the object, the one who must deliver in order to fulfill her demands. When she states that "one prick alone was never worth much to me," this woman speaks rationally about an irrational desire. And as a result, substantial and visible change is inaugurated in the stereotypical male mode of existence. Not only do the wife's words order a restructuring of her husband's anatomy, calling for a plurality of penises where normally there is only one, they also reshape his voice. Tellingly, in this bawdy contest of one-upmanship, the woman speaks first and the beleaguered husband responds by following his wife's verbal lead, patterning his speech after hers: "Je n'avoie preu en .I. con," he explains. "Puis que tant vit me doniiez" (I didn't see any value in one cunt since you had given me so many pricks, MR V, 206; N IV, 215).[51] This reconstructed male voice issues from a reconstructed male body that the wife has created through her speech.[52]

Indeed her voice has produced a most graphic depiction of how knowledge and pleasure might merge. When the wife in the "Four Wishes" asks for "more pricks," causing extra sexual members to break out in unexpected places on her husband's body, they appear significantly on his face and head as well as his limbs. The concentration of penises on the man's forehead, eyes, nose, and mouth soundly disrupts the pat medieval distinction between the thinking head and the sensual body. This reformulated male anatomy provides a striking visual conflation of the traditional sites of knowledge and pleasure, demonstrating graphically that these functions need not necessarily be held apart. The female speaking "subject" here generates an image that suggests, beneath its comic veneer, something quite serious: that one can know pleasure, that knowledge can take shape in a way that differs from knowing something in the abstract or with the rational mind.

If woman's speech here proves literally valueless because it dashes the couple's chance to get rich quickly, its greater threat is to question the very logic of a system that reduces women to body parts while granting ultimate authority to the male head. Despite the typically conservative endings of Old French fabliaux, which reinstate male wisdom and authority over the wanton chaos of female pleasure, these texts demonstrate vividly how woman can shake up the standard scenario of male/female relations by the very exercise of those orifices used traditionally to typecast and dismiss her.

If the voices of the outspoken female protagonists in medieval fabliaux do not become the dominant voices in the texts that contain them, their words play a crucial role in that dominant structure, infiltrating it in ways that reveal its essential weakness and vulnerability. When female protagonists take control verbally and actually "wear the pants" in the family, the very role and function of those pants as a literal covering for the male sex organs and a metaphorical emblem of conjugal authority undergoes a radical reformulation. By revealing the inadequate performance of her husband in bed, the disobedient wife of the "Four Wishes" also lays bare the insufficience of philosophical and rational systems that privilege one true answer over the possibility of competing truths. In insisting that "one prick alone was never worth much to me," she rejects not only her husband's meager sexual member but the binary logic that enshrines the male head/phallus, a logic that pits men against women and knowledge against pleasure only to privilege the first term of each binary pair.

In asking for "more pricks," the fabliau woman's voice sounds a richly ambivalent note that has been replayed for us much more recently in the purposefully ambiguous title of Luce Irigaray's *This Sex Which Is Not One*. Depending on how one reads it, "This Sex Which Is Not One" can appear to echo the rationale of specular logic that grants primacy to the male phallus while relegating female genitalia to the status of an absence or a lack: His is the model sex while hers exists only as an impoverished reflection of the potent phallus. If her vagina is but a hole or envelope for the male organ, cast as the "negative, the other, the reverse of the only visible and morphologically designateable sex organ" (26), then woman's sex is not number one, not primary, not really even a sex in its own right at all (23). But conversely, "This Sex Which Is Not One" can proclaim that, unlike the monolithic status of the male phallus, the female sex is not limited by the constraints of a single sexual member or a single erogenous zone. Female sexuality "is not one" because it derives not from the unitary phallus but from the two lips of the vagina. And the subject speaking from this anatomical configuration is similarly not monolithic but multiple, for it speaks, as does the wife in the "Four Wishes," as an object of desire and a desiring subject simultaneously in a way that engages Irigaray's now-famous rhetorical question: "But what if the 'object' started to speak? Which also means beginning to 'see,' etc. What disaggregation of the subject would that entail?" (*Speculum*, 135).

This is precisely the question posed, some 500 years earlier, by the "Four Wishes of St. Martin" and related fabliau narratives. What happens when the socially constrained, philosophically silenced, metaphorically de-capitated female speaks? What are the consequences of acknowledging that women have two mouths instead of one: a facial mouth complete with the teeth and tongue necessary to emit speech and a vaginal mouth bearing erotic lips that do not speak? Even in the fabliaux, the female mouth re-duced to a vagina still speaks, and herein lies the problem. These tales show us, in the most bawdy and exaggerated way, how a double con-struction of a speaking and sexualized woman cannot be tolerated by the specular logic that views anatomy in terms of the presence or absence of the phallus. From the perspective of the penis-eye, there can be only one head as there is only one penis. Acknowledgment of the female head along with her body would threaten the very logic that sets man up as the master in his house, head of the household, wearer of the proverbial pants.

In that fleeting moment of asking for more pricks, the wife in the "Four Wishes" challenges this view by asserting, in the language of Old French fabliaux, that "this sex is not one, but two," not reducible to a body without voice or a talking cunt. This female sex, represented by the seem-ingly libidinous body of the fabliau wife, is paradoxically a body endowed with a voice, an object of desire that speaks also as a subject, an erotic sexual mouth and a toothed virile one simultaneously. Standing outside the limits of either/or logic that constructs woman as man's necessary and inferior opposite, this speaking female body can question the hierarchy that privileges one over two, can call for a new understanding of the relation between head and body, can ask for new rules of the game.

In saying "I want more pricks," this fabliau wife says in essence, "I want more than one prick, more than the monolithic phallus, more than this phallocentric world view."

Notes

1. For a recent assessment of the problem of antifeminism in the fabliau and a recap of previous studies, see Norris J. Lacy, "Fabliau Women." On the dozen or so fabliaux that treat female sexuality explicitly, see Sarah Melhado White, "Sexual Language and Human Conflict in Old French Fabliaux." Leslie Johnson has argued convincingly for the ways women come out "on top" in certain fabliaux, thereby mitigating the wholesale antifeminism most often found in the morals to these tales ("Women on Top: Antifeminism in the Fabliaux?").

2. R. Howard Bloch has shown that the fabliaux are more than naturalistic tales about sex and bodies. But his analysis remains remarkably blind to issues of gender. See *The Scandal of the Fabliaux*; and in partial response E. Jane Burns, "Knowing Women: Female Orifices in the Old French Farce and Fabliau" and "This Prick Which Is Not One: How Women Talk Back in Old French Fabliaux."

3. Anatole de Montaiglon and Gaston Raynaud, *Recueil général et complet des fabliaux*, V, 206, and Willem Noomen and Nico Van den Boogaard, *Nouveau recueil complet des fabliaux (NRCF)*, IV, 215. I will indicate volume and page from Montaiglon's edition (e.g., MR V, 206) and from Noomen's edition where available (e.g., N IV, 215). Translations of Old French works appearing in this chapter are mine unless otherwise indicated. I have drawn sometimes on Robert L. Harrison's inspired translation of the fabliaux, *Gallic Salt: Eighteen Fabliaux Translated from the Old French*.

4. Problems of origin, audience, and reception of works in these reputedly "realist" genres remain unsolved. See especially Joseph Bédier, *Les fabliaux: Études de littérature populaire et d'histoire littéraire du Moyen Âge*; Jean Rychner, *Contribution à l'étude des fabliaux*; Per Nykrog, *Les Fabliaux*. For a thorough discussion of the arguments on both sides regarding the fabliau's provenance and delivery, see Charles Muscatine, *The Old French Fabliaux*; Muscatine himself argues that the fabliaux should be taken seriously as evidence in medieval French cultural history (152–69). On farce see Gustave Cohen, ed., *Recueil de farces françaises inédites du 15e siècle*; André Tissier, ed., *Recueil de farces (1450–1550)*; Barbara Bowen, *Les caractéristiques essentielles de la farce française*.

5. On sexuality and obscenity generally in the fabliaux, see Muscatine, *Old French Fabliaux*, 105–51.

6. Alice Jardine, *Gynesis: Configurations of Woman and Modernity*.

7. Luce Irigaray, *Spéculum de l'autre femme*, 18–20; Hélène Cixous, "Castration or Decapitation?"

8. *Nouveau recueil de farces françaises des XVe et XVIe siècles*, ed. Émile Picot

and Christophe Nyrop, 126, vv. 154–55; translation mine. The text edited by Picot and Nyrop represents, according to Tissier, a later version of a British Museum manuscript dating 1532–50. Tissier edits this text as "Les Deux maris et leurs deux femmes," *Recueil de farces*, 395–474.

9. See R. Howard Bloch, "Medieval Misogyny." And for a series of feminist commentaries on Bloch's piece, see *Medieval Feminist Newsletter* 6 (Fall 1988) and Bloch's response in *Medieval Feminist Newsletter* 7 (Spring 1989).

10. On censure of the vagina, see Irigaray, *Spéculum*, 30, and Karen Horney, *Feminine Psychology*, 145–61.

11. The farce "Tarabin-Tarabas" provides an interesting variation on the association of men with the head and women with the ass: the wife here complains of her husband's ill-functioning head—he's stubborn, never stops speaking, is full of hot air. The husband attacks his wife's ass—it farts and stinks, is dirty and bestial. Although the recurring lament, "Ha! teste! / Ha! cul!" signals both body parts as problematic, the head remains the representative characteristic for men, while the woman is marked by the lower and wholly corporeal *cul* (Cohen, 95–101).

12. Philippe Ménard, *Les Fabliaux: Contes à rire du Moyen Âge*, 155. The confusion provides the subject matter for several fabliaux to be discussed here: "De Berangier au long cul" (MR III, 252–62; N IV, 245–77) and "Du Sot chevalier" (MR I, 220–30; N V, 313–36).

13. Pierre Payer, *Sex in the Penitentials: The Development of a Sexual Code 550–1150*, 29, 30, 118. The tendency to efface crucial distinctions in female anatomy is not limited to the Middle Ages. Pierre Guiraud notes that in the erotic literature of modern France vulva and vagina are often subsumed under the single rubric *con*, *Dictionnaire érotique*, 38.

14. See James A. Brundage, *Law, Sex, and Christian Society in Medieval Europe*, 161, 286, 367, 452.

15. *Speculum of the Other Woman*, 22. To savor the playful punning of Irigaray's prose, see the original text, "Hors scène, hors représentation, hors jeu, hors je," *Spéculum de l'autre femme*, 21.

16. See Ian Maclean, *The Renaissance Notion of Woman*, which details Aristotle's explanation of woman's physiognomy—her large hips and narrow shoulders—as resulting from her colder humors that lack sufficient energy to drive matter up toward the head (30–35). Maclean also discusses Aristotle's allied theory that female irrationality resulted from a cranial suture preventing the humors from escaping (41).

17. I do not mean here to take an essentialist position that would read the inscribed woman's voice as an expression of female identity or full-bodied "presence" in the text. Nor do I consider Irigaray herself to be an essentialist. For a discussion of the difficulties inherent in Irigaray's critique of male subjective hegemony, see Shoshana Felman, "Women and Madness: The Critical Phallacy"; Jane Gallop, "The Father's Seduction"; Toril Moi, *Sexual/Textual Politics*, 116; Domna Stanton, "Difference on Trial: A Critique of the Maternal Metaphor in Cixous, Irigaray, and Kristeva." For an explanation of why Irigaray is not an essentialist, see Jane Gallop, "Lip Service" in *Thinking Through the Body*; Margaret Whitford, "Rereading Irigaray"; Naomi Schor, "This Essentialism Which Is Not

One"; Diana Fuss, *Essentially Speaking*, 55–72; Elizabeth A. Grosz, *Jacques Lacan: A Feminist Introduction*.

18. For a discussion of how one might read the female voice as located within another, dominant voice, see Nina Auerbach, "Engorging the Patriarchy"; and Jane Gallop, "*Writing and Sexual Difference*: The Difference Within."

19. See Irigaray's comments on Freud's essay on the uncanny, *Spéculum de l'autre femme*, 52–56.

20. Noomen's text varies significantly in the last line: "Prenez lo quel que vos volez / De cez jeus, ice vos covient!" (Pick whichever game you wish, as it suits you, vv. 228–29).

21. Noomen gives the following for line 289: "De moi, par l'ame vostre pere."

22. In Noomen's reading the unfortunate husband does not know what a cunt is nor why he has a prick, "Ne ne savoit que cons estoit: / Non por uec li vis li estoit," vv. 33–34).

23. Gustave Cohen, ed. *Recueil de farces françaises inédites du 15e siècle*, 283–86.

24. Mary Jane Stearns Schenck, *The Fabliaux: Tales of Wit and Deception*, 117–20.

25. Marie-Thérèse Lorcin, *Façons de sentir et de penser: Les fabliaux français*, 110.

26. R. Howard Bloch, *The Scandal of the Fabliaux*, 109. The Lacanian analysis of fabliaux offered by Alexandre Leupin's *Barbarolexis: Medieval Writing and Sexuality* provides an incisive reading of the problem of the book in the Middle Ages that also unfortunately reduces female sexuality to pure textuality: "Since it governs all activities of art and skill, every desire to write, the female sexual organ is not a mere addendum to the corpus but, rather, its bottomless bottom—the Other whose whiteness writing always approaches yet invariably does not reach." The homophony cultivated by Gautier Le Leu between *con* and *comme* is alleged further to point up "the secondary metaphoricity of all literature" (131–32).

27. Noomen's text omits the wife's mention of service and merit and supplies instead the following exchange: "Mes amis, me dites vos voir? / —Oil, ma bele suer, por voir!" (My dear, is that true?—Yes, dear it is, vv. 59–60).

28. *Esploit* can mean action or execution; success, ardor, or passion; advantage, profit, gain, or revenue. The wife in the "Four Wishes" is getting none of these.

29. Noomen's text substitutes "nose" for "face" (*nariz* for *viz*): "Que tot soiez chargiez de viz: / Ne remaigne oil ne nariz," vv. 95–96.

30. In Noomen's version, the pricks are even colored: "Sor lui avoit maint vit carré, / Et grant et grox et rebolé / Maint noir, / maint blanc et maint vermoil" (On him there were many square pricks, large, thick and puffy ones / Many black, many white, many red, vv. 115–17).

31. "Sire," dist ele, "souhaidiez / Le quart souhait qu'encore avon, / Qu'aiez .I. vit et je .I. con; / Si ert ausi comme devant, / Et si n'avrons perdu noiant" ("Sir," she said, "use the fourth wish remaining to us to wish that you have one prick and I one cunt. Then we will be as before and will have lost nothing." MR V, 207; N IV, 215).

32. In "Du Chevalier confesseur" the wife explains the rarity of women who are content with their husbands alone and offers infidelity as the obvious solution

(Menard, 178). Other fabliaux that reiterate this image are "De Porcelet" (MR IV, 144; N VI, 185), "Du Vallet aus XII fames (MR III 186; N IV, 131), "De la Morel sa provende avoit" (MR I, 318), "La Veuve" (ed. Livingston, vv. 432–88), "Du Pescheor de pont seur Saine" (MR III, 68; N IV, 107), "De Cele qui se fist foutre sur la fosse de son mari" (MR III, 118), "Le Chevalier qui fist sa fame confesse" (MR I, 178; N IV, 227).

33. In Noomen's edition the word *savoir* appears in the A text only, N IV, 208. A similar moral ends "Du Vilain de bailleul" (MR IV, 212; N V, 223), in which the wife deceives her foolish husband to have an affair with a priest. Rather than expressing her sexual desire outright as does the wife in the "Four Wishes," this woman cajoles and tricks her husband into allowing her to exercise her sexual prerogative. The moral, "C'on doit por fol tenir celui / Qui mieus croit sa fame que lui" (He who believes his wife instead of himself should be considered crazy, MR IV, 216; N V, 249) underscores the loss of control in conjugal affairs as a loss of reason, a falling into folly.

34. "Tost demanderiez .III. fusées / De chanvre, de laine ou de lin" ("You will ask for three bobbins of thread: hemp, wool, and linen." MR V, 203, N IV, 213).

35. See Jane Gallop, "Snatches of Conversation"; and Catherine Belsey, *The Subject of Tragedy: Identity and Difference in Renaissance Drama*, introduction and chapter 6.

36. Catherine Belsey, *The Subject of Tragedy*, chapter 3; and Hélène Cixous, "They [women] always inhabit the place of silence, or at most make it echo with their singing. And neither is to their benefit, for they remain outside knowledge" ("Castration or Decapitation," 49).

37. Thomas Laqueur explains how metaphorical connections between the throat and the cervix/vagina/pudenda are common in antiquity and persist through the nineteenth century. He offers a particularly striking nineteenth-century illustration of the larynx that bears strong resemblance to female genitalia (*Making Sex: Body and Gender from the Greeks to Freud*, 37). For a specifically medieval attribution of a vaginal function to the woman's mouth, see depictions of the birth of the Antichrist contained in Renate Blumenfeld-Kosinski's *Not of Woman Born: Representations of Caesarean Birth in Medieval and Renaissance Culture*, plates 23, 24.

38. "Le Fabliau du moigne," ed. A. Lanfors, 562 v. 116.

39. For a rapid survey of psychoanalytic commentary linking the female mouth and vagina, see Kaja Silverman, *The Acoustic Mirror: The Female Voice in Psychoanalysis and Cinema*, 67. In *Trubert*, a woman's detached genitals are claimed to be the mouth and nose of a man, "la bouche i est / de Goulias et les narilles," *Trubert*, ed. G. Renaud de Lage, v. 1968, and "Des deux vilains," ed. Livingston).

40. Sarah White, "Sexual Language and Human Conflict in Old French Fabliaux," 185–210.

41. She laments only to herself, "Qu'il deüst veillier, et il dort!" ("He should be awake but he's sleeping!" MR V, 186; N VI, 268).

42. "De la Coille noire" (MR VI, 90; N V, 186).

43. "De la Sorisete des estopes" (MR IV, 158; N VI, 178). As the moral states, "Qant el viaut ome decevoir / Plus l'an deçoit et plus l'afole / Tot solemant par sa parole" (When she wants to deceive a man, she tricks and bedevils him by her

speech alone, MR IV, 165; N VI, 183). Alexandre Leupin offers a very different reading of this fabliau and the "Four Wishes" itself in his *Barbarolexis*, 100, claiming that castration, "symbolized by the whiteness of asexuality, is the irrefutable figure through which the text touches the real, inscribing on it the missing signifier. Castration marks that moment when the text must begin to speak in infinite metaphor." And woman is erased: "the woman's body is thus the symptom of a lack."

44. A similar scenario structures "Du Fol Vilain," ed. Charles H. Livingston.

45. More often they threaten man's sexual prowess as they critique his ability to perform. The wife in the "Souhaiz desvez" says pointedly to her husband that his penis cannot measure up to even the smallest in her dream, "Mès li vit à la povre gent / Estoient tel que uns toz seus / En vaudroit largemant ces deus / Teus con il est" ("But the pricks of the least-well endowed men were such that one alone would be worth two of his as it was," MR V, 190; N VI, 272). The wife in "Black Balls" avers more aggressively, "Je ne gerra mais delez moi / Li vilains qui tel hernois porte!" ("I will not have lying next to me a guy with equipment like that." MR VI, 91). Noomen's text is even more explicit, "Ja ne gerra mais avoc moi / Li vilains qui tes coilles porte," ("I will not have lying next to me a guy with balls like that," N V, 186).

46. "J'ai les denz et granz et lons, / Et mon cons n'en a encor nus," (MR V, 113; N IV, 32).

47. See Wendy O'Flaherty, *Women, Androgynes, and Other Mythical Beasts*, 53–57, 81, 90; Wolfgang Lederer, *Fear of Women*, chapter 1; Karen Horney, "The Dread of Woman" and "The Denial of the Vagina," in *Feminine Psychology*. For a mythic tale that bears striking resemblance to the "Four Wishes," see "Long Tongue the Demoness" in *Tales of Sex and Violence: Folklore, Sacrifice, and Danger in the Jaiminīya Brāhmāna*, trans. Wendy O'Flaherty.

48. That the cotton which the countess stuffs in her mouth to control her speech also marks her resistance to possible vaginal penetration is made clear in other tales like "Du Pescheor du pont seur Saine," where stuffing of the woman's mouth is paired with sexual stuffing of her vagina, "A well-fed young woman often wants to have sex," MR III, 69; N IV, 124.

49. For a critique of Foucault's *History of Sexuality* demonstrating how his reading misses this essential point, see Victor Seidler, "Reason, Desire, and Male Sexuality." Seidler aptly observes how Foucault, who recognized in his *History of Madness* the extent to which rationality served historically as a means of establishing sociopolitical superiority, failed surprisingly to see how reason is also inextricably linked to historical definitions of masculinity.

50. That the voice of the fabliau's talking "cunt" (or in this case, its anal equivalent) produces not female speech but a conversation between men is reiterated in the concluding scenes of this tale. The knight, stymied by the cotton stuffing, uses his third boon to request that the woman's anus speak because the vagina cannot. After the anus reveals why the cunt is speechless, "Qu'il a la gueule tote plaine" (Because its mouth is full, MR VI, 87; N III, 172), the "cunt" repeats the explanation: "Ge ne pooie, / Por ce que encombrez estoie, / Du coton que ma dame i mist" (I couldn't [speak] because I was impeded by the cotton that my lady

put there, MR VI, 88; N III, 173). On hearing this, the countess's husband laughs heartily, "Quand li quens l'ot, forment s'en rist," underwriting the joke between himself and the knight. Subsequently, at the knight's request for just treatment, the count asks the countess to unpack her vagina (MR VI, 87–88; N III, 173), thus bringing her lips back under male control.

51. These lines, omitted from Noomen's text (IV, 215), appear in Manuscript A, which he cites on p. 206.

52. "Si ot vit lonc et vit quarré, / vit gros, vit cort, vit reboulé, / vit corbe, vit agu, vit gros (Thus he has long pricks and square ones, fat pricks, short pricks, puffy pricks, curved pricks, sharp pricks, thick pricks, MR V, 204–5; N IV, 214).

2. A Taste of Knowledge: Genesis and Generation in the Old French *Jeu d'Adam*

> The fact that philosophy presents woman as that which relentlessly
> undermines man's rational endeavors is not an ideological
> coincidence.
>
> —Toril Moi

The privileged intertext for the issues of knowledge and pleasure played
out in the Old French farce and fabliau that we discussed in the preceding
chapter lies in the biblical creation story and the church fathers' commentaries on it. Adam and Eve's interaction in Genesis provides a platform for
addressing not only questions of wifely obedience and disobedience, but
also questions about female speech, silence, and seduction from Tertullian
to St. Thomas. The key issue for many patristic commentators of the
Genesis narrative, not unlike that of the husbands in the "Farce moralisée
à quatre personnaiges" and related fabliaux, resides in the gendered hierarchy they perceive in the mind/body split. Since man, deriving from
Adam in the view of the church fathers, has a rational mind, while woman,
descended from Eve, is identified by her wantonly irrational body, male
domination of women becomes a logical extension of the necessary triumph of mind over matter. That triumph is typically assured in patristic
commentaries on Genesis, as in thirteenth- and fourteenth-century French
comic portrayals of female sexuality, by attempts to control what were
considered to be the two principal means of irrational female expression:
woman's sexuality and her speech.

By looking back to the church fathers, we can see how the elaborate
excursus on the problems of the deficient female "head" and lascivious
"ass" in the "Farce moralisée à quatre personnaiges" is conditioned by a
larger medieval theological debate on sin and salvation that pits the thinking male mind against the pleasure-seeking woman's body. In rereading in
particular the highly informative comments of Augustine on Genesis along
with Platonic and Aristotelian works that informed medieval theological

views on anatomy and generation, we can see further what the fathers' varied arguments for the social dominance of man over woman masks. What the Genesis story hides, and Old French farce and fabliau continue to cover up, is how the hierarchical imposition of mind over matter, a move that places man over woman intellectually and socially, displaces a more fundamental concern with biological precedence. The fathers' repeated insistence that man must dominate woman so that the mind can control the body obscures a more troubling preoccupation with the process of human reproduction. Since man originates in woman biologically, her body provides the ultimate source for his privileged subjectivity. The fact that her physical matter necessarily precedes the creation of his mind undercuts the neat hierarchy of mind over matter in ways that the fathers' serious pronouncements on female sexuality and Old French comic constructions of "head" and "ass" work hard to deny.

If we turn back in French literature from late medieval comic texts to the twelfth-century French mystery play of Adam and Eve, *Le Jeu d'Adam*, we find an intriguing secular recasting of the Genesis narrative that, though it follows scripture and Augustinian commentary to a great extent, also provides a countervoice to these views. That resistant voice emerges most strongly in the troublesome statements of a vernacular Eve whose speech is notably absent from patristic commentaries about woman's sexuality and voice. The words of the "first woman" in the Old French theatrical rendition of the creation story subtly reveal how the dichotomy between knowledge and pleasure that structures the founding Western myth of male/female relations actually co-opts female reproductive capacity to bolster the monolith of male subjectivity. This vernacular Eve thus provides a particularly cogent example of how constructed female speech can challenge from within a philosophical system that suppresses and devalues woman's words. Like the hypothetical female speaker posited in Michèle LeDoeuff's critique of Western thought, this Eve can be heard at key moments in the Old French play to speak "not from that other position produced by philosophy as a preserve of purely negative otherness. Nor from within metaphysics since this founds the duality of masculine rationality and feminine disorder."[1] Her voice calls for "other possibilities" ("Women and Philosophy," 198).

In this chapter we will look at the different ways woman has been constructed as a body in patriarchal discourses from Plato and Aristotle to the church fathers, examining in particular how the female body has been figured between the extremes of womanly flesh that threatens to efface the male mind and a female body that can produce life in the flesh. In attempting to discern the relation between these two views of femininity, we will turn repeatedly to "other possibilities" figured in the Old French *Jeu d'Adam*, which provides a counterpoint to the ancient and medieval constructions of femininity. Listening to the words of this theatrical Eve, we can see how the impetus to control the female body with the male mind, as it is outlined first in the fathers' comments on woman's digressive nature and Augustine's reactions to the biblical creation story and later in the head/ass dichotomy of the "Farce moralisée à quatre personnaiges," derives from the problematic issue of biological reproduction. Behind the politics of mind over matter and knowledge over pleasure that so often structures medieval comic portraits of female sexuality lies a more fundamental concern with human creation, that is to say: procreation. Eve's voice in the Old French *Jeu d'Adam* reveals just what is at stake in both antique and medieval constructions of woman as flesh. It is through her voice that the paradox of the corporeal but wombless woman emerges.

We will begin by looking at medieval theological constructions of woman as wholly corporeal in the first section of this chapter, entitled "Mind Over Matter: Why Women Should Be Silent," and then move to discussions of woman's role in reproduction in the second, "Matter Before Mind: How Women Came First."

MIND OVER MATTER: WHY WOMEN SHOULD BE SILENT

Augustine's Singing Asshole

One does not expect St. Augustine, one of the most influential church fathers, bishop of Hippo, author of the *Confessions* and the *City of God*, to write in the bawdy mode of the Old French fabliau. But he does so on at least two occasions, perhaps not surprisingly when addressing the issue of human sexuality in his series of commentaries on Genesis. Departing significantly from prior interpretations by Ambrose, Jerome, and Gregory of Nyssa, who found marriage and sexual intercourse to be incompatible with paradise, and diverging slightly from his own earlier writings on the subject,[2] Augustine argues in the *City of God* that there could have been physical intercourse, marriage, even childbirth in the Garden of Eden. But the marriage of Adam and Eve would have been a harmonious friendship undisrupted by the torments of lust.[3] In Eden sexual intercourse could have taken place without sin, Augustine contends, because the arousal of the sexual members and sexual desire and activity would all have fallen under the purview of the will: "Then (had there been no sin) the man would have sowed the seed and the woman would have conceived the child when their sexual organs had been aroused by the will, at the appropriate time and in the necessary degree, and had not been excited by lust."[4] To convince unbelievers that such an occurrence might have been possible, Augustine cites other human organs that were known to be under willful control:

> For we set in motion, at our command, not only those members which are fitted with bones and joints, like the hands, feet and fingers, but also those which are loosely constructed of pliant tissues and muscles, which we can move, when we choose, by shaking, which we extend by stretching, which we twist and flex, contract and harden—such parts, I mean, as those of the mouth and face, which the will moves, as far as it can. In fact, even the lungs, which are the softest of all the internal organs and for that reason are protected in the cavity of the chest, are controlled by the will for the purpose of drawing breath and expelling it, and for producing and modulating the vocal sounds. In the same way as bellows serve the purpose of smiths and of organists, the lungs are obedient to the will of a man when he breathes out or breathes in, or speaks or shouts or sings. (587–88)

Augustine then passes to extraordinary examples of the rare and remarkable but natural abilities possessed by some individuals in order to show how the body can be an obedient servant, beyond the normal limitations of nature, even in people living this present, troubled life in the corruptible flesh. It is here that his prose anticipates the ribald tone of the fabliau:

> Some people can even move their ears, either one at a time or both together. Others without moving the head can bring the whole scalp—all the part covered with hair—down towards the forehead and bring it back again at will. Some can swallow an incredible number of various articles and then with a slight contraction of the diaphragm, can produce, as if out of a bag, any article they please, in perfect condition. There are others who imitate the cries of birds and

beasts and the voices of any other men, reproducing them so accurately so as to be quite indistinguishable from the originals, unless they are seen. A number of people produce at will such musical sounds from their behind (without any stink) that they seem to be singing from that region. (588)

If reference to the human body—the ears and head—are to be expected here, allusion to the behind or literally "the lowest part," a euphemism for the anus, prefigures in a particularly striking way the discussion of head and ass found in the fifteenth-century "Farce moralisée à quatre personnaiges."[5] When Augustine refers to the odorless singing asshole in order to demonstrate the control of mind over matter, his argument depends on a key distinction between voluntary and involuntary bodily functions that parallels the farce's differentiation between the rational, thinking head and the irrational, chaotic body. Arguing that a sinless, lustless intercourse could have united Adam and Eve in Eden, Augustine distinguishes song and whistling, willful functions of the head, from farting, a lower body function that, like the activities of the sex organs, remains beyond the mind's control. Under normal circumstances the mouth differs from the asshole, according to this view, because the former is governed by the will while the latter remains purely corporeal.

Even more importantly however for Augustine, as for the anonymous author of the "Farce moralisée" writing 1,000 years later, the poles of the mind/body split are clearly gendered. Forming part of a larger binary scheme that pits spirit against flesh, contemplative virtue against active virtue, the intellectual power of the mind against the body's perception and pleasure (14, 22 ; 584), Augustine's argument for lustless sex identifies reason (*ratio*), the mind (*mens*), and the soul (*animus*) as male features, while associating femaleness with the wildly chaotic body. In pondering Adam's fall, for example, Augustine wonders how the first man "endowed with a spiritual mind" could possibly have allowed himself to be seduced by the serpent. "Was it because the man would not have been able to believe this, that the woman was employed on the supposition that she had limited understanding, and also perhaps that she was living according to the spirit of the flesh and not according to the spirit of the mind?"[6]

In this view, the woman occupies a corporeal space significantly apart from that of the more knowledgeable male. Whereas he cogitates, mulling over thoughts in his mind, she devours her sexual prey, taking it in as food to be consumed. Her flesh is lascivious, desiring, and mindless. Eve's sin in this reading of Genesis is not only that she possessed a body that could be seduced and then seduce in turn. More specifically, this woman erred by bringing knowledge too close to pleasure, mixing mind and body through the activity of *cognoscere* that the Bible so often evokes: "And then they knew each other."[7] Offering knowledge only in the form of carnal knowledge, Eve pulled the rational, thinking man away from his covenant with the all-knowledgeable God into the realm of lust, thus rashly collapsing the sacrosanct distinction between mind and body. Once Adam's head was contaminated by Eve's mindless flesh, the paradigm of their gendered body parts carried over to individual men and women after the Fall. Outside of Eden, as Augustine observes, when the asshole farts and stinks, blindly obeying nature's call, and the sex organs respond only to lust, such corporeal functions represent a kind of feminized bodily defiance of the more rational masculinized will.

Mind Over Matter: Woman's Headless Body

The emphasis on seduction and the seducibility of the woman's body, not found in the Genesis story itself, originates in Jewish apocalyptic and rabbinic commentaries, where the biblical account of the Fall is combined with a tale of female seduction from the watcher myth. The latter, found in 1 Enoch, a Jewish exegesis on Genesis from the second century B.C., and in a later version in chapter 5 of the Testament of the Twelve Patriarchs, portrays women as sirens who use cosmetics, physical adornment, and "feminine" wiles to seduce the angels of God. Used to explain the origin of evil, this tale signals female seduction resulting from the allure of the woman's body as the ultimate danger to salvation.[8]

Biblical women—with the exception of good women like Judith, Esther, and Ruth, who represent impersonal abstractions beyond bodily concerns—are typically allied with the weaknesses of the body through seduction and sexuality. As figures like Delilah and Potiphar's wife square off against virtuous women representing the church, female identity is located either in the menacing body or safely and miraculously beyond it. Neither pole overlaps the sacrosanct male preserve of the mind. Those women deemed fleshly are typically linked to the body by medieval commentators in two ways: either as mother or temptress. For Isidore of Seville, following Aristotle, "mother is the matter, father the cause."[9] A creature so strongly associated with matter must naturally, according to the binary logic that dominated medieval commentaries on woman's nature, be concomitantly weak in mind and hence wayward and lustful. Gregory's *Moralia in Job* goes so far as to characterize the male mind as "female" when it appears unstable and changeable, easily alarmed, agitated, open to deception. He explains how the minds of men who serve God with yielding purpose are called women, whereas those who follow the Lord with firm and steady steps are men.[10] To be a full-fledged man in this scenario requires the straightforward commitment of a rational mind.

This view of female sexuality emerges perhaps most tellingly in Abelard's famous description of his love affair with Heloise, where the male pursuit of philosophical thinking stands in precise opposition to the woman's seductive flesh. As Abelard puts it, "I began to think myself the only philosopher in the world, with nothing to fear from anyone and so I yielded to the lusts of the flesh."[11] When Heloise later rejects Abelard's proposal to marry her, she echoes this sentiment, urging him to preserve his energies and interests for philosophy, "to guard against being sucked down headlong into this Charybdis, there to lose all sense of shame and be plunged forever into a whirlpool of [philosophical] impurity (73)."[12] She is the lustful and fleshy Charybdis, provider of dangerous pleasure; he the purveyor of savoir.

Abelard's own commentary on Genesis reiterates Augustine's position: while man and woman were created equal, she became subservient after the Fall because of her greater role in sin. Man, who resisted the serpent's seduction, exceeded woman not only in love and power but especially in reason and wisdom.[13] When Thomas Aquinas later combines Augustine's reading of Genesis in the *De Genesi ad litteram* with Aristotle's pronouncements on women in the *De generatione animalium*, he further reinforces the contention that man's superiority over woman resides in his intellectual knowledge: "Such is the subjection in which woman is by nature subordinate to man, because the power of rational discernment is by nature stronger in man."[14]

But an additional factor complicates the picture. For this fleshly, mindless female creature also manages to speak. Long before Aquinas or Abelard, what is perceived to be the problem of female sexuality is linked to the issue of woman's threatening voice. Indeed woman's speech is central to the medieval theological debate on feminine nature that views woman's talkative "head," to borrow a term from the later Old French farce, to be as problematic as her seductive "ass."

For Augustine, the problem with the female body—reminiscent of the asshole lacking a mind to guide it—is that it needs a governing head, one that can not only think but also speak for it. Augustine's interpretation of the Genesis story, emphasizing as it does the problem of sexuality, marked a crucial shift in interpretation that colored all subsequent readings. Elaine Pagels has shown how the majority of Jewish and Christian interpreters preceding Augustine took Genesis as a story of human freedom to choose good or evil. But for Augustine, Adam's misuse of moral freedom caused not only the mortality of humankind but the corruption of sexuality.[15] As Peter Brown explains it, Augustine placed sexuality at the center of the human person, registering *concupiscentia carnis* as a permanent flaw in the soul of humans after the fall. Concupiscence here glimpsed especially in the sex drive becomes a problem of all people, even those who are married, a *poena reciproca* standing as a permanent symptom of Adam's fall.[16] Pagels rehearses the scholarly discussion that explains how Augustine came to this interpretation of Genesis by misreading Paul's comments in Romans 5:12. Whereas the Greek text states that death came upon all humanity because of Adam, in that all humans sinned, Augustine's Latin translation conveyed to him a different meaning: death came upon all humanity because of Adam *in whom* all sinned (*Adam, Eve*, 143, esp. n.51).

But Augustine's reading of the creation myth as proof of the female body's inability to know and think derives more specifically from the commentary in 1 Timothy 2:11–14 falsely attributed to Paul that is taken up in *De Genesi ad litteram*. There Augustine explains woman's susceptibility to the devil's seduction as follows:

> But perhaps the woman had not yet received the gift of the knowledge of God, but under the direction and tutelage of her husband she was to acquire it gradually. It is not without reason that St. Paul said, "For Adam was formed first, then Eve, and Adam was not seduced (deceived), but the woman was seduced (deceived) and fell into sin (became a transgressor)." (11, 42:58)[17]

The full quotation from 1 Timothy, excerpted in Augustine's discussion of Adam's fall reads as follows: "Woman is to keep silent. For Adam was formed first, then Eve; and Adam was not deceived, but the woman was deceived and became a transgressor." Silence is here invoked as the remedy for woman's wayward seducibility because her speech is thought to seduce or lead astray as mindlessly as her body. Thus in a section of the First Epistle to Timothy mistakenly attributed to Paul, the author states: "I permit no woman to teach or to have authority over men; she is to keep silent." This advice is prefigured in Ecclesiasticus: "from a woman sin had its beginning, and because of her we all die" and the consequent advice that one "allow no outlet to water, and no boldness of speech in an evil wife."[18] Both texts associate female sexuality with the power of the female voice, suggesting silence as a cure for sexual transgression, as do many patristic warnings against woman's speech.

Clement of Alexandria and Tertullian limit their comments to the body, advising that woman's face be covered in church and her beauty obscured, hoping thereby to prevent the kind of temptation that caused the Fall.[19] But covering the woman's head actually solves two problems, as Paul makes clear in 1 Corinthians. In veiling her physical beauty, the head-covering also curtails her unwanted speech, for as Paul explains, "any woman who prays or prophesies with her head unveiled dishonors her head" (1 Cor. 11:4–10) and "women should keep silence in the churches. For they are not permitted to speak, but should be subordinate, even as the law says. If there is anything they desire to know, let them ask their husbands at home" (1 Cor. 14:34–35).

Husbands thus become the "head" of the family, dispensing knowledge and wisdom to their potentially alluring wives, much as the church fathers themselves issue wise pronouncements to curtail the seductive effects of the woman's body and speech. Augustine goes so far as to suggest that women have no heads of their own. Using the reference to women's veiled heads in 1 Cor 11:3–12, he asserts that man alone is made in God's image and that woman can attain this image only when taken together with the male who is her "head."[20] Following the serial hierarchy that makes God the head of Christ, Christ the head of man, and man the head of woman,[21] Augustine admonishes Ecdicia for having acted independently of her husband, explaining that woman should not make decisions without consulting her "head," here understood to be her spouse.[22]

How Eve Talks Back in the *Jeu d'Adam*

Functioning much like the disparaging comments of perturbed husbands in the "Farce moralisée à quatre personnaiges," patristic commentaries on the Genesis story reduce woman to a silent, irrational body, providing no words from female voices that might counter, resist, or correct the misogynous portrait. But in vernacular literature of the High Middle Ages in France, women's varied responses to this phallocentric portrait of femininity can more readily be found. One particularly strong voice emerges in the Old French theatrical enactment of the Adam and Eve story, where the female object of discussion in the fathers' writings becomes an embodied protagonist who pointedly questions the logic underwriting the mind/body split.

The Adam and Eve story was best known in the French Middle Ages through a twelfth-century vernacular dramatization, *Jeu d'Adam*.[23] Eve here figures as a major actor whose speech plays as prominent a role as her body, providing a theatrical illustration of the dangerous woman's voice we are warned against in 1 Timothy. When Adam curses Eve in the Old French mystery play, he condemns her mouth along with her sexualized body, pairing the flawed rib that betrayed him, "My rib betrayed my whole body," with woman's evil speech: "Now I am lost because of your advice. On account of your advice I have fallen into evil."[24] Woman's public speaking lips and private genital labia are here equally to blame for man's moral and social downfall.

The seduction itself, as in the biblical account, is cast in terms of voice. When God castigates the fallen Adam, he blames him specifically for having listened to his wife, for having chosen to believe her words instead of God's: "You believed your wife instead of me."[25] The dramatic crisis is staged as a battle between rival speechmakers. Although God's sermon promises to procure pleasure (*deduit*), Adam chooses Eve's *mal conseil*, inspired by the devil's devious speech, over God's counsel."[26] Having given her *word* to the devil in making a secret pact with him,[27] Eve uses her own alluring words to draw Adam away from God's *commandement*, "I abandoned my maker because of my wife's advice."[28] Cast as a "tendre chose" (v. 227), she, like the tender-assed wife in the "Farce moralisée," can destroy her husband's mastery of conjugal affairs by attacking his intellect and his reason. In words that prefigure the lament of the downcast husband in "The Four Wishes of St. Martin," Adam bemoans his fate at the hands of woman, exclaiming to her, "Oh, evil woman [wife] full of treason! / You quickly pushed me to perdition! / How you snatched away my sense and reason!" (vv. 535–37).[29]

What the devil promises, through his mouthpiece Eve, is a kind of *savoir* that derives from tasting the forbidden fruit. If the rational Adam is not tempted by the devil's query, "Vols le tu saver?" (Do you want to know? v. 115) and his proposed solution, "Guste le fruit" (Taste the fruit, v. 169), Eve is willing to listen to a voice claiming that for Adam to love and fear God "n'est pas saveir" (is not wise, v. 136). She is tempted by the possibility of an alternative *savoir* that contains its own pleasure, a knowledge providing an alternative to Adam's subservience and obedience to God. In the contractual agreement originally outlined between God and Eve, pleasure is his alone. When the dutiful prelapsarian wife agrees to follow God's instruction by bowing to her husband, never stepping out from under control, "A lui soies tot tens encline, / Nen issir de sa discipline" (Always bend to him; do not contest his rules, vv. 35–36), she does so according to God's pleasure, "Jol frai, sire, a ton plaisir" (I will do it, Lord, as it pleases you, v. 41). Acting in his service means doing what pleases him: "Le ton pleisir, le ton servise / Frai, sire, en tote guise" (I will do your bidding and serve you in every way, vv. 47–48).[30] Eve, in this vernacular dramatization, however, is ready to displease, or more accurately to challenge the terms of the biblical and patristic equation that posit pleasure and displeasure as irreconcilable extremes.

She launches the challenge through a pointed question that cuts to the heart of the mind/body hierarchy that this play underwrites. The devil attempts to entice Eve with promises of God's total knowledge, with the fruit of *sapience:* "This is the fruit of wisdom. It gives knowledge of all knowledge."[31] Eve, however, does not make the obvious play for total mastery. We hear no claims to the effect of "I'll take it." To the devil's assertion that the fruit contains "all knowledge, good and evil" (tut saver, bien et mal, v. 251) Eve inquires about its flavor. Faced with the possibility of acquiring total knowledge, she wants to know what it tastes like: "Quel savor a?" (v. 252).

Whereas we might at first hear in these words the stereotype of woman as the irrational, inferior thinker, incapable of discerning the importance of "knowledge" in contrast to more ephemeral "pleasure," Eve's seemingly mindless question about the taste of knowledge does more than underwrite that standard dichotomy. Although her query illustrates on the one hand Michèle LeDoeuff's contention that the privileging of the rational male voice necessarily generates and then denigrates its opposite as something to define itself *against* ("Women and Philosophy," 196). Eve's allusion to taste also calls into question the very terms of the binary pair it seems at first to illustrate. Punning on the etymological link between knowledge and pleasure—*saver* and *savor* descend from the same Latin root (*sapio, sapere*)—Eve's retort to the devil's offer of total knowledge boldly conflates the realms of knowledge and pleasure, thereby radically revising the basic structuring mechanism of the whole of Genesis I. That narrative establishes a series of opposite categories, separating light from darkness, heaven from earth, land from sea, seed trees from fruit trees, sun from moon, fish from fowl, and finally man from woman. Defying God's plenary word and her husband's terrestrial authority, the Old French Eve substitutes for both of these hierarchical and univocal traditions a world where opposites can coexist as equally valid alternatives, where light is not necessarily valued over darkness, sun over moon, man over woman. This female protagonist's words provide a subtly humorous send-up of the "double braid" that for Hélène Cixous structures the world according to the binary pairs of "activity/passivity, sun/moon, culture/nature, day/night, father/mother, head/heart, intelligible/palpable, logos/pathos" and their gendered equivalents in "Form/Matter" and "Man/Woman."[32]

In a more specifically medieval context, this literary Eve recasts—through her ambiguous question—the misognyous portrait that makes the properly silent woman subservient to the thinking, speaking man. Her voice reminds us in a significant way that women have heads and mouths too. And that those mouths do not exist independently of the body and its senses. Eve's speech in this theatrical piece says not only that woman is more than body, but that the body should be an essential part of knowledge and understanding. She shows the limitations of conceiving of mind apart from body. In contradistinction to God's position in this text—Adam must choose between his voice and Eve's, between divine orders and woman's seduction—Eve asserts that the choice need not be made in such stark either/or terms. Her probing question implies that we can "know pleasure" or "taste knowledge" without having to impose a reductive hierarchy upon the two terms.[33]

By asking what knowledge tastes like, or asking for a taste of knowledge as if it were an ice cream cone or a piece of cake, this literary Eve speaks against a long tradition of misogynous discourse that promotes the conception of a mind/body split specifically by silencing woman. In effect, the slyly joking words of the Old French theatrical Eve offer a deft critique of the statement in 1 Timothy that "woman should be silent." For here she is not. But they also address the apostle's second proposition, the idea that "man came first."

MATTER BEFORE MIND: HOW WOMEN CAME FIRST

Augustine's Birth from the Pores

We have seen how the construction of male and female relations in Augustine's readings of the Genesis story provides a striking anticipation of the head/ass dichotomy governing the "Farce moralisée à quatre personnaiges" and related Old French fabliaux. But Augustine's glosses on the Adam and Eve narrative also highlight an essential feature of the mind/body split that the later Old French farce and fabliau deftly conceal. That is, the role of female genitalia in reproduction, and especially in childbirth. Jane Gallop has shown in her provocative *Thinking Through the Body* how in eighteenth-century French thought the rational male philosopher, emblematized in her analysis by the Marquis de Sade, constructs his identity in opposition to the mother, as the processes of thinking and childbirth become polarized around the mind/body split (55–71). The tradition has deep roots in Christian thought, going back to the beginning, to the Genesis narrative that establishes Eve as the mother of all mankind, source of human life for generations to come. And this is precisely where the issue of female flesh, of woman as body, becomes complicated for Augustine and later interpreters of the biblical creation story.

In a second surprisingly fabliau-like passage, this one taken from his *Opus imperfectum contra Julianum*, Augustine initially develops his argument for sinless intercourse in Eden by describing the human birth process, via the pointed objections of his Pelagian opponent Julian of Eclanum.[34] Making fun of Augustine's prior description of Edenic sex as the pastoral activity of a farmer sowing seeds in this "field of generation" (*City of God* 14, 23: 586–87), Julian imagines a scenario of reproduction that took place wholly in the absence of physical contact with woman. This, he says, is what Augustine's interpretation of Genesis suggests:

> If Adam had not sinned, then the woman could have been made ready
> for fecundity just as the soil is. Perhaps sheaves of children would
> shoot forth through all the joints and through the small conduits of
> the body which doctors call pores. Thus fertile in all parts, she would
> sweat forth offspring instead of lice! And if some of them should
> break forth through her eyes, they would take away the sight of
> the one who brought them forth; if a helmeted swarm marches

forth from the sphere of the pupil, without doubt blindness would curse the wretched woman. Nor would it be hard to slay the off-spring—not born, but sweated.[35]

This sexless Eve oozing forth children from her pores, a woman apparently without womb, vagina, or other reproductive organs normally possessed by biological women, constitutes the logical extension of the mind/body hierarchy Augustine invokes to portray female flesh as the dreaded rival of male will. Yet Julian's comments reveal a curious twist of logic in Augustine's construction of the archetypal female. For if woman in Augustine's gloss on Genesis in the *De Genesi ad litteram* (*On the Literal Meaning of Genesis*) emerges as a creature thoroughly mired in the realm of the flesh, she appears here as a being devoid of the most fundamental womanly and flesh-bound activity: creating new flesh by giving birth. In evoking the image of offspring that were sweated forth, "not born," Julian reveals, perhaps unwittingly, how Augustine's desire for lustless intercourse effectively denatures female biology. The broader implications of Julian's insight point toward a birth process that is ungendered, indeed generic, recalling Augustine's argument in the *Confessions* (8, 24: 37) that the exhortation in Genesis 1:28 to "reproduce and multiply" refers not to physical reproductive activity but only to diverse thoughts and expressions produced by the fertile human *mind*. Reproduction in the mind or birth through the body's pores could both conceivably be accomplished by members of either sex. Augustine's logic has thus displaced the physical act of giving birth away from its biological grounding in the female body while insisting at the same time on the necessary corporeality of that female body. In moving from *De Genesi ad litteram* to the *Opus Imperfectum*, we see curiously how the very argument that constructs woman as tempting flesh implies a related desire to deny woman her most basic flesh-bound activity in childbirth.[36]

The issue for Augustine comes down to a question of precedence, cast blatantly as a rivalry between man and woman in the crucial process of human reproduction. Discussing the creation of woman in *De Genesi ad litteram*, Augustine asks rhetorically, "Are we to say that without any sexual embrace a man could have been made from a woman but not a woman from a man?" (9, 16: 91). Defending the possibility of creating Eve from Adam's side, he casts the act of generation in Genesis 2 as a specifically male version of woman's delivery from the womb. "Did the womb of the Virgin have the power to produce a Man whereas the side of the man had no power to produce a woman?" (9, 16: 91). Augustine here invokes a female model of generation only to elide female reproductive capacity altogether. His comments on the processes of generation in Genesis are then not only, and perhaps not principally, about how bodies couple in sex (lustful or not). In arguing that before the Fall the rational male mind could have dominated the flesh gendered as female, Augustine explains similarly how the production of life from female flesh could be appropriated to male control. Indeed his insistence on the necessary hierarchizing of mind over body emerges as a strategy to compensate for the disquieting biological fact that in reproduction woman comes first.

When Augustine quotes the Epistle to Timothy in order to substantiate his view of woman's mental deficiency, he grounds his claim, like the writer of the epistle before him, on the question of precedence: "For Adam was formed first, then Eve; and Adam was not deceived, but the woman was deceived and became a transgressor."[37] Woman had less knowledge, was more fleshly, more easily seduced and hence required silencing *because* she was formed second in the process of creation. Patricia Parker has shown how Genesis 2 and the interpretations of it attributed to Paul and Peter (1 Cor. 11; Eph. 5:22–31; 1 Peter 3:1–7) combined with Aristotle's notion of woman as a deformity or lack conditions a long tradition of placing woman second: in Milton, Rousseau, and Freud in particular. Freud's contention that in the beginning the little girl was a little boy constitutes, according to Parker, a psychoanalytic rewriting of the story of generation and human creation that preserves the fundamental chronology at work in Genesis 2: man was created first and woman came afterward.[38] But what precisely is at stake for Paul and for Augustine, and other medieval philosophers who take up the argument for Adam's precedence? And what does the silencing of woman have to do with the role of the first woman, Eve, as mother of all humanity?

Medieval medical treatises from the thirteenth century on helped to substantiate theological claims of woman's natural inferiority through graphic descriptions of her biological inferiority.[39] The woman who lacks a head metaphorically is shown concretely to lack male genitalia. Galen's view of female anatomy dominated medieval thought, perpetrating among other notions the idea that women have the same sex organs as men but in a lesser, altered, invisible form. The uterus was considered equivalent to the scrotum, with the ovaries mimicking the testes, the neck of the vagina replicating the penis, and the vulva replacing the foreskin. In woman's case these male organs were thought simply to be concealed, internalized, a view that gave rise to the fabliau-like scenario that women who made the mistake of spreading their legs too far apart would risk having their sex organs fall out, thereby becoming men.[40]

We recognize here an obvious example of Irigaray's logic-of-the-same whereby women appear as failed men. But the detail of this pseudoanatomical account is significant in regard to the issue of human reproduction and Augustine's concern with how man "sows the seed and woman conceives the child" in the narrative of sexless intercourse in Eden with which we began. When Galen calls the uterus a scrotum and the vagina a penis, the effect of his pseudo-physiology is not only to stage woman as a lesser male—one whose defining sexual organs are invisible. More importantly, this construction of female anatomy displaces and erases the potential functioning of female reproductive organs (gestation in the uterus and birth from the vagina) altogether, much as Augustine's alleged birth from the pores appropriates woman's reproductive capacity in Julian's account.

The Christian Middle Ages inherited its traditions of privileging mind over matter in part from Platonic and Aristotelian views on anatomy, generation, and metaphysics. Both systems align women with matter, the material, baser, sensate realm because of her role in reproduction. But both ultimately also recast woman's predominant role in childbirth, transfering the primary function of reproduction to men. Through examination of these accounts, we can see how the ideological hierarchy that places mind over matter in both antique and medieval writings about feminine nature masks a problem of biological precedence. That is to say, biological sequence positions female matter, in the form of a reproductive, mothering body not after but chronologically *before* the (male) mind that can only exist within a body.

Plato's Womb of the Mind

In a founding gesture that could not be more opposite from Eve's conflation of *savoir* and *saveur* in the Old French *Jeu d'Adam*, the Platonic construction of the universe isolates knowledge in the realm of a soul, far from the sensate deceptions of the material body. Socrates makes the hierarchy clear when exhorting the Athenians to "make your first and chief concern not for your bodies nor for your possessions, but for the highest welfare of your souls" (*Apology*, 30a–b).[41] In developing the radical and desired decoupling of mind and body that would lead to the cultivation of this pure, bodiless soul,[42] Plato locates women firmly in the lesser bodily realm. If women are beautiful, that beauty is but a pale reflection of real Beauty, that "everlasting loveliness which neither comes nor goes, which neither flowers nor fades" (*Symposium*, 221a, "Woman as Body," 112). Plato uses the lives of women, as Elizabeth Spelman has shown, to provide a negative example for the nascent philosopher who seeks to soar above the body to the realm of the thinking soul (114–15). Women constitute a special liability because, like boys, they fail to distinguish the realms of body and soul exemplified by abstract Beauty on the one hand and beautiful things on the other (*Republic*, 557c). As Spelman has so aptly put it, "They don't realize that it is not through one's senses that one knows about beauty or anything else, for real beauty is eternal and invisible and unchangeable and can only be known through the soul" (116). Women in short resemble Eve in the *Jeu d'Adam*, who thinks that one can "taste" knowledge.

Women's key role in giving birth to children similarly creates mere bodies, products inferior to procreation of the spirit that concocts "something lovelier and less mortal than human seed" (*Symposium*, 209c). The privileged creation, as Plato makes clear in the *Timaeus*, occurs not in the female womb but the male head. The soul, we are told, as a guiding genius dwells in the highest part of the body. From its location in the head, the brain emits marrow or "seed," which it sends down the spinal column and out through the penis.[43] The seed's appetite for egress is called an eros of begetting, the most sublime form of eros, an eros that escapes the bodily contamination because of its higher source. Plato compares this mind/soul generator of life to a plant whose roots are not on earth but in the heavens (90A), suggesting that our own human root lies in the male head, not the lower body, the umbilicus or the female womb. When God created humans, Plato explains, he made marrow and added to it various kinds of souls, then he "moulded into spherical shape the ploughland, so to speak, that was to contain the divine seed" (73B). But this ploughland is not the "ploughland of the womb" that Plato later describes; it is the male head, patterned after the round shape of the universe (44D) and reflecting also the principal organ of female reproduction whose functions it partially usurps. Just as, in the creation narrative, God created the head first, later building the other parts of the body around this essential root (73D), so too the life of every individual is thought to originate in that privileged, male head.

Thus Plato effectively elevates reproduction above the lower body functions of female anatomy. The divine soul, in his view, is protected against contamination from these lower functions by the physiological division that separates head from chest: "Fearing, no doubt, to pollute the divine part on their account, except in so far as was absolutely inevitable, they lodged the mortal apart therefrom in a different dwelling place in the body, building between head and breast, as an isthmus and boundary, the neck, which they placed between the two to keep them asunder" (69D–E). A further division provided by the diaphragm isolates the breast from the even baser genital area: "And since part of it (the trunk) has a nobler nature, part a baser, they built another partition across the cavity of the trunk, as if marking off the men's quarter's from the women's, and set the midriff as a screen between them" (70A).

The philosopher's path to the realm of forms ascends from the sensible to the intelligible in a movement that parallels Plato's own transfer of the site of reproduction from the lower abdomen to the head, or from the women's quarter to the men's.[44] Irigaray's complex reading of the cave analogy in *Speculum of the Other Woman* has demonstrated how the philosopher's ascent to an ideal mirror (a form that reflects objects) casts the cave as a metaphor for inner space, for the den, the womb, the *hystera* that must be transcended, abandoned by the philosopher whose journey carries him away from this image of female reproduction. Leaving behind his biological origin in matter and the female womb-body that exemplifies it, he rises toward what is posited as an alternate origin: the idea. The philosopher seeking immortality substitutes for his origins in the mother an origin outside the darkness of the cave, in the light at its mouth that the seated, chained prisoners hope in vain to attain.[45]

In Irigaray's reading the *hystera*/cave is an appropriation, both formally and functionally, of the womb whose vaginal passage links outside to inside. But the cave analogy inverts the shape of the womb, making it point upward to the transcendent light rather than down toward the earth. In the process of metaphorization, the *hystera* itself is forgotten, obscured. As the theater in which Platonic representation takes place from the light of a fire projected onto a screen that the seated figures watch, the *hystera* englobes every sight but cannot itself ever be represented (245). The "unrepresentable origin of all forms" (253), its role is obscured by the light of the fire that visibly creates forms on the screen and by the light of the sun outside the cave, both of which participate in a miming of reproduction (255). In place of real human offspring, the image of the sun engenders sham offspring, copies of copies, artificial images, shadows.

Irigaray shows ultimately how Plato's cave analogy displaces the process of reproduction that has its origin in woman onto a process of representation whose origin and base lie outside of woman. "Conception" then finds "its 'proper' meaning only in the re-birth into truth. And truth, in order to escape any hint of verisimilitude, will be situated in a time that predates birth" (355). A battle of precedence is thus set up. The *hystera* becomes the ground on which man already constitutes or represents himself, creating his subjectivity through a play of likenesses—between ideal forms and their concrete realizations. The male subject existed in the perfection of self-identity from before the *hystera*'s operation, from before birth (355). The biological fact that every male mind must come initially out of a female body is thus effectively camouflaged by claiming prior existence for the ideal realm. If female matter precedes male mind, that mind has a prior origin beyond woman's body.

Aristotle's Messy Matter

A similar struggle against woman's primacy in the birth process lies at the heart of Aristotle's theories of reproduction. Irigaray has explained cogently how Aristotle's commentary on the biological conception of a girl-child founders most significantly on the metaphysical problem of imagining how a girl-child could exist. The latter process entails imagining the fleshbound female sex not only as a potentially thinking and knowing subject, but more importantly, as the very source, biologically speaking, of male subjectivity itself. In terms of generation and human creation, the dreaded female flesh actually comes before the male mind.[46] Aristotle acknowledges this, curiously, in *De generatione animalium*, where he refers to the menses as prime matter, "the catamenia have in their nature an affinity to the primitive matter."[47] Although female matter may be viewed by Aristotle as radically impotent in comparison to the moving, logos-creating male principle, the prime matter of the menses remains nonetheless the ground for the logos's development. Aristotle thus concedes implicitly that at least from a biological point of view all being comes from the material mother. Her body provides the physical source of the logos itself.

But elsewhere Aristotle characterizes the female as a "mutilated male" because her impure semen lacks one essential ingredient, the "principle of the soul" (737a).[48] The central question of *De generatione animalium* concerns how the soul is transferred or created to give life to flesh. Since only the male produces true semen, the female contributes the material for generation in the menses. The male imparts motion and form to the female matter, adding soul to the body, "What the male contributes to generation is the form and the efficient cause (principle of motion), while the female contributes the material (729a). But the female as female is passive, and the male, as male, active, and the principle of the movement comes from him" (729b).[49] In reproduction, woman's most perfect functioning involves giving birth to a male child, creating the conditions in which the male element—more perfect than the female—will prevail. Woman then becomes an organ or contributing part of male physiology, matter set into motion by and for the soul of the unified male offspring.[50]

But if the female contributes nutritive and sensitive souls—living organizations of matter—"it remains for the reason alone so to enter and alone to be divine" (736b).[51] The hierarchy is clear-cut: man as the cause of initial movement holds a privileged position in human generation.

> Again, as the first efficient or moving cause, to which belong the definition and the form, is better and more divine in its nature than the material on which it works, it is better that the superior principle should be separated from the inferior. Therefore, wherever it is possible and insofar as it is possible, the male is separated from the female. For the first principle or efficient cause whereby that which comes into being is male, is better and more divine than the material whereby it is female.[52]

The male takes precedence hierarchically because he precedes chronologically, as initial cause.[53]

In contrast to Freud, who, in Sarah Kofman's reading, locates the enigma of woman in the baffling process of her transformation from a "little boy" into a woman, Plato and Aristotle situate the troubling female enigma in the mechanics of the birth process itself. For these ancient philosophers, as for Augustine and the author of 1 Timothy, the concern is not with how "woman becomes a woman"—how she moves from a supposedly male erogenous zone to a female one—but with the less sexual and more overtly biological process of how man comes into being.[54] The nagging question does not concern how woman develops out of man but how man issues from woman. Both scenarios involve significant hierarchical reversal, but of different sorts. Whereas in Freud's account of female development the woman moves from a kind of bisexual equality to a position of inferiority, thereby bolstering the primacy of the penis, the reversal for medieval Christian thinkers and their ancient predecessors concerns a switch from Eve as the source of all life to Eve as the root of disobedience.

Life Emerging from the Body

We have seen how, in the reading of Genesis 2 attributed to Paul and later taken up by Augustine, woman was deceived and became a transgressor by implication because she was created second. She must remain thus forever second to her husband, whose head and mind will rightfully dominate her body. If Mieke Bal is right, the reading of Genesis reflected in Timothy may derive from a retrospective fallacy.[55] Reading backward from Genesis 3, where God assigns sex roles to Adam and Eve, the writer mistakenly understands woman to have come from man. Bal contends to the contrary that the creation story in Genesis 2 describes the formation of the first body as an unnamed and unsexed neutral body, an earth-body or thing "made of clay" that would have included woman too. From this undifferentiated matter, the word for woman appears first, meaning she was first to exist. Her existence transforms the meaning of the earth-body into earth man. Evidence from the Gnostic Gospels also suggests that early church writings may have been much less sexist than the canon of Orthodox Christian teachings and biblical commentaries of the fathers have led us to believe.[56]

The fact remains, however, that most religious communities in the western empire headed by Rome followed the Pauline tradition reflected in the letter to Timothy. They denied the authority to teach or speak to women because Adam was formed first. But what does this mean? A look at Paul's letter to the Corinthians reveals the hierarchical reversal at play in his use of Genesis 2 rather than the more egalitarian formulation of Genesis 1—"male and female God created them." In 1 Corinthians 11:7–9, Paul asserts that man "is the image and glory of God; but woman is the glory of man. (For man was not made from woman, but woman from man. Neither was man created for woman but woman for man.)" Here the description of God corresponds to a description of human interaction that authorizes a social pattern of male dominance, as Elaine Pagels has pointed out (105). But that social dominance is predicated, as Paul's aside makes clear, on a denial of woman's preeminent role in reproduction: "For man was not made from woman." Like Augustine and Plato, Paul here explicates the process of human generation by reversing an essential chronology. The biological fact that men are born of women's bodies, making women come first, not second, in a very important sense, is here masked by an ideology of female subservience. Man's biological dependence on woman is denied and replaced by the notion of her necessary social dependence on him. The ideology that elevated male mind over female matter emerges here as a compensatory gesture for a biological reality in which female matter (mother) necessarily precedes the generation and proper functioning of any individual mind.

Indeed Augustine did not need Julian of Eclanum's wildly imaginative scenario of the fecund Eve sweating forth children from her pores in order to construct an image of reproduction without woman. The Bible itself gave Augustine the most useful paradigm for sexless reproduction in Genesis 2, where woman's role in childbirth is even more thoroughly displaced. As Augustine interprets the emergence of Eve from Adam's body, "woman with the appearances and distinctive physical characteristics of her sex was made for man from man" (*De Genesi ad litteram*, 9, 11: 19). No blood, no sex, no mother. Augustine's assertion elsewhere that woman was created by God for the sole purpose of producing children, "I do not see for what goal woman would have been given to man as a helpmate if not for generating children,"[57] pales considerably when juxtaposed with his insistence that woman herself was born of man. Indeed, the true mother in Augustine's schema is not the biological female but a less corporeal Mother Church, "the Mother who begot you and formed you in her womb."[58] Where then is woman to be found in Augustine's narrative of human sexuality and generation?

Male Disobedience: Adam's Rib and Augustine's Penis

If we return for a moment to Augustine's argument for the singing asshole, we are reminded that the central issue at stake in these remarks, as in the comments in 1 Timothy, is that of disobedience. It is precisely because woman transgressed, in Augustine's reasoning, that the flesh later disobeys through lust. When Adam and Eve gained the knowledge of good and evil, Augustine explains, "the consequence was that they were embarrassed by the insubordination of their flesh, the punishment which was a kind of evidence of their disobedience, and they 'sewed together fig leaves and made aprons for themselves' " (*City of God* 14, 17: 579). As punishment for disobeying God's will, the Edenic couple and all human beings thereafter are plagued by sexual organs that disobey their own willful control: "Thus modesty, from a sense of shame, covered what was excited to disobedience by lust, in defiance of a will which had been condemned for the guilt of disobedience" (14, 17: 579). Disobedience of the sexual members is then a retribution for the first disobedience, which was prompted, as we know from Genesis, by a woman (14, 20: 582). It was, Augustine concludes, because man forsook God by pleasing himself that he was handed over to himself, and because he did not obey God he could not obey himself (14, 24: 589). But whose disobedience is at issue here, woman's or man's?

Augustine's fabliau-like comments on the function of body parts in Book 14, Chapters 23 and 24, of the *City of God* reveal a significant slippage in the master theologian's reasoning.

> We move our hands and feet to perform their special functions, when we so will; this involves no reluctance on their part, and the movements are performed with all the ease we observe in our own case and in that of others. And we observe it particularly in craftsmen engaged in all kinds of physical tasks, where natural powers which lack strength and speed are developed by active training. Then why should we not believe that the sexual organs (*illa membra*) could have been the obedient servants of mankind, at the bidding of the will, in the same way as the other, if there had been no lust, which came in as the retribution for the sin of disobedience?" (14, 23: 585).

But what sexual organs is Augustine referring to, here and throughout Book 14, which provides the subject of our current discussion? His general references to "sexual organs" (*membra, genitales corporis*) often suggest that both male and female genitalia are at issue, that both escape problematically the control of the will. "Anyone who utters a word in anger, anyone who goes so far as to strike another person, could not do so if his tongue or hand were not put in motion at the command, as one may say, of his will; and those members (*membra*) are set in motion by the same will even when there is no anger. But the genital organs (*genitales corporis*) have become, as it were, the private property of lust" (14, 19: 581).

If we return to the passage with which we began, where Augustine characterizes parts of the body that respond to the will, it becomes clear that his preoccupation and sole point of reference is the male sexual member. The vagina would fall reasonably, and in fact stereotypically, into the category of the mouth and face, described by Augustine as "loosely con-structed of pliant tissues and muscles, which we can move, when we choose by shaking, which we extend by stretching, which we twist and flex, contract and harden" (14, 24: 587). The problem Augustine addresses in his commentary on Genesis is then less a problem of female than of male sexuality. The dilemma he describes is one of man at the mercy of his own body during sexual arousal and intercourse; it is a case of male flesh disobedient to the male mind.[59]

Other passages in Augustine's text reveal how his example of a man capable of whistling from his asshole explains how pre-lapsarian man, not woman, could have exercised control over his sexual organs. God could have made it so: "It would not have been difficult for God to fashion him in such a way that even what is now set in motion in his flesh only by lust should have been moved only by his will" (14, 24: 588). Knowledge of God ensures domination of the mind over man's sexualized body: "Now surely any friend of wisdom and holy joys (*amicus sapientiae sanctorumque gaudiorum*) who lives a married life but knows, in the words of the Apostle's warning, 'how to possess his bodily instrument in holiness and honour, not in the sickness of desire, like the Gentiles who have no knowledge of God'—surely such a man would prefer, if possible, to beget his children without lust of this kind. For then the parts created for this task would be the servants of the mind" (14, 16: 577). The problem is not only one of sexual arousal, but also at times, lack thereof, "sometimes the impulse [of lust] is an unwanted intruder, sometimes it abandons the eager lover, and desire cools off in the body while it is at boiling heat in the mind. Thus strangely does lust refuse to be servant not only of the will to beget but even to the lust for lascivious indulgence . . . on the whole it is totally opposed to the mind's control" (14, 16: 577).

In arguing that because of the first sin of disobedience, prompted by Eve's alliance with the devil, man's flesh, through lust, becomes disobedient to his mind, Augustine has effectively turned a biological model on its head. Did the moral wrong of Eve's disobedience prompt the physio-logical reality of male erection or did the unruliness of male erection prompt the narrative of Eve's disobedience?

Ample evidence in the *Confessions* suggests Augustine's own troubled experience with nocturnal emissions, which defy control by the rational mind: "So great a power have these deep images over my soul and my flesh that these false visions persuade me when asleep to do what true sights cannot persuade me to when awake. . . . At such times, where is reason, by which a man awake resists those suggestions, and remains un-shaken even if the very deeds themselves are urged upon him?" (*Confessions* 10, 30). And in *De Genesi ad litteram*, "Moreover, when the image that arises in the thoughts of the speaker becomes so vivid in the dream of the sleeper that it is indistinguishable from actual intercourse, it immediately moves the flesh and the natural result follows. . . . But a right disposition of the soul, purified by a desire for what is more perfect, kills many desires that have no connection with the natural motions of the flesh" (12, 15: 31). Augustine characterizes the uncontrolled wanderings of his flesh as a result of seduction: "See with what companions I ran about the streets of Baby-lon, and how I wallowed in its mire as in cinnamon and precious oint-ments! That I might cling even more firmly to its very navel, my invisible enemy crushed me underfoot and seduced me, for I was easy to seduce" (*Confessions* 2, 3). And later too a perpetrator of seduction. "Caught fast in a disease of the flesh with its deadly sweetness" (*Confessions* 6, 12), the young Augustine rejects the advice of his friend Alypius, who counsels continence. Echoing Genesis 3:1, Augustine explains, "Through me the serpent spoke to Alypius; by my tongue he wove sweet snares and placed them on his path so that his feet might be entangled by them" (*Confessions* 6, 12). This abhorrence of the unruly male flesh persists throughout Au-gustine's writings, pushing him to argue consistently that Adam's sin brought mortality and sexual desire upon the human race, depriving them of the freedom to choose not to sin. Amplifying his argument in the *Opus imperfectum contra Julianum*, Augustine critiques Julian's characterization of uncontrollable sexual desire as a "diabolical excitement of the genitals" (2:33, *PL* 45, 1155), calling it a "vital fire that does not obey the soul's decision but, for the most part, rises up against the soul's desire in disor-derly and ugly movements" *Adam, Eve*, 140–41). For the intensely Neo-platonic Augustine, this "rising up" of the male genitals constitutes an unacceptable descent into the flesh. It represents that "other" law Paul describes: "I see in my members another law at war with my mind and making me captive to the law of sin which dwells in my members" (Rom. 7:22–25).[60]

In Plato's *Timaeus* we can see, similarly, how the philosopher's project of escaping the female body attempts to resolve a problem centered ulti-mately in male, not female, anatomy. If in rising from the sensible to the intelligible, the Platonic seeker of wisdom overcomes the carnality of fe-male reproductive organs, he also evades the more troubling resistance and unruliness of male genitalia. In Plato's description of human generation,

sexual organs for both men and women are conceived of as animate creatures that exist independently of rational control. If the female womb,
seeking to reproduce, is said to wander around the interior body cavity, it
is the male reproductive organ whose movements are clearly visible. Plato
categorizes them in opposition to the privileged orderliness of the mind:
"Hence it is that in men the genital organ is disobedient and self-willed,
like a creature deaf to reason and determined, because of frenzied appetite,
to carry all before it" (*Timaeus*, 91B). The problem with the body, overtly
cast off on woman in the *Republic* and related dialogues and less directly
passed onto her in the cave analogy, resides ultimately in the disobedient
male flesh. The quintessential Platonic project of rising up from the sensible to the intelligible is jeopardized most specifically by the rising up of
the male sexual organ that holds man in the sensate realm distant from the
soul's knowledge. Locating reproduction in the mind would then be a
compensatory gesture; an attempt to control the unruly male body.

*   *   *

Augustine's comments on human sexuality discussed in this chapter
reveal how the Adam and Eve story deftly conceals two biological realities
behind narratives of female subservience. We have seen, first of all, how
the physiological disobedience of man's flesh is displaced in the narrative
of the Fall onto the reputed act of woman's disobedience, which emerges
as prior cause. Secondly, woman's biological role in childbirth is eclipsed
in Genesis 2 by a tale of male creation. The ideological hierarchy that
places mind over matter in medieval Christian thought thus works to hide
the fact that *biologically* matter actually supersedes mind in at least two
important ways: through the unruly male member's irrational wanderings
and the generative female womb's productive creation. The logic that
emerges from Paul's exhortation in 1 Timothy to silence women and control their sexual digression reads then as a compensatory gesture for a
doubled male lack. In the passages discussed above, we hear Paul, and
Augustine after him, advising men who cannot exercise adequate control
over their sexual organ to exercise dominion over women instead. And we
hear them advocating simultaneously that men, who cannot bear children,
should make women into their children or their childlike wards. Thus
when Augustine distinguishes between the male *spiritus* and female *anima*,
explaining that woman represents the appetite of the soul, which must be
subject to virile reasoning, he characterizes her as a dependent and subser-

vient part of the male being: "And even as in his soul there is one power which is master by virtue of counsel and another made its subject so as to obey, so also for man in the corporeal order there was made woman . . . as to bodily sex she would be subject to the male sex, just as the active appetite is made subject, so as to conceive right and prudent conduct from the rational mind" (*Confessions*, 13, 32).

When the Mother Speaks: Returning to the *Jeu d'Adam*

It is the logic underwriting these moves to make woman second in the hierarchy of mind and body that Eve's inquiring voice in the Old French *Jeu d'Adam* calls radically into question. Deconstructing the concept of woman as flesh, she reveals simultaneously woman as the source of life rather than the root of disobedience. When she responds to the devil's offer of knowledge (*saveir*) by asking "Quel savor a?" (What does it taste like?, v. 252), the heroine in this paraliturgical drama subtly dislodges the very hierarchy that holds knowledge above pleasure, undermining the necessary privileging of *saver* over *savor* and penis over vagina as an embodied locus of both sex and birth. Eve's remarks in the *Jeu d'Adam* are set within a relatively conservative retelling of the creation story from Genesis; in the play's final scenes we witness Eve condemned for disobedience and the fallen couple punished with expulsion from paradise. The play begins with a creation narrative that parallels Genesis 2 as God explains to Adam that his social superiority over Eve results from biological precedence. She was born of him: "De ta coste l'ai fourmee, / N'est pas estrange, de tei est nee. / Jo la plasmai de ton cors, / De tei eissit, non pas de fors. / Tu la governe par raison" (I formed her from your rib. She is not a foreigner, but born from you. I molded her from your body. She issued from you, not from outside. You control her through reason, vv. 17–21). The Old French text plays on the double meaning of the verb *issir* (to issue forth, to leave) as it underscores the biblical message: Because Eve issued from Adam's body, she must not leave his control but remain subservient to his governance, "A lui soies tot tens encline, / Nen issir de sa discipline" (Always bend to him; do not defy his rules, vv. 35–36).

Born of man, not woman, this female creature becomes subservient to her two male progenitors as woman's role generally in biological creation—through the process of giving birth—is displaced and eclipsed. From the opening scene of the *Jeu d'Adam*, emphasis falls on God's creative powers as he who fashioned the earth (*terre*) and heavens, formed Adam out of that earth and then made Adam in his own image (vv. 91, 99–100, 105). This succession of specular likenesses culminates in the figure of Eve, whom God formed from Adam's body (v. 19). She stands here as the last result in the chain of creation, rather than the initial source of life that simple biology would dictate. After the couple's expulsion from paradise, the displacement of woman's reproductive function onto a male Godhead resurfaces when the prophet Aaron enters holding his flowering rod. The rod, he explains, can bear flower and fruit without being planted. God produces this spiritual fruit, the fruit of salvation without "carnal engendering" (vv. 775–80). This is reproduction without vagina or womb; birth that takes place without the woman giving birth. When the fallen Adam laments that no one will be able to help him now, he refers specifically to fleshly creatures, to a "man who has been born" (N'en serrai trait por home né, v. 377), which is to say "man born of woman." It is only Christ, born miraculously from the Virgin (v. 382), who can save men. Woman's role in giving birth is again effaced in the name of a higher, male principle of generation through the defeminized woman, the Virgin, a female whose full reproductive capacity has been usurped and appropriated by the ultimate creator, God. Rather than the source of all life, Eve becomes the root of disobedience. Speaking in the register of patriarchal discourse that constructs her as female deviance, she says to Adam, "Tu mesfesis, mes jo sui la racine" (You behaved improperly, but I am the root cause, v. 581).

But this vernacular scenario of failed female reproduction, not unlike Aristotle's confused account of female biology or Galen's depiction of the woman's masculinized reproductive organs, also situates the unproductive female body at the origin of life, here the origin of mankind. Repeated references to the lineage that will "come out of" this first woman return us via the Old French verb *issir* to prior references to Eve coming out of Adam's body and therefore not being able to rightfully leave his side. But the connotations have changed in this instance. In condemning all of Eve's lineage as the future bearers of her sin, the text proclaims this first woman to be nonetheless the source of future generations: "Toit ceals qui de tei istront" (All those who will come from you, v. 459). They will issue from her, not Adam. She remains, even here, a kind of prime matter from which all human beings descend.

What precisely then is the role of Eve's body and flesh in this vernacular adaptation of the Genesis story? Following Augustine's reading of Paul, the *Jeu d'Adam* casts Eve as the weaker vessel who was seduced by the serpent: "Si jo mesfis," she says, "ne fu merveille grant, / Quant traï moi le serpent suduiant. / Mult set de mal." (It should come as no surprise that I behaved improperly, since I was betrayed by the seductive serpent. He's full of evil, vv. 465–67). Adam, though influenced by the words of his wife, was not seduced per se: "Jo ai mesfait par ma mollier" (I sinned because of my wife, v. 422). We might want to ask here in what way was Eve seduced and by whom, really? If her body is synonymous with the flesh, whose flesh is in question or at stake? What exactly is the sin of disobedience that Eve personifies in this paraliturgical version of the creation story?

After eating the forbidden fruit, Adam voices a long lament for having allowed his wife to come between himself and his creator (vv. 315–56) that culminates in a passage of direct address to Eve. The regret expressed by the fallen man is curiously not over Eve's disobedient speech or actions. Adam's initial lament concerns rather a struggle that he waged against a member of his own body, here represented by the missing rib. He blames woman specifically for having been born from his body, "Ai! femme deavee! / Mal fussez vus de moi nee!" (Oh! Bewitched woman! How unfortunate that you were born from me, vv. 357–58), wishing that the rib taken from his side had been burned and destroyed so that it could not launch such an attack against him, "Car fust arse iceste coste / Qui m'ad mis en si male poste! / Car fust la coste en fu brudlee / Qui m'ad basti si grant meslee!" (Would that this rib, which has put me in such a sorry state and which launched such a struggle against me, had been burned, vv. 359–62). It is the rib here, not the woman, that is decried for having betrayed the whole body, making it crazy or senseless, "La coste ad tut le cors traï / E afolé e mal bailli" (The rib betrayed the entire body and made it crazy and mistreated it, vv. 365–66). The use of *afolé* to characterize the wayward rib echoes an earlier passage in which disobedience to God's will and command emerge as *folie*. God tells Adam early in the play that if Eve fails to listen to his commandment, she will lack wisdom: "Se nel entent, donc s'afoloie" (If she does not listen, she'll be crazy, v. 60). Yet we can see in Adam's prolonged lament that the problem lies not with Eve per se, but with a part of Adam's own anatomy that has gone awry, disobeyed, escaped voluntary control of his mind and reason. We are reminded of Augustine's unruly member that escapes the will's authority.

The Old French text emphasizes at every turn that the persona of Eve functions less as an independent being than as a representative part of

Adam's body. In the lines we quoted earlier, God specifies that she is not a foreign being but was born of Adam; God formed her from Adam's body, and she came out of him, not from elsewhere (vv. 17–20). Eve is Adam's *pareil*, his likeness, resembling him, (vv. 11, 373). At one point God tells Adam that he has put both good and evil in his body and that the obedient man should leave the bad and pursue only the good, "En vostre cors vus met e bien e mal: / . . . Laisse le mal e si te pren al bien" (I put both good and evil in your body; leave the evil and engage the good, vv. 65, 69). But how, one wonders, can Adam leave behind something that is a part of him? We are confronted here with two competing narratives: one locating the problem of sin and disobedience within Adam's body, the other displacing that internal, perhaps biological, dilemma of the disobedient "rib" onto Eve's *conseil*, "Ele me dona mal conseil" (She gave me bad advice, v. 356). Adam's fourteen-line harangue against his troublesome rib segues finally into a direct denunciation of Eve as his likeness/equal whose advice destroys him: "Ai, Eve! cum a mal ore! / Cume grant peine me curut sore / Quant onches fustes mi parail! / Ore sui perriz par ton conseil" (Oh Eve! How unfortunate! What great troubles surround me now. Whereas earlier you were my equal, now I am lost on account of your advice, vv. 371–73). But this advice, as in the biblical account, originates from another source, outside of Eve, independent of her: the serpent. Representative of the *folie* that stands in opposition to God's wisdom and reason, it is through the serpent that Eve succeeds in robbing Adam of his sense and reason: "Cum me tolis le sens e la raison!" (How you took away my good sense and reason, v. 537). Adam's own speech has been closely allied with that of the serpent/devil all along. The dialogue is structured so that we often hear the words issuing from Adam's voice echoed immediately in the devil's response, as if the serpent were another part of him, a second voice. One form of repetition occurs in the rhyme scheme where Adam sets the pattern and the devil follows—"Adam: 'Jo ne sai quant.' / Diabolus: 'Nel te dirrai pas en curant.'" (Adam: I don't know when"; Devil: I won't tell you hastily, vv. 119–20 and elsewhere vv. 123–24, 135–36, 138–39, 152–53, 171–72, 179–80). Another is in the repetition of words mid-line such as "Adam: 'Ne puis *saver* coment.' Diabolus: 'Vols le tu *saver*?'" (vv. 115–16, my emphasis) or "Adam: 'Quant son precept *trespasserai*.' / Diabolus: 'Quel est cist grant *trepassement*?'" (vv. 142–43, my emphasis, and elsewhere vv. 120–21, 170–71). What is this diabolical part of the archetypal man if not the troublesome, life generative "rib" that rises up against him in echo of Augustine's diabolical rising up of the flesh?

Adam's dilemma as he outlines it here is to have moved, through contact with Eve, from the world of comfortable binary oppositions that unequivocally pit God's knowledge against man's subservience, *sagesse* against *folie*, to Eve's world that mingles *savoir* with *saveur*. As Adam earlier predicted, listening to the devil "te ferra changer saver" (will change your knowledge/understanding, v. 284). But in what way? What does it mean that after eating the apple Eve sees clearly: "Or sunt mi oil tant cler veant" (Now my eyes see so clearly, v. 307) and knows all: "Sai jo trestut" (v. 310)? The knowledge gained from the apple derives only from tasting it, as Eve explains. Responding to Adam's "Est il tant bon?" (Is it good, v. 295) she says "Tu le saveras. / Nel poez saver si'n gusteras" (You will find out. You can't know until you taste it, vv. 295–96) and later "Manjue! Ten! / Par co saveras e mal e bien" (Here, eat! Then you will know about good and evil, vv. 299–300). Knowledge and the mastery that accompanies it here come from sense perception in the mouth. "Manjue, Adam!" Eve declares, "Ne faz demore! / Tu le prendras en mult bon ore." (Eat, Adam! Don't delay. Eat some soon, vv. 310–12). Although this female voice later disappears from the narrative that finally deems Eve's thoughts and acts to be transgressive and intolerable, we can hear in that text's midsection a suggestion that alternate ways of structuring knowledge exist. With her provocative query this heroine raises a question that is generally silenced as it falls into the blindspot of Western thought.

Standing at that in-between point that characterizes the neck of the cave in Plato's *hystera*, the forgotten vagina, the locus of female sexuality and reproductive capacity under erasure, Eve in this vernacular rendering of the Genesis story raises what Irigaray has called "the difficult relation of man's relation to the other" (361). As if speaking to the Latin Fathers that preceded her, to Augustine in particular whose theological writings so infuse the lines of this vernacular play, and to his philosophical ancestors in Aristotelian and Platonic thought, this Old French Eve raises an old question in a new way. When she asks what relation exists between knowledge and pleasure, the intelligible and the sensible, the rational and the irrational, the will and the body, she asks whether we cannot perhaps define these relations anew, otherwise, differently. Can we circumvent the dichotomies of binary logic that value precedence over succession: the precedence of creator over created, for example, that leads inevitably to a hierarchizing of the male head, mind, and reason over the woman's body? Can we recast the logic that remakes female biology in the service of ideology, obscuring sexual difference and female reproductive capacity behind the monolith of male subjectivity?

In asking what knowledge tastes like, this heroine opens the possibility that knowledge might exist side by side with pleasure, that obedience might be mixed with disobedience, and order with disorder, in relational dynamics that escape the polarization of rational mind and irrational body. Conflating *savoir* with *saveur*, Eve defies God's plenary word and her husband's terrestrial authority, substituting for both of these hierarchical and univocal traditions the vision of a world where opposites might coexist in a dialogic and relational dynamic. Woman's irreverent and inquiring speech here debunks Augustine's wished-for sexless Eden where the asshole could rise above farting to the heights of speech or song as the will triumphed over bodily urges. In Eve's scenario the asshole could fart *and* sing, stink and speak simultaneously. Her words, issuing from a body operating equally as matter and mind, a body that can both give birth and think, a female body not obsessed by the male desire to control unruly and unpredictable genitalia, suggest the possibility that one might live and know and think and speak *from* the body rather than feeling compelled to rise above or escape from it.

Notes

1. Michèle LeDoeuff, "Women and Philosophy," 198.

2. In earlier spiritualized and thoroughly asexual readings of Genesis, Augustine contended that there was no fleshly union before the Fall (*On Genesis Against the Manichees* and *Confessions* 13: 24). See Elizabeth Clark, "Adam's Only Companion: Augustine and the Early Christian Debate on Marriage" and "Vitiated Seeds and Holy Vessels: Augustine's Manichean Past."

3. See especially Peter Brown, *Body and Society*, chapter 19. Thomas Aquinas concurs in the *Summa Theologica*, Part I, Question 98, article 2, "Whether in the State of Innocence There Would Have Been Generation by Coition?" See also Elizabeth Clark and Herbert Richardson, *Women and Religion: A Feminist Sourcebook of Christian Thought*, 91.

4. Augustine, *Concerning the City of God Against the Pagans*, Book 14, 24: 587. This view is reiterated by Aquinas in terms of reason rather than will, *Summa Theologica*, Part I, Question 98, article 2, "Beasts are without reason. In this way man becomes, as it were, like them in coition, because he cannot moderate concupiscence. In the state of innocence nothing of this would have happened that was not regulated by reason." See Clark and Richardson, *Women and Religion*, 93.

5. "Non nollui *ab imo* sine paedore ullo ita numerosos pro arbitrio sonitus edunt," Augustine, "La Cité de Dieu," 35: 452.

6. Augustine, *The Literal Meaning of Genesis*, Book 11, 42: 58. The dichotomy recurs in many ways, as in the following excerpt from the *City of God*: "So intense is the pleasure that when it reaches its climax there is an almost total extinction of

mental alertness; the intellectual sentries, as it were, are overwhelmed" (14, 16: 577). For a discussion of how the Christian West viewed woman's wickedness as stemming directly from her body, evidenced especially in the artistic decoration of historical monuments, see Margaret Miles, *Carnal Knowing: Female Nakedness and Religious Meaning in the Christian West*, 117–44. An alternative twelfth-century view of female sexual identity can be found in Hildegard of Bingen's writings. See Prudence Allen, "Hildegard of Bingen's Philosophy of Sex Identity."

7. The Hebrew term *jada* means to know and to have sex, making the tree of knowledge and the tree of life or generation one and the same.

8. The seduction element of the watcher legend is also blended into the version of the Adam and Eve story found in the Latin *Life of Adam and Eve*. See Bernard P. Prusak, "Woman: Seductive Siren and Source of Sin? Pseudepigraphal Myth and Christian Origins." There was considerable confusion in patristic thought over the sexual character of the risen body. If woman was essentially body, she could be redeemed only by transcending her female nature. Hence Augustine's contention in the *City of God* (22, 17: 1057) that woman is restored to God only when there is no sexual differentiation of bodies. See Rosemary Radford Ruether, "Mysogynism and Virginal Feminism in the Fathers of the Church," 160–61.

9. "Mater enim quasi materia. Nam causa pater est." *Etymologies*, IX, V, 5–6.

10. Quoted in Joan Ferrante, *Woman as Image in Medieval Literature*, 20–21. Chapter 1 contains one of the earliest discussions of medieval theologians' commentaries on women. A more recent and fuller discussion can be found in R. Howard Bloch, *Medieval Misogyny and the Invention of Western Romantic Love*, esp. Chapter 3.

11. *The Letters of Abelard and Heloise*, trans. and ed. Betty Radice. This stereotypically antifeminist characterization of male/female relations seems at first an inappropriate stance for Abelard, who was known for his "evangelical feminism," a remarkably liberal and consistent theological support of women. But Abelard's personal rapport with Heloise reveals a more domineering and manipulative side to the benevolent patriarch, as Peggy Kamuf has shown, a side also evident in his comments on Genesis, perhaps not surprisingly the most anti-feminist of Abelard's writings. See Peggy Kamuf, *Fictions of Feminine Desire: Disclosures of Heloise*; and Mary Martin McLaughlin, "Abelard and the Dignity of Women."

12. Augustine locates the dilemma even more specifically in marriage because "Nothing casts down the manly mind from its heights as the fondling of women, and those bodily contacts which belong to the married state," Thomas Aquinas quoting Augustine in the *Summa Theologiae*. Cited by Eleanor Commo McLaughlin, "Equality of Souls, Inequality of Sexes: Woman in Medieval Theology," 233.

13. McLaughlin, "Abelard and the Dignity of Women," 306.

14. Thomas Aquinas, "Et sic ex tali subjectione naturaliter femina subjecta est viro, quia naturaliter in homine magis abundat discretio rationis" *Summa Theologiae* (1, Question 92, Article 2), vol. 13, p. 38.

15. Elaine Pagels, *Adam, Eve, and the Serpent*, 78–97.

16. Brown, *Body and Society*, 408, 418, 422.

17. See Ian Maclean, *The Renaissance Notion of Woman*, 9, for an explanation

of how Peter 3:7, referring to woman as the "weaker vessel," prompted scholastic thinkers among others to deduce diminished mental powers, especially reason, in the female.

18. Ecclesiasticus (or the Wisdom of Jesus ben Sirach) 25:24–26. See Bernard Prusak, "Woman," 96.

19. Prusak, "Woman," 102, 104.

20. See *De Trinitate* 6:12, where Augustine fuses Genesis with 1 Corinthians 11:3–12 (*PL* 42, 946).

21. See 1 Cor 11:3, "But I want you to understand that the head of every man is Christ, the head of a woman is her husband, and the head of Christ is God."

22. Augustine, Epistle 262 to Ecdicia and the following references to women obeying their husbands: 1 Peter 3:1–7, Ephesians 5:21–6:9.

23. *Le Jeu d'Adam*, ed. Willem Noomen. This paraliturgical drama has traditionally been interpreted by French commentators as highly profane, even a precursor to the later Old French farce (Gustave Cohen, *Histoire de la mise en scène dans le théâtre religieux du Moyen Âge*, esp. 57), whereas scholars of English literature tend to give the play a more orthodox reading. Steven Justice argues, for example, that the play demonstrates to the laity the need for salvation and penance during the Lenten season, and he provides, in the process, a thorough account of arguments on both sides, "The Authority of Ritual in the *Jeu d'Adam*." Joseph Dane's sociohistorical reading sees the play as promoting the rise of the clerical class, "Clerical Propaganda in the Anglo-Norman *Representacio Ade (Mystère d'Adam)*." For a more recent and very incisive reading that preserves the ambiguities and inherent contradictions in the very project of transposing a biblical narrative into vernacular drama, see Jonathan Beck, "Genesis, Sexual Antagonism, and the Defective Couple of the Twelfth-Century *Jeu d'Adam*."

24. "La coste ad tut le cors trai" (v. 365); "Ore sui perriz par ton conseil. / Par ton conseil sui mis a mal" (vv. 374–75). For an explanation of how the play's author follows an exegetical tradition stemming from Augustine's *De Genesi contra Manichaeos*, see Larry Crist, "*Le Jeu d'Adam* et l'exégèse de la chute."

25. "Ta moiller creïstes plus que moi" (v. 423).

26. vv. 188, 197, 356 vs. v. 71.

27. "Bien te pois creire a ma parole" (v. 219).

28. "Jo ai guerpi mun criator / Par le conseil de mal uxor" (vv. 321–22). The discussion of woman's dangerous speech is cast here significantly in dialogue, highlighting speech acts of female and male protagonists. See Eugene Vance, "The Apple as Feather," in his *Mervelous Signals*; and on the *Jeu d'Adam* more generally, see Sarah White, "The Old French *Jeu d'Adam*: Latin *ordo*, Vernacular Play."

29. "Oï, male femme, plaine de traïson! / Tant m'as mis tost en perdicion! / Cum me tolis le sens e la raison!" (vv. 535–37).

30. Maurice Accarie has argued cogently that Eve's sin in this play is to break with woman's subordinate role and insist on sexual equality ("Féminisme et anti-féminisme dans le *Jeu d'Adam*).

31. "Ço est le fruit de sapience, / De tut saveir done science" (vv. 157–58).

32. Hélène Cixous and Catherine Clément, *The Newly Born Woman*, 63.

33. I do not mean to imply here that Eve in the *Jeu d'Adam* illustrates a female

mode of knowing based on a fixed gender identity such as that found in the analyses of Evelyn Fox Keller, Nancy Chodorow, Carol Gilligan, and Susan Bordo, where cognition and emotion remain separate poles. Rather I want to suggest that Eve's words in the *Jeu d'Adam* outline the possibility of a dialogic relation between cognition and emotion, knowledge and pleasure. For a critique of the aforementioned readings of female knowing, see Toril Moi, "Patriarchal Thought and the Drive for Knowledge," 189–205.

34. Elizabeth Clark explains that from 418 or 419 until Augustine's death in 430, Julian charged him with Manichean-like beliefs in the body as evil. Augustine's protracted response to Julian is found in his *On Marriage and Concupiscence*, Book II; *Against Two Epistles of the Pelagians*; *Against Julian*; and finally in the *Opus imperfectum* quoted below, where Augustine cites passages from Julian's *To Florus*. See Clark's introduction to her translation, *Julian of Eclanum, Ad Florum*.

35. Elizabeth Clark's translation of *Julian of Eclanum, to Florus*, 156–68.

36. For a study of caesarean birth in the Middle Ages that includes a section on medieval attitudes toward childbirth generally, see Renate Blumenfeld-Kosinski, *Not of Woman Born: Representations of Caesarean Birth in Medieval and Renaissance Culture*, esp. chapter 1.

37. 1 Tim 2:12–14. For a fascinating, if problematic, rereading of Genesis 1–3 that argues for the equal status of Adam and Eve during creation and the Fall, demonstrating how Paul and subsequent commentators misread the biblical text, see Mieke Bal, "Sexuality, Sin, and Sorrow: The Emergence of Female Character (A Reading of Genesis 1–3)"; and Teresa de Lauretis's review of this essay, *Semiotica* 67, 3–4 (1987).

38. Patricia Parker, "Coming Second: Woman's Place."

39. See Vern Bullough, "Medieval Medical and Scientific Views of Women"; Helen Rodnite Lemay, "Human Sexuality in Twelfth- Through Fifteenth-Century Scientific Writings," and "Some Thirteenth- and Fourteenth-Century Lectures on Female Sexuality." For a compact discussion of how medieval theological views of women derive from antique sources, see Elizabeth Robertson, "Medieval Views of Female Spirituality," in her *Early English Devotional Prose and the Female Audience*; and on the subject more generally, Thomas Laqueur, *Making Sex: Body and Gender from the Greeks to Freud*.

40. See Vern Bullough, "Medieval Views," 492.

41. See Elizabeth Spelman, "Woman as Body: Ancient and Contemporary Views," 111.

42. See Jane Flax, "Political Philosophy and the Patriarchal Unconscious: A Psychoanalytic Perspective on Epistemology and Metaphysics," 258.

43. Plato, *Timaeus*, 91A–B.

44. For a more detailed analysis of how Plato transfers the female's power of reproduction to the art of the male philosopher, see Page duBois, *Sowing the Body: Psychoanalysis and Ancient Representations of Women*, 169–83.

45. Luce Irigaray, *Speculum of the Other Woman*, 243–364.

46. Irigaray, "How to Conceive (of) a Girl," *Speculum of the Other Woman*, 160–68.

47. Aristotle, *De generatione animalium*, vol. 5 of *The Works of Aristotle*, 729 a.

48. A lesser male, woman is also portrayed in this view as a failed, nonvirile male because she lacks semen: "the woman is, as it were, an impotent male, for it is through a certain incapacity that the female is female, being incapable of concocting the nutriment in its last stage into semen" (*De generatione animalium*, 728A).

49. See Lynda Lange, "Woman is Not a Rational Animal: On Aristotle's Biology of Reproduction."

50. On Aristotle's writings about women generally, see Prudence Allen, *The Concept of Woman: The Aristotelian Revolution 750 BC–AD 1250*, 251–478; and Fernand van Steenberghen, *La philosophie au XIIIe siècle*, chapters 4, 6, 8.

51. Aristotle also states, "no bodily activity has any connection with reason," 736b.

52. Aristotle, *De generatione animalium*, 731b.

53. In Aristotle's *Politics* and *Nichomachean Ethics*, the social implications of this theory of generation become explicit when he argues that men, by nature, should be the rulers of women. The rational part of the soul should rightfully rule over the irrational part, except in women, slaves, and children, who often lack the capacity to deliberate, he claims. (See Elizabeth Spelman, "Aristotle and the Politicization of the Soul," 23).

54. Sarah Kofman, *L'Énigme de la femme: La femme dans les textes de Freud*, 132, 170–72, 226.

55. Mieke Bal, "Sexuality, Sin, and Sorrow."

56. Pagels, *Adam, Eve, and the Serpent*, 57–77.

57. Augustine, *De Genesi ad litteram* 9, 5: 9. See also 9, 9: 15 and *City of God* 14, 22.

58. Augustine, *Letters*, No. 243.

59. I see here a more fundamental hierarchical reversal than the process of "gender switching" outlined by Stephen G. Nichols, who contends that Augustine "makes Eve's desire the model for masculine (adulterous) concupiscence. In other words, Augustine sees carnality as mimetic gender switching: men may lust, but in so doing they cast themselves in a feminine image" ("Rewriting Marriage in the Middle Ages," especially 47–48).

60. The Gnostic interpretations of Genesis, long suppressed by Orthodox Christianity, offer alternative scenarios. Although Philo of Alexandria casts Adam as the nobler, rational element made in God's image and Eve as body and sensation, the majority of known Gnostic texts depict Adam as the psyche and Eve as the higher principle, the spiritual itself. See Elaine Pagels, *Adam, Eve, and the Serpent*, chapter 3.

PART II

Desiring Ladies

T he authors of Old French courtly romance could be said without
exaggeration to have suffered from the Pygmalion complex. Miming
the work of Ovid's model artist and mastercraftsman, twelfth-century romance narrators often paint portraits of idealized feminine beauty that
suggest posed statues rather than living flesh. The fetishized bodies of romance heroines are typically frozen in descriptions of isolated body parts,
descriptions that most often descend from an initial focus on the woman's
hair to a sustained look at the face and its features, passing quickly past
the neck and chest to glimpse the hands and hips.[1] Dismembered and
objectified by the gaze of the male narrator and/or protagonist whose observation constructs the desired and desirable female, these women's bodies, though they appear in public and are presumed to be clothed, are
described nonetheless as if they were naked. The eyes of the beholder seem
magically to undress the beautiful anatomy they perceive, or rather imagine. Emphasis falls throughout the standard portrait of medieval beauty
on the whiteness of the woman's exposed skin, whether of the face, hands,
chest, shoulders, or bosom, and we typically hear of her round, firm—and
seemingly bare—breasts. Such portraits recall most directly the sexually
charged image of Pygmalion's ivory statue, who was said in the Ovidian
tale to be "even more lovely naked" than if she were wearing clothes.[2]
Ovid's text and its medieval descendants, however, while suggesting the
allure of an unclothed female body, never actually expose the woman's
nakedness or the sexual difference it would entail.

In an opposing gesture Pygmalion later dresses his statue, further
fetishizing the beloved "body he has fashioned" (*Metamorphoses*, 242) by
covering the skin with lavish decoration: "He decks her limbs with dresses,
and her fingers / With rings which he puts on, and he brings a neck-
lace, / And earrings, and a ribbon for her bosom" (242), only to prefer the
naked body finally to the sumptuously adorned one. And romance authors, despite the general absence of allusions to clothing in the standard
medieval catalogue of isolated body parts, do elsewhere typically indulge
in lengthy descriptions of the heroine's dress. At these moments we confront a female body that seems oddly without flesh, as the sexual difference

marking the heroine's anatomy recedes yet again, this time to disappear altogether behind abundant layers of clothing that both adorn and conceal it. The most extreme example of this phenomenon is provided by Chrétien de Troyes's protracted description of the dress and cloak given to Enide by Queen Guenevere on the occasion of the young heroine's wedding in *Erec et Enide*. We hear over the course of some eighty-five lines the intricate details of this heroine's garb: the rich green, patterned cloth that makes up the dress, its sleeves lined with ermine, the gold trim inlaid with stones of violet, green, deep blue and grey-brown. We learn of the cloak's golden fasteners, its double sable collar and lining of rich cloth worked with criss-cross designs in violet, red, indigo, white, green, blue, and yellow (vv. 1575–1660). But where is the woman in this elaborate portrait of femininity?

Whether excessively overdressed or metaphorically undressed, the beautiful, idolized female body in Old French tales of love and romance attracts and seduces, ironically, to the extent that it is "not where it is." I borrow the formulation from Hélène Cixous's reading of fairy tales in which she defines female beauty as less an attribute of woman's anatomy than a product of male erotic fantasy. The fairy tale heroine in Cixous's terms is

> Absent, hence desirable, a dependent nonentity, hence adorable. Because she isn't there where she is. As long as she isn't where she is.[3]

For the medieval heroine whose fetishized body functions as an object of exchange between men—Philomena between her father and the ravisher Tereus, Enide between her father and her future husband Erec, Iseut between King Marc and her lover Tristan—desirability derives from two criteria: the extent to which the female anatomy is first eroticized by the male gaze that constructs it as a collection of seemingly naked body parts and the extent to which that same body is then desexualized beneath extravagant and sumptuous clothing. Irigaray has cogently explained, for bodies of later historical periods, the import of such a double play that appears to reveal the woman's sexuality while actually hiding her sex:

> Though her body is beautiful and she is decked out in gold for him and by him, woman will still be reserved, modest, shameful, as far as her sexed organs are concerned. She will discreetly assist in hiding them. Ensuring this *double game* of flaunting her body, her jewels, in

order to hide her sex organs all the better. For woman's "body" has some "usefulness," represents some "value" only on condition that her sex organs are hidden. Since they are something and nothing in consumer terms.[4]

This is Irigaray's ironic response to Freud's comment about weaving and female narcissism: woman's sole contribution to the history of civilization—the craft of weaving—constitutes a natural extension of woman's lack. Through weaving, Freud contends, women repeat the gesture of the pubic hairs that hide the specificity of female genitalia. In beautifying her own body with elegant clothing, the woman attempts to conceal a deficient body, to cover over her castration. But Irigaray explains how this view of corporeal vanity in the female results from a prior male desire to establish the woman as an object worthy of his desire, one that shows no obvious lack. If "woman weaves to sustain the disavowal of her sex" (*Speculum*, 116), she does so only as an extension and reification of the effect of the male gaze that tries to reshape her body by hiding its genital difference.

The importance of Irigaray's insight for readers of courtly romance is that it explains the relation between gestures of fetishizing the naked female body on the one hand and moves to cover it up on the other. To metaphorically undress the heroine with a gaze that displaces erotic interest from the female genitalia onto other body parts, produces the same effect as covering up the woman's body with clothes that make it all the more attractive. Both gestures deny sexual difference while eroticizing the heroine into a seductive and desirable Beauty.

It is in this sense that courtly romance most closely resembles what Cixous has referred to as stories of "once upon a time," fairy tales where heroines follow the paradigm of Sleeping Beauty, who "has the perfection of something finished. Or not begun. However, she is breathing. Just enough life—and not too much. Then he will kiss her. So that when she opens her eyes she will see only *him*; him in place of everything, all-him" (*Newly Born Woman*, 66). This dream plot of the beautiful woman falling in love leaves no more room for female subjectivity (67) than does Ovid's awakening of Pygmalion's "ivory girl" : "The lips he kisses / are real indeed, the ivory girl can feel them, / And blushes and responds, and the eyes open, / At once on lover and heaven" (*Metamorphoses*, 243). Once awakened, neither of these slumbering beauties—Ovid's rendition of Galatea nor Cixous's depiction of Sleeping Beauty—is fully alive, for neither one speaks. Indeed, as Cixous reminds us, the Sleeping Beauty scenario ends when the woman wakes up: "He leans over her. . . . Cut. The tale is finished. Curtain. Once awake (him or her), it would be an entirely different story. Then there would be two people, perhaps. You never know with women" (66).

But courtly romance diverges from the Pygmalion and Sleeping Beauty narratives in a significant way: romance heroines are fully awake. However fetishized the bodies of courtly heroines may be, however frozen at certain moments into rigidifying portraits of perfection—they also move and talk, enacting and telling "a different story" from the one that their otherwise stereotyped and codified bodies underwrite. Within the dominant fairy story about the love of beautifully elegant courtly ladies, romance contains a rival narrative of wakeful women who, despite their arresting beauty, also speak.

I have chosen to examine in the pages that follow three twelfth-century romances whose principal heroines offer a stereotypical array of desirable and coveted female bodies: the eroticized virgin Philomena, the courtly wife and lover Enide, and the adulterous queen Iseut. As we move back in time from the exaggerated portraits of lascivious female bodies in Old French farce and fabliau, with their roots in the seductive biblical Eve, to the more delicate and beautiful heroines of courtly romance, we can begin to see how the ideology of courtly beauty provides yet another strategy for addressing the threat of female sexuality that the farce and fabliau stage more overtly. If the later, comic genres tend to reduce women to mindless, gaping orifices, bodies whose speech can be dismissed as petty harassment or idle chatter, romance constructs strikingly beautiful heroines whose perfected bodies appear to have no sexualized orifices at all. And their courtly, measured speech proves generally more alluring than hostile. Yet female sexuality and woman's corporeal nature are still very much at issue.

As the "knowing" women of fabliau, farce, and the *Jeu d'Adam* can be heard effectively to talk back to the theologically based conceptions of feminine nature that construct women as mindless bodies, so too the heroines of Old French romance talk back at key moments to their Ovidian intertext, redefining the terms of courtly love, passion, and desire that typically structure male/female relations in romance narrative. If these tales show us at great length how men desire women within an ideology of courtly love, they give us as well the inscribed voices of "desiring ladies," female protagonists whose words redefine the very terms of the medieval love scenario that constructs them as objects of desire.

We will examine in the pages that follow how medieval romance narratives from twelfth-century France play out, in a variety of ways, the paradox of the speaking statue that the tales of Pygmalion and Sleeping Beauty set up but do not explore. We will investigate, in so doing, how the medieval French love story constructs the sexualized female body, remembering along with Denise Riley that there is no "bedrock biological womanness" but always some characterization at play.[5] Keeping in mind Riley's cautionary note that constructions of the female body, whether in a historical or literary context, are historically mutable (*Am I That Name?* 104), we will ask more specifically how the anatomically gendered body is established and interpreted as "female" in twelfth-century romance. As we follow that body's fluctuations of identity and the different densities of sexed being that it takes on at different moments in the narrative, we will be asking how various literary strategies chart and categorize the "attributed being of woman" in relation to her speech (*Am I That Name?* 1, 6). In turning to Old French romance narratives featuring Philomena, Enide, and Iseut, we will see how three tales of courtly romance formulate a question reminiscent of Philomena's provocative query to Tereus, as they ask, in different ways, "what if the beautiful body constructed by the desiring male gaze could speak?" How would it tell the story differently?

3. Beauty in the Blindspot: Philomena's Talking Hands

Philomena appears in the Old French reworking of a tale from Ovid's *Metamorphoses* as a classic medieval beauty possessing all the requisite attributes of the typically gorgeous heroine in courtly romance.[6] But her portrait differs substantially from the standard depiction of the courtly lady. No extended description of this heroine's clothing is to be found in the Old French text. Indeed the lengthy and stereotypical passage attesting to Philomena's beauty begins with an unusual detail, an overt reference to the absence of clothing, at least to the absence of a nun's habit that might have otherwise veiled this woman's extraordinary physical perfection. "Ne sanbloit pas nonain velee (She did not appear as a veiled nun, v. 126), we are told, before hearing the requisite catalogue of comely anatomical features: her beautiful body and bright face are accompanied by shiny golden hair; a smooth white forehead; clear, wide-set eyes; well-formed eyebrows; a long straight nose; a pink and white complexion; a smiling mouth with full, slightly red lips; sweet breath; small white teeth closely set; a chin, neck, throat, and chest whiter than ermine; two small breasts like apples, thin long white hands; thin thighs and slightly curving hips. In contrast to the Ovidian tale, which links the heroine's beauty directly to clothes, the Old French narrative includes a single line that mentions offhandedly that Philomena was wearing a silk dress. To Ovid's "Here Philomena came, in rich apparel, / In richer grace, as lovely as the naiads, / As lovely as the dryads of the woodlands, / As lovely, rather, as they would be, if only / They had such clothes as hers" (vv. 143–44), the French text says simply: "An un samit estoit laciee."[7] The only other reference to female clothing throughout the poem occurs when Philomena's sister Progne announces that she will dress in mourning for the sister she believes to have died (v. 1005).

Fabric of various kinds, woven cloth, and weaving do play, however, a crucial role in this narrative of love, rape, and mutilation. Of all the

romances to be discussed in this study, the *Philomena* makes most explicit
the link between the female orifices of mouth and vagina and does so
through the agency of textiles. Following Ovid's plot, the Old French
Tereus savagely rapes his wife's sister, Philomena, and to prevent her from
recounting the act, cuts out her tongue. The ravaged Philomena, enclosed
in a hut where no outsider can see or hear her, then uses her womanly
skills at weaving to "write her story" into a tapestry (Tot ot escrit an la
cortine, v. 1131) that she sends to her unsuspecting sister, Progne.[8] From
the very beginning of the tale, the cloth and clothing that typically conceal
the fetishized female body in courtly romance, while obscuring the role of
women as weavers who might produce that cloth, perform a different
function. Serving as a means of communication rather than decorative
adornment, weaving here enables Philomena to speak without speaking,
to tell her silenced story in colored pictures that lead eventually to the
sisters' joint plot of revenge. Rather than producing cloth that might hide
or deny the detail of female genitalia, weaving works in this narrative to
tell the suppressed story of what can happen to female genitalia, the tale
of Tereus's handiwork—referred to repeatedly as his *oeuvre*. In fact Philomena's *cortine*, different from the clothing Freud alludes to as the product
of woman's weaving, refers most obviously to a tapestry or wall hanging.
But the Old French *cortine* also carries the more specific meaning of "bed
curtain": a tapestry that enclosed the medieval bed to produce both privacy and warmth. Upending the traditional medieval function of the
rideau de lit that would have covered lovers and hidden them from view,
Philomena's tapestry reveals Tereus's vile sexual maneuvers in a way that
also explains the "restless sleep" he suffered after gazing longingly at the
beautiful Philomena when he visited her father Pandion's castle: "Ne prist
au lit pes ne repos, / N'onques por dormir n'ot l'uel clos; / Tant con tote
la nuit dura / Tote nuit son lit mesura" (He took no rest or peace in sleep,
nor did he close his eyes in sleep. The whole night through he tossed and
turned, vv. 645–48). Others who slept soundly at the castle are said to
have known nothing of Tereus's nocturnal torment in bed: "A mout grant
eise se dormoient / Et de tot ce mot ne savoient" (They slept calmly and
knew nothing of this, vv. 655–56). Not, that is, until Philomena's bed curtain tells the tale of Tereus's sexual obsessions.

If in the Ovidian tale Philomena's weaving "threatens to retrieve from
obscurity," as Patricia Joplin has explained, "all that her culture defines as
outside the bounds of allowable discourse, whether sexual, spiritual, or

literary,"[9] the Old French *cortine* does this and more. Lengthy narrative additions in the medieval reworking of Ovid's myth allow the anonymous Old French author to focus in particular on issues of female agency. The question with which we began this study, Philomena's deft query to Tereus that asks pointedly "what women's words might be worth," is absent from the Ovidian tale, as are sustained discussions about female knowledge, skills, and talents that feed into an elaborate economy of women's collective work grounded in sight, hearing, and touch as alternatives to speech. These key features of the Old French *Philomena* are set against an extended discussion of love that, in typical medieval fashion, saps the afflicted male viewer of knowledge and self-control. As a result, Philomena's tapestry in the Old French version of the tale not only redefines the terms of female expression through speech and writing, it also recasts the standard function attributed to the beautiful body in courtly romance. Outlining an economy of seeing and knowing based on women's work that is defined in terms of gesture rather than speech, Philomena's tapestry offers a concerted challenge to the male gaze that constructs female beauty throughout the romance, displacing the beauty fashioned by Tereus's eyes to a beautiful pictorial message crafted by Philomena's hands.

To understand how this transformation occurs, we need to read the story depicted in Philomena's tapestry against the story emblematized in her sister Progne's brutal infanticide. To do so will be to practice what Nancy K. Miller, in another context, has called reading for the underread.[10] The tendency among readers of the Ovidian "Philomel" at least has been to privilege the liberating and peaceful artistry of this heroine over the male-inspired violence and brutality of her sister.[11] Indeed it is difficult to accept Progne's savage decapitation of her own son, whose body parts she subsequently cooks and serves to the unsuspecting Tereus, or to understand this act as anything but a hopeless repetition of the mutilation and dismemberment earlier visited upon Philomena.

And yet the Old French version of Ovid's tale encourages us at every turn to read these women's stories as two parallel accounts of seduction, abduction, and silencing: one of a beautiful virgin, the other a nurturing mother. We are moved by the interaction of these female protagonists to ask how rape and motherhood are related. Or more specifically, in terms of narrative outcome, we are encouraged to ponder how infanticide on Progne's part might compensate for the rape of her virgin sister. Although it is true, as Jane Marcus points out for the Ovidian version of the tale, that Philomena plays the creator/writer to her sister's role as reader/receiver of the fateful message (79), there is also an important way in which both women, especially in the French text, can be seen as writers who recast standard narrative plots. They do so not with words—written or oral— but by using their hands to draw portraits that must be seen in order to be read. Philomena's tapestry retells the story of erotic beauty that typically features a seductive virgin who guarantees male pleasure. Progne's barbaric meal recasts the narrative of unfaltering maternal love that focuses traditionally on the mother who guarantees male patrimony and the husband's legal right to possess offspring. Repetition of the words *issir* (to issue forth, come out of, be born) and *norreture* (nourishment, feeding) links these two projects by pairing the female orifices of vagina and mouth in a way that Tereus in his roles as rapist and husband/father could never have imagined.

In the Introduction we discussed the effects of Philomena's speech to Tereus. This chapter will examine the silent gestures of Philomena and her sister Progne, showing how the stories they tell with their hands redefine the parameters of woman's speech. Taken together, these women's stories provide an unexpected answer to Philomena's probing question about what woman's words could be worth.

Beauty and Knowledge

The portrait of Philomena's extraordinarily lovely body described above does not provide a complete picture of her beauty. To the standard medieval catalogue of fetishized female body parts, the Old French text appends a list of things that this heroine knows how to do, thereby imputing agency to that same fetishized object. But initially, we hear only of a beautiful body carefully fashioned by the text's narrator[12] along with God and Nature, who function as parallel creators of the heroine's beauty.[13] The opening description is governed tellingly by repeated use of the verb *avoir*, which constructs Philomena as an alluring object of desire who *has* a smooth white forehead, a lady who *has* a high long straight nose or who *has* small close set teeth (Le front *ot* blanc et plain sanz fronce . . . Le nes *ot* haut et lonc et droit, . . . Danz *ot* petiz, serrez et blans, vv. 145, 149, 158). This standard usage of the verb *avoir* suggests to the attentive listener not that Philomena possesses these qualities herself, but that she "has" them in the eye of the beholder. Indeed Philomena's beauty derives in this instance from Tereus's gaze as he observes her stately entrance into the room.

The subsequent cataloguing of the extraordinary beauty that the ravisher's sight constructs, focuses in typical medieval fashion on the heroine's head and face: sixteen out of twenty-one lines (vv. 143–58) are devoted to these uppermost body parts. Most significantly, however, special attention is paid within this portrait to the heroine's mouth, which receives nearly half of those sixteen lines:

> Boche riant, levres grossettes
> Et un petitet vermeillettes
> Plus que samiz vermaus an grainne,
> Et plus soef oloit s'alainne
> Que pimanz ne basmes d'ancans;
> Danz ot petiz, serrez et blans
>
> (vv. 153–58)

(A smiling mouth, plump lips, a little reddish. Redder than red silk cloth. And her breath smelled sweeter than spice and incense. She had small white teeth, close together).

Philomena's other attributes are allotted only an average of one or two lines apiece. This heroine's mouth is, interestingly, an alluring, erotic, and seductive mouth, a smiling mouth with plump reddish lips that evoke the other erotic female lips unmentioned here except as they appear euphemistically as *le sorplus* (v. 165), meaning generally "all the rest" and more specifically the unspeakable "female genitalia." Philomena's teeth are typically small: delicate and not menacing (v. 158). But most importantly her tongue, which is necessary for speech, is absent. This is the beautiful body that speaks the language of seduction without speaking at all,[14] a body whose beauty allures, even compels, Tereus to fall hopelessly, helplessly in love with it.

In its utter silence this beautifully constructed body differs little from the body of the heroine subjected to rape a few scenes later. There, Tereus's uncontestable power as subject of the action is rendered most clearly in the reduction of the female object of desire to its smallest and most objectified linguistic unit. The desired woman becomes no more than the direct object pronoun "la":

> Car cil totes voies l'assaut,
> Si l'esforce tant et justise
> Que tot a force l'a conquise
> Et trestot son buen an a fet
>   (vv. 836–39, my emphasis)

(He attacks her immediately, he so overpowers and dominates her that he conquers her by force. And he takes his pleasure from her)

There is no Beauty here. Only body remains as a haunting echo of the more subtle reduction of woman to body parts charted in the preceding glorified image of femininity.

A crucial feature of this speechless body is that it lacks not only a mouth to articulate thoughts but even a brain to conceive them. We are reminded repeatedly of Philomena's naive ignorance. She suspected nothing of Tereus's ulterior motive:

> Cele ne set que ce puet estre
> Ne ne se puet aparcevoir
> Que cil la vueille decevoir
>   (vv. 746–48)

(She does not know what this might mean. She cannot imagine that he wants to trick her)

She cannot conceive of Tereus's plot:

> Mout cuidoit bien estre seure
> D'aler bien et de revenir.
> Et comant poïst ç'avenir
> Que s'apansast de la mervoille
> Que li tiranz li aparoille?
>   (vv. 678–82)

(She thought she would be safe in going and returning. How could she have imagined the incredible incident that the tyrant was preparing for her?)

She later laments her inability to perceive his ruse:

> Ha, lasse, por quoi ne conui
> La feintise et la traïson
>   (vv. 826–27)[15]

(Alas, why didn't I recognize his dissembling and betrayal?)

The second half of Philomena's portrait offers an altogether different image of the heroine's reputed beauty, as repetition of the verb *avoir* gives way to phrases dominated instead by *savoir*. Two pivotal lines make the transition:

> Avuec la grant biaute qu'ele *ot*
> *Sot* quanque doit savoir pucele
>   (vv. 170–71)

(Along with the great beauty she possessed, she knew everything a young woman should know)

Philomena's beauty is rivaled only her knowledge (*sagesse*), we are told, "Ne fu pas mains sage que bele" (She was no less wise than beautiful), in a second portrait that grants to the quintessentially beautiful heroine a subjectivity missing from the earlier account:

> Plus sot de joie et de deport
> Qu'Apoloines ne que Tristanz,
> Plus an sot voire voir dis tanz.
> Des tables sot et des eschas,
> Del vieil jeu et del "sis et as",
> De la bufe et de la hamee.
> Por son deduit esoit amee
> Et requise de hauz barons.
> D'espreviers sot et de faucons
> Et del jantil et del lanier;
> Bien sot feire un faucon muiier
> Et un ostor et un tercuel.
>   (vv. 174–85)

(She knew more about games and pleasure—ten times more—than Apollonius or Tristan. She knew how to play chess, backgammon, and the old six and ace game. She knew the slap and trap game too. Because of her delight in games she was loved and sought after by noble lords. She knew about sparrowhawks and falcons, gentles and lanners. She knew how to moult a falcon, a goshawk or a tercel.)

Here and in the following nineteen lines (vv. 186–204) the silent and statuesque female body comes to life. Philomena knows more about joy and amusement than Apollonius and Tristan, acclaimed in the twelfth and thirteenth centuries as accomplished performers and musicians. Her skill at games—she knows dice, chess, backgammon—is matched by a specialized knowledge of hawking and hunting. Along with these, she has unparalleled talents of weaving and working cloth: "Avuec c'iert si bone ovriere / D'ovrer une porpre vermoille / Qu'an tot le mont n'ot sa paroille" (In addition, she was such an accomplished weaver/embroiderer that no one in the world could equal her at weaving/embroidering red cloth, vv. 188–90).

So skilled is Philomena at weaving, moreover, that in addition to creating the complicated patterns of figured silk, she can depict Hellequin's troop. That is to say that she can make cloth talk:

Un diaspre ou un baudequin
Nes la mesniee Hellequin
Seust ele an un drap portreire
                    vv. 191–93

(On patterned or rich silk, she knew how to depict in cloth even Hellequin's followers)

This harlequin's troop was thought in the Middle Ages to be a band of suffering souls who, under the guidance of Hellequin, wandered through the night making a hideous racket. To portray them fully would require images and sounds, to relay voice through weaving or to make cloth speak much in the way Philomena uses the famed tapestry later in the tale to convey her own speech. We also learn from this portrait that Philomena's knowledge of the authors and grammar enables her to write verse and prose. She knows how to play the psaltery, the lyre, the mandolin, and the rote and can reproduce any sound or note on the medieval stringed instrument called the *viol*.

More than simply imputing agency to the beautiful body of the preceding portrait, this long list of talents significantly rewrites the earlier account by shifting the previous focus on the woman's face, as a surrogate for female genitalia, to another emblematic body part: the hands.[16] What is implied by the repeated invocation of *savoir* to describe Philomena's gameplaying, hawking, writing, and music playing is the activity of able hands that carry out these tasks. The heroine's hands here differ radically in their role and function from the "thin white delicate hands" that were cast in a studied immobility in the first portrait, making them seem incapable of action.

The list of activities that Philomena *knows* how to carry out ends, significantly, with a reference to her accomplished speech: so well (knowledgeably) does she speak that she could teach others the art of speaking:[17]

Et tant sot sagement parler
Que solemant de sa parole
Seust ele tenir escole
(vv. 202–4)

(And she knew how to speak so well that she could teach oratory
to others)

Speaking, one might think initially, differs from the other activities comprising Philomena's *sagesse* in that it does not require use of the hands. And yet that is the very point of this tale in one respect at least: that one can speak with the hands to produce images in weaving as one might also produce sounds in music, gestures in hawking, words in writing, all of which could substitute for meaningful speech and voice. The point is especially cogent for female protagonists so often constructed in the standard portrait of medieval beauty as the artistic product of male hands. If in Chrétien's *Yvain*, Laudine's great beauty comes from the hand of God, "Don fust si grant biaute venue? / Ja la fist *Dex, de sa main* nue" (Where did such great beauty come from? God made it with his own hands, vv. 1501–2, my emphasis), Blancheflor emerges in the *Perceval* as a double of Pygmalion's well-crafted statue:

> Le front ot haut et blanc et plain
> Come s'il fust *ovrez a main*,
> Et que de *main d'ome* ovrez fust
> De pierre ou d'yvoire ou de fust.
> (vv. 1815–18, my emphasis)

(She had a high, white, smooth forehead as if worked by hand, the way a man's hand fashions stone or ivory or wood.)

If Philomena is fashioned by Nature's touch and the narrator's words, she also writes and tells her own story in a tapestry made by hand.

In a very subtle way, Philomena's talent at speaking through pictures, cast in the second portrait as an uncanny ability to weave or work costly red silk like no one else (vv. 189–90), is itself woven into the initial portrait of her silent face. In a highly atypical line, used to describe this heroine's slightly reddish lips, those very lips that will soon be unable to send any message, we learn that they are redder than cloth. They are redder even than scarlet samite dyed expensively with cochineal:

> Boche riant, levres grossettes
> Et un petitet vermeillettes
> Plus que samiz vermauz an grainne.
> (vv. 153–55)

(A smiling mouth, plump lips and slightly reddish, redder than red silk cloth.)

This allusion to colored cloth announces very early in the tale how the heroine's lovely lips might later be replaced by skilled hands that tell a woven story, much as the reference to her portraying Hellequin's troops implies an uncanny skill at speaking without words.

The Politics of the Male Gaze

If this message regarding Philomena's exceptional gifts is given to us, the reader/listener, from the outset of the tale, its import remains well hidden from Tereus, who imagines confidently that depriving Philomena of her tongue will effectively prevent her from recounting her tale. That Tereus sees only the lovely and powerless Philomena as constructed by the initial catalogue of her physical beauty is made especially clear when the lengthy indexing of all the heroine's features comes to an end. As Philomena advances to embrace her father and Tereus, the accomplished heroine said to be amply endowed with knowledge and diverse skills dissolves for a brief moment into thin air. In her stead the beautified and disembodied face of the earlier portrait emerges to represent her. "Vermoille" now refers only to the heroine's complexion and "samit" to the silk cloth enveloping her eroticized body:

> La pucele vint a son pere
> Qui la face ot vermoille et clere;
> An un samit estoit laciee
> Et Tereus l'a anbraciee,
> Si la salue et beise ansanble.
> Si granz biautez son cuer li anble
> Et sa tres bele contenance.
>
> (vv. 205–11)

(The young girl came to her father, her light skin blushing. She was laced in silk and Tereus embraced her. He greeted her and they kissed. Her great beauty and beautiful looks stole his heart.)

The "tres bele contenance" that Tereus sees and kisses has none of the attributes so carefully laid out in the preceding description of Philomena's *sagesse*. Unlike the earlier account, this portrait of Philomena's beauty results as much from Tereus's longing gaze as from the narrator's creative words. In typical medieval fashion, Tereus's attraction to Philomena derives from visual observation:

> Mes Tereus ne se deduit
> An nul servise qu'an li face
> S'au jant cors non et an la face
> De la pucele regarder.
>
> (vv. 596–99)

(Tereus takes no pleasure in anything they do for him. He derives pleasure only from looking at the beautiful body and face of the young woman).

His all-consuming look replaces even the consumption of food and drink:

A grant mervoille la regarde
Qu'a nule autre rien n'est pansis.
Au mangier ont longuemant sis
Et mout li pleisoit a seoir,
Plus por la pucele veoir
Que por boivre ne por mangier.
                    (vv. 608–13)

(He looks at her in wonder thinking of nothing else. They sat a long time while eating and it pleased him to sit there more in order to look at the young woman than to eat or drink.)

Similar sentiments are expressed by Philomena's father Pandion. When Philomena is about to leave for Thrace, her father begs her to return promptly because seeing her brings him such great pleasure, "Car tant sui liez quant je te voi / Et tant ai de joie et de bien" (I am so delighted when I see you. It gives me such joy and well-being, vv. 692–93).[18] The sexual connotations of this remark, well hidden behind the pose of a concerned parent, become more obvious in another passage where Pandion explains his reluctance to let his daughter depart. It is the way Philomena serves him, he says, that pleases him so much, the way she waits on him day and night, putting on his shoes and dressing him, "Que ma fille me garde et sert / Et nuit et jor et soir et main; . . . Ma douce fille m'a tant chier / Qu'ele me chauce, ele me vest, / Et son servise tant me plest" (My daughter takes care of me and serves me night and day, evening and morning . . . My sweet daughter holds me so dear that she dresses me and puts on my shoes. Her service pleases me so, vv. 370–71, 374–76). In effect both men, despite their diverse characterizations as treacherous tyrant and loving father, want to have Philomena in their company so they can watch her as she pleases and serves them. That is what makes her beautiful in their eyes.

Denise Riley has taught us how "the body becomes visible as a body and as a female body only under some particular gaze," a historicized gaze specific in time and place (106). Tereus's gaze is that of the medieval lover conditioned by that particular brand of Ovidian passion that typically makes the suitor ill, crazy, and speechless, reducing him to utter helplessness. Love in this formulation reverses the standard male/female relation by making women into warriors who hunt their male prey. Tereus thus falls victim to a love that attacks him, "Qu'Amors a vers lui prise guerre" (Love made war on him, v. 238), a love that temporarily vanquishes and destroys the most valiant of men: "Folie? Mes Amors, ce cuit, / Cele qui tot vaint et destruit" (Was it madness? No, Love, I think, who vanquishes and destroys all, vv. 393–94).

In a curious reversal of gender roles, love is shown here to empower women with the amorous equivalent of the military might generally reserved for medieval knights. The suitors themselves become concomitantly more womanlike, losing their strength, their wits, and often their rational speech. As Tereus falls prey to Philomena's alluring body, emotion overtakes his intellect, "Sa folie son savoir vaint," forcing him to adopt behaviors appropriate to the stereotypical female.[19] In a desperate attempt to gain possession of his "beloved," Tereus lies, cajoles, begs, and pleads: "Tant a li fel tiranz luitie / Par fiancier et par jurer / Et par proiier et par plorer / Qu'il espleita si con li plot" (The treacherous tyrant had battled so long, promising, swearing, begging, and crying, manipulating in every way he could, vv. 548–51). Having fallen under the spell of love, this powerful monarch falls apart emotionally, sobbing uncontrollably at his initial inability to satisfy his desire. One thinks here of the distraught husbands in the "Farce moralisée," men who are powerless to bring their wives' bodies under their control, or of the impassioned husband in the "Four Wishes of Saint Martin," who is utterly at the mercy of his wife's whimsical wish. All are scrambling to maintain *savoir* in their camp alone, to keep the female body in a position of intellectual subservience.

When we hear in Tereus's case that it is specifically the sight of woman, the very woman his gaze constructs, that supposedly robs the male subject of the control and mastery that typically accompany his *savoir*, the claim rings false. "Knowing" for Tereus, as for the ogling Pandion, means controlling the female body through the desiring look they cast upon it, freezing it as an object of their gaze much as the medieval narrator does in his standard portrait of feminine beauty. When we are told that even the tongues of Plato, Homer, and Cato, men "de grant savoir," would not have been able to narrate the "granz biaute" of Philomena, our credulity wanes further. The woman's *granz biaute* is precisely what fills the pages of ancient and medieval accounts of female protagonists. It is woman's *savoir* in all the complexity suggested by this narrator's second portrait of Philomena that typically escapes the pen or voice of the knowledgeable male creator, whose desiring eyes read the body alone, much as Tereus reads only beauty.

The Economy of Women's Work

Atypically, the Old French *Philomena* offers, against the politics of the male gaze on female beauty, an alternate economy of seeing and knowing cast in terms of women's work. Sight more than speech connects the female protagonists throughout this tale but it is a sight moving between women that restructures the abuse of power enshrined in the classic male gaze. Progne's initial request to Tereus articulates a desire not only to visit but specifically to see her sister: "De Philomena sa seror / Ot talant que veoir l'alast" (She wanted to go see Philomena her sister, vv. 52–53). Tereus denies this request in two lines that exploit the homophony between the Old French *voie* referring to the path one travels and *voie* meaning sight:

> Et si il li deffant la voie
> Tant qu'ele sa seror ne voie.
> > (vv. 61–62)

(And he forbid her passage (the path) to see her sister.)

The sisters work throughout the narrative to establish and pursue that *voie* that will enable them to see each other again. Progne's disappointment at not seeing Philomena when Tereus returns from Athens, "Car tot maintenant qu'ele vit / Son seignor et sa compaignie / Et de sa seror ne vit mie" (Now she saw her husband and his retinue / but she did not see her sister, vv. 890–92), echoes in Philomena's melancholic gaze at the distant city where Progne lives in ignorance of her sister's fate: "Antre les bois et la riviere / Vit la cite ou sa suer iere / Si comance a plorer mout fort" (Between the woods and the stream she saw the city where her sister was. / She began to sob heavily, vv. 1167–69).[20] Prevented from traveling the path (*voie*) to Progne's home, Philomena sends the tapestry via her female guardian, who in turn passes it to her daughter: "Mes el ne set mie par cui / Se sa mestre n'anprant la voie / Ou se sa fille n'i anvoie" (But she does not know via whom [to send the tapestry] unless her mistress shows her the way or unless the mistress's daughter takes it, vv. 1140–42). Contact between the sisters is reestablished initially when Progne sees the visual images woven by her ravished sister and through this woman's work learns of Tereus's mutilating deed (*uevre*): "Si li a la cortine oferte, / Et la reïne l'a overte, / Si la regarde et conut l'uevre" (She gave the queen the woven curtain, and she opened it, and learned of the deed the handiwork, vv. 1235–37). But Progne must then visually follow the sight of the female messenger, stealthily, along the path leading back to Philomena's prison hut: "Cele s'on va et cest apres, / Ne de trop loing ne de trop pres, / Si qu'onques n'an pert la veüe" (She [the messenger] left and the queen followed, not too closely nor too far behind, so that she would not lose sight of her, vv. 1241–43). Tracing this visual thread made by the woman's body moving through the forest, Progne weaves her way back to the sight of a lost sister in partial imitation of Philomena's own woven thread sent forth for Progne to see and read.[21] Thus do the two meanings of the Old French *voie*—signifying both "path" and "sight"—conjoin to produce a homophonic echo and semantic restructuring of the third meaning that the same sound in another spelling (*voix*) could evoke: that of "voice."

Threads of weaving and sight connect all the female protagonists in this tale that refigures woman's speech. Different from Ovid's heroine, the Old French Philomena has not fashioned her tapestry alone. The *vilaine* stationed in the forest hideaway to prevent Philomena's escape is an accomplished weaver, as is her daughter in residence:

> Car filer et tistre savoit
> Et une soe fille avoit
> Qu'ele aprenoit a son mestier.
>   (vv. 871–73)

(She knew how to spin and weave and she had a daughter to whom she taught her craft.)

Though in ignorance of the tapestry's message, both women help to create and transmit the meaningful cloth. In addition to providing colored thread and other supplies, the old woman weaves a pattern into one of the tapestry's corners or borders:

La vieille ne li contredist
Mes mout volantiers li eida
Et trestot quanqu'ele cuida
Qui a tel uevre convenist
Porchacier et querre li fist.
Trestot li quist son aparoil,
Tant que fil inde et fil vermoil
Et jaune et vert a plante ot,
Mes ele ne conut ne ne sot
Rien de quanque cele tissoit;
Mes l'uevre li abelissoit
Qui mout estoit a feire gries,
Car tissu ot a l'un des chies
Que Philomena l'avoit feite.

(vv. 1108–21)

(The old woman did not impede her but gladly helped her. She sought out and tracked down everything she thought would be appropriate to such a work. Soon Philomena asked to use the loom and attached to it blue, red, yellow, and green threads. The woman knew or understood nothing of what Philomena was weaving. Yet she made the piece more attractive, added to the work, with some difficulty, by weaving one of the edges that Philomena had prepared.)

Just as they work together on this joint project that will "talk" to Progne in the absence of words, these female protagonists "speak" to each other in visual gestures, Philomena making signs that the old woman reads effortlessly without ever misunderstanding:

La cortine qu'ele ot tissue
Prist, puis est arriere venue
La ou sa mestre l'atandoit
Qui toz ses signes antandoit
Que ja n'i mespreïst de rien,
Ainz l'antandoit pres d'aussi bien
Con s'ele li deïst de boche.

(vv. 1185–91)[22]

(She took the tapestry she had woven and came to her mistress who understood all her signals without mistaking anything about them. The woman understood her as well as if she spoke from the mouth.)

This collaborative woman's work substantially redefines the intersection of knowledge and sight that constructs the medieval portrait of female beauty under a desiring male gaze. The tapestry's visual depiction of Tereus's actions designed for Progne's eyes to read, makes the lascivious male viewer into the silent object of a female gaze. Progne *sees* how he crosses the sea to arrive in Athens, brings Philomena to Trace, rapes her, cuts out her tongue, and imprisons her in the secluded hut (vv. 1122–33). She sees the action without having to hear Tereus speak. Significantly, the woven surrogate for Philomena's words contains no representation of Tereus's imposing voice.

But the woman's gaze in this scenario does not simply mimic the imprisoning look of the empowered male observer who created Philomena's beauty in his own eyes. In place of Tereus's one-way look that constructs his subjectivity in opposition to the object of desire, the female gaze circulates between women as a means of communication, carrying messages back and forth in a motion that resembles instead the passage of thread between two poles of the weaver's loom. As the *vilaine* reads Progne's gestures, so too Progne then reads the images in her sister's tapestry and later follows with her eyes the path of the *vilaine*'s daughter moving back through the forest to establish final contact with the sister whose voice has been cut off from her.

Yet Philomena's tapestry does more than make the silent woman speak. It also transfers the terms of embodiment and beauty from the lovely woman to her newly found woven "speech," a speech that is now embodied within an object, a speech given material form in fabric. This significant shift allows Philomena to write the body instead of being the body,[23] to act upon a body of writing rather than having her body acted upon by others. As an example of work done with woman's hands, hands that extend out from the female body to make contact with other women, this tapestry emblematizes a kind of woman's narrative that comes not solely from the disembodied voice, which in the traditional formulation proceeds from the male mind, but through the hands. As these women's hands work, the role and function of the female body changes radically from a desired object without voice to a body producing a visible and beautiful narrative, itself a woven body that speaks to another woman, though without sound or words.

Women's knowledge, defined here as the knowledge of weaving cloth possessed jointly by Philomena, the old woman, and her daughter, implies agency and cognition in terms very different from those structuring the masterful, speaking subject that Tereus represents.[24] And Tereus fails utterly to perceive the existence of this alternate form of knowledge. After taking drastic precautions to conceal his crime—isolating his captive in a secluded forest and cutting out her tongue—this tyrant foolishly selects, according to the narrator, a female guard who knows how to weave:

> Mes Tereus folie fist
> Qui avuec Philomena mist
> Por la garder une vilainne
> Qui vivoit de sa propre painne,
> Car filer et tistre savoit.
> (vv. 867–71)

(But Tereus made a foolish mistake when he chose as Philomena's guardian a peasant woman who made her living by spinning and weaving.)

The very presence of this skilled woman and her apprentice daughter call forth from the beautifully embodied heroine a crucial knowledge—depicted in the earlier portrait of her own *savoir*—that Tereus previously failed to see. When Tereus mutilates Philomena's tongue so that she will not be able to "conter a home" (tell any man/person) the shame and attack she has suffered, vv. 847–49), he does not imagine she might tell the tale to women through an economy of seeing and knowing so radically different from his. He cannot conceive that her handiwork might respond to or correct his master *oeuvre*. But that is precisely what takes place as Philomena puts her own *savoir* to work.[25]

The Revenge Plot

Commentators of both Ovidian and Old French versions of the Philomena story have generally found the narrative of Progne more problematic than that of her sister.[26] Certainly it is more complex. In contrast to Philomena's single, peaceful, and constructive action of weaving cloth, Progne performs two violent and destructive deeds: decapitating her son and cooking parts of his chopped-up body into a stew while roasting the rest. Cooking, no less a traditionally woman's craft than weaving, seems here to have been caught up in a cycle of male violence that only mimics and prolongs the damage of Tereus's initial crime. This perception results in part because Philomena's woven tale circulates unproblematically within a female economy, passing from the ravaged heroine to her guardian and the guardian's daughter to arrive finally at the distanced sister without ever confronting or engaging the eyes of the male ravisher. Progne's response to the rape, by contrast, reenters the patriarchal world by addressing Tereus directly.

But in so doing Progne's actions in the Old French tale reveal the impossibility of their own professed goal of avenging a rape. What can women do to men, they seem to ask, that would parallel the savage violation of rape? Murder of the rapist would be repayment in kind for murder of the female victim. But that is not what Tereus has done to Philomena. It is in this sense that Progne's response to Tereus's *oeuvre*, however bloody and violent it may be, can never function neatly, unproblematically, in the cycle of male violence that demands equal retribution for crimes committed, requiring an eye for an eye, a tooth for a tooth, one human body for another. The part of Philomena's body that has been violated in rape has no equivalent in the male anatomy. Or does it?

I want to suggest here that Progne's actions of mutilation and cooking can be read as a continuation of the narrative begun in Philomena's tapestry. If Progne functions first as a reader of her sister's text, she can also be seen as writing a text of her own, or rather composing a visual sequel to the images she saw in Philomena's woven story. In fact the sisters work together to forge a new narrative plot, much as the *vilaine* and her daughter helped earlier to make and circulate Philomena's tapestry. In helping Philomena to rewrite the suppressed story of her rape along with the fictions of courtly love and beauty that accompany it, Progne also rewrites her own gruesome past: the tale of her marriage to Tereus and the motherhood that followed it. Taken together the stories woven by Philomena and Progne rework two myths of female nature: that of the beloved beauty, which conditions Tereus's classic line to Philomena, "sachiez bien, / Que je vos aim" ("Know this that I love you," vv. 766–67) and the tale of the loving mother emblematized in the narrator's comment, "Que mere ne doit son anfant / Ne ocire ne desmanbrer" (A mother should not kill or dismember her child, vv. 1318–19).

Seduction and Food

Progne's careful words inviting Tereus to partake of the fateful stew she
has prepared from his son's body read, curiously, as a seduction scene.
Suggesting that he come without companions so that the two of them can
be alone together when she "serves him completely," Progne holds out the
promise of something akin to the erotic pleasure Tereus sought from
Philomena:

> Au roi qui de rien ne se gueite
> Vient, si li prie et le semont
> Que de la rien an tot le mont
> Qu'ele cuide que il plus aint
> Vaingne mangier et si n'amaint
> Ne conpaingnon ne escuiïer,
> Mes que li ne doie enuiier
> Car ja n'i avra que aus deus:
> Ele iert sole et il iert seus
> Et ele del tot servira
> (vv. 1342–51)

(She comes to the king, who suspects nothing. She begs and
implores him to come and eat the thing that she believes him to love
most in all the world. She implores that he not bring along any
companion or squire. He needn't worry; there will be no one there
but the two of them. She will be alone and he will be alone/safe. She
will serve him completely)

Progne's allusions to an intimate setting—that there would only be
the two of them, she alone and he alone (vv. 1349–51),—echo hauntingly
the isolation of Tereus and Philomena in the rape scene:

> Et quant il sont leanz andui,
> Seul antre la pucele et lui,
> Que nus ne les voit ne ne ot
> (vv. 741–43)

(And when they are both there alone, the young woman and him,
such that no one can see or hear them)

Indeed, before raping Philomena, Tereus attempted a fake seduction similar to the one that Progne stages here by promising a different kind of secret liaison:

Bele, fet il, or sachiez bien
Que je vos aim et si vos pri
Que de moi façoiz vostre ami,
Et ceste chose soit celee
Se vos volez qu'ele et duree
(vv. 766−70)

(Beautiful one, he said, know that I love you and thus ask you to make me your lover. It will be a secret if you want it to last)

But why the use of food and its gory preparation in Progne's recasting of the ill-fated love story? As Progne replays the scene of Philomena's seduction and violation, she substitutes for the tyrant's pleasure in raping Philomena (vv. 836−39) the pleasure that Tereus expects to derive from eating. But Progne's rewriting of the rape scene reverses the gendered roles of its key participants so that Tereus no longer occupies the subject position. His "pleasure" is now no longer his. Throughout the revenge sequence, emphasis falls ironically on the delight Tereus will have in consuming his camouflaged meal. He will be eating the thing he loves most in all the world, Progne assures him: ("Que de la rien an tot le mont / Qu'ele cuide que il plus aint / Vaingne mangier" vv. 1344−46). The erotic overtones of her claim that Tereus will eat this meal with pleasure, "Que vos mangeroiz a deduit" (You will eat with pleasure, v. 1364) echo in the narrator's description of the scene, "Progne l'an mainne et si l'assiet / Mout pleisammant et a grant eise / Por ce que li mangiers li pleise" (Progne leads him and seats him, pleasantly and comfortably, so that the meal will please him, vv. 1372−74).

When we come to the moment where Tereus savagely cuts the flesh on his plate and puts it in his mouth, we realize how feeding the tyrant this chilling meal aptly reverses the terms of the original rape. As retribution for Tereus having forced his body into Philomena's, Progne here forces another body into Tereus's open mouth. And as with the rape of Philomena, the putative "pleasure" is attributed to him alone.[27] The appropriateness of feeding as retribution for rape is further reinforced when we remember how Tereus himself was said previously to feed off the pleasurable sight of Philomena rather than partaking of the banquet offered at Pandion's palace:

> Au mangier ont longuemant sis
> Et mout li pleisoit a seoir,
> Plus por la pucele veoir
> Que por boivre ne por mangier.
> (vv. 610–13) [28]

(They remained seated and ate for a long time. It pleased him to sit there, more so in order to watch the young woman than to eat or drink.)

Now Progne feeds Tereus, though not according to his desire or pleasure.

But why involve the innocent son, Itys, in this plot of mutilation and perverse meal planning? Through a subtle word play on *norreture* (meaning food and feeding) and *issir* (meaning to come out of, issue from), the narrator tells us how Tereus's mutilation of Philomena's tongue follows from the rape just as one evil deed generates another to feed and nourish itself:

> Voir dist qui dist: 'Toz jorz atret
> Li uns maus l'autre et sel norrist.'
> (vv. 840–41)

(He speaks the truth who says: "One evil attracts another and feeds off of it.")

The result of this process is a "male norreture" that issues forth as a kind of deformed offspring:

> Et male norreture an ist,
> Si male come issir an doit.
> (vv. 842–43)

(Evil nourishment/offspring is born of this, as bad as can come from it.)

What Progne engineers in her cooking of Itys's innocent flesh is an apt transformation of this "male norreture" (evil offspring/offshoot) into a "norreture male" (male offspring/nourishment). The mutilated mouth that emerges as the bad offspring of Tereus's having raped Philomena is matched appropriately by a literal offspring made monstrous through mutilation. At this juncture Progne's rewriting of the plot of the lovely virgin turns tellingly to recast the myth of the loving mother.

Progne's Marriage to Tereus or The Abduction and Silencing of the Second Sister

When Progne discovers her ravaged sister in the forest hideaway, a woman abducted, raped, silenced, and forcefully kept from seeing her family, the distraught sister's first words allude curiously not to Philomena's plight but to her own marriage to Tereus:

> Suer, dist ele, venez vos an,
> Car trop avez ci sejorne.
> Tant mar veïstes ajorne
> Le jor que li fel m'esposa
> (vv. 1270–73)

(Sister, she said, come away, you have stayed here too long. Cursed is the day you saw the sunrise when the traitor married me)

Indeed the Old French *Philomena* itself begins with an account of Tereus and Progne's marriage that makes reference to Itys's unfortunate end, then detours into the Philomena story only after promising to return to Itys: "Ithis ot non. Ce fu diaus granz / Qu'il ne vesqui plus longuemant. / Je vos dirai assez comant / De lui avint a la parclose, / Mes ainz vos dirai autre chose" (His name is Itys. It was tragic that he did not live longer. I will tell you what happened to him at the end of my tale. But first I will speak of something else, vv. 44–48). Philomena's rape stands as a subsidiary part, a detour to "something else" within the companion story of Progne's marriage and her son Itys from which it draws its meaning.

And in fact Progne's liaison with Tereus parallels Philomena's brutal encounter with the ravisher more fully than one might initially suspect.

Traded in a marriage deal struck between Pandion and Tereus, Progne was given away by her father (Cele fu a mari *donee*, v. 6) and carried off by her husband (S'an *mena* Tereus sa fame, v. 33), much as Philomena is later bartered away temporarily by Pandion, "Que sa fille li a *bailliee*" (He gave him his daughter, v. 673) and led off as a virgin ripe for ravishing, "La pucele que il an *mainne*" (the maiden that he led away with him, v. 717).[29] No textual evidence attests to whether Progne was raped by Tereus, either before or during her marriage. That he used force against her, to counter her wishes, however, is made explicit by Tereus himself when he tells Philomena why Progne did not accompany him on the sea voyage to Athens:

> Se je li leissasse venir
> Ele fust ça a vos venue,
> Mes je l'ai de la retenue
> Tot a force contre son cuer.
>   (vv. 252–55)

(If I had let her come, she would have come here to see you. But I restrained (retained) her, forcefully, against her wishes.)

The line describing how Tereus prevented Progne from traveling to her sister, "Tot a force contre son cuer" (Forcefully against her wishes, v. 255) prepares tellingly for the subsequent "Que tot a force l'a conquise" (Forcefully he overcame her) as Tereus rapes Philomena against her "heart" to please himself (v. 839).

Both women are thus subjected to the ravisher's imposing force. And though Tereus does not literally cut out Progne's tongue he does effectively eliminate her speech in a crucial scene at the outset of the tale. When Tereus comes to Athens as Progne's messenger, he comes in order to speak for her, ostensibly on her behalf. But he also speaks in her place, substituting his words for hers. Tereus thus silences the female voice that had wanted to communicate directly with his sister (v. 108).[30] Although Tereus mouths the same request to Philomena that Progne would have made, the simple presence of his male body critically deforms the female voice it represents:

La pucele antre ses braz prant
Et si li dist: 'Ma douce amie,
Vostre suer vos salue et prie
Que vos veigniez deduire o li'
        (vv. 242–45)

(He takes the maiden [Philomena] in his arms and says, "Sweet one, your sister sends greetings and begs you to come enjoy yourself with her")

Delivering Progne's purely verbal message with a physical embrace that echoes the designs of his own carnal desire for Philomena, Tereus effectively transforms the expression of friendship between sisters into a more sinister message between ravisher and victim. "Deduire" in Old French carries the dual meaning of enjoying oneself in the company of others and enjoying oneself sexually. Progne's words suggest the first meaning, that the sisters will enjoy each other's company, while Tereus's delivery implies the second, that he will amuse himself, taking pleasure in Philomena. Speaking ostensibly for Progne, Tereus makes her voice speak only for him as if she, like Philomena, had no voice at all.

Progne remains significantly different from Philomena, however, to the extent that she exerts no seductive influence over Tereus. Nowhere in the tale do we hear of Tereus taking pleasure in Progne's body or beauty. His gaze never rests on her physiognomy, which goes unnoticed, unmentioned altogether. Neither does Progne profess any interest in him. When Tereus returns empty-handed from Athens and approaches his wife, it is she who looks at him, remarks the absence of Philomena, and without a word of greeting for her husband expresses concern for her sister alone:

Car tot maintenant qu'ele vit
Son seignor et sa compaignie
Et de sa seror ne vit mie
Qu'ele cuidoit mout conjoïr
Ne li plot rien nule a oïr
Ne de respondre ne li chaut,
Ne "Bien veingniez", ne "Deus vos saut".

Ainz demande come esfreee
Quant il l'orent tuit saluee:
"Ou est ma suer? Por quoi ne vient?"
(vv. 890–99)

(Now she sees her husband and his retinue but she does not see her
sister whom she had planned to greet joyously. Nothing she hears
can please her and she takes no interest in speaking, not even to say
"welcome back" or "thank God." Rather she asks as if in distress,
after they all greet her, "Where is my sister? Why hasn't she come?")

The lavish kisses exchanged between Tereus and Pandion (vv. 93–95,
711–12) and the ravisher's deceptively delicate hugging and kissing of Philomena (v. 749) find no equivalent expression of affection between Tereus
and his wife. Rather, as Progne herself explains, the thing Tereus "loves
best in all the world" is his son, Itys (vv. 1345–46). The virgin bride that
Progne once was—in an earlier mode of existence now symbolized by
Philomena's virginal innocence—serves only as a procreative vessel to produce the cherished male heir. Whereas the imprisoned Philomena guarantees the tyrant's sexual pleasure, his wife, restrained at home, secures his
legal patrimony.

A Murderer or a Mother?

That women who kill their children are rare in literature as in life makes
Progne's decapitation and murder of her own son both shocking and powerful. For recent examples of similar maternal violence, one has only to
recall Toni Morrison's compelling novel *Beloved*, based on the plight of
nameless escaped slavewomen in the American South known to have murdered their own children, or Adrienne Rich's reference to the suburban
housewife Joanne Michulski's having decapitated and chopped up the
bodies of her two youngest children in 1974.[31] Both narratives make us wonder what could push mothers, the quintessential givers of life, traditional
nourishers of children and families—whether in the womb, through breast
milk or later cooking—to kill? A slave woman's bloody attempt to prevent
her children from returning to slavery constituted, in Morrison's reading
of it, a savage indictment of racial oppression. Joanne Michulski's crime,
in Rich's narrative, stands as a woman's angry response to the clean-cut

and quiet but still devastating oppression sometimes endured by the suburban housewife. But why protest oppressive institutions by killing one's own children? What is the relation between motherhood and infanticide that Morrison's slave mother, Joanne Michulski, and the Old French Progne play out on different historical stages and in significantly different ways?

For Progne the killing of Itys (made frequently to rhyme with *fils* [son] in this tale) redirects the murderous male gaze, which led to Philomena's rape, away from the beautiful and innocent female body and onto an equally beautiful and innocent male heir. Indeed it is precisely when Progne, previously at a loss to know how to avenge her ravished sister,[32] *sees* her son approach that the murder plot comes to her mind. The child's extraordinary beauty, reminiscent of Philomena's own attractiveness, helps spark the thought:

> Atant ses fiz devant li vint
> Qui biaus estoit a desmesure
> Si l'amena mesavanture
> Qui li estoit a avenir.
> La mere voit son fil venir.
>
> (vv. 1292–96)

(Her son, who was exceedingly handsome/beautiful, came to her. Thus did he bring forth the misfortune that he would suffer. The mother saw her son approach.)

As the loving mother fondles her son ("Si con la tenoit acolee / Li petiz anfes par chierte"; As she held her young son tightly and lovingly, vv. 1328–29) in an echo of Tereus's earlier gentle hugging of Philomena "doucement l'acole et baise," v. 749), Progne lays plans for the action that will turn the tables on Tereus in a most unexpected way. Progne's murder plot eventually provokes the erstwhile ravisher to echo the hauntingly unanswered question she herself posed to him earlier in the tale. The gruesome feast remakes Progne's previous "ou est ma suer?" (Where is my sister?) into Tereus's stupefyingly naive and fateful, "ou est Itis?" (Where is Itys? where is my son? v. 1381).

But Progne's decapitation of her own son also rewrites the story of her marriage to Tereus, her role as the faceless procreator of heirs that will only repeat their fathers' savage ways. The killing of Itys in this sense would put an end—albeit violent—to the cycle of brutality and vilification that hallmarks Tereus's relations to women, a cycle that Progne has been made to participate in, to foster and further by producing, from her own body, one such future male. By killing Itys, Progne can extricate herself from an unwitting collusion in producing ravishers of women, and she can also effectively stop the cycle of abuse. Tereus has no other children; he can produce no future legitimate heir alone. This is perhaps the most cogent point made by Progne's murder of their son.

When considered from this perspective, Progne's act, cast as a message to her savage husband, might read less as a mother's senselessly brutal infanticide than as a move on the part of a complicitous procreator to take back the child she gave in birth. It is almost as if in killing Itys Progne unravels the threads of time, reversing the course of past events to return to a moment before the birth of her child, a moment perhaps even before her marriage, a time when she, like Philomena, was an innocent *pucele*. In undoing the story of her own abduction and metaphorical imprisonment, which led her to help perpetuate a tyrant's family line, Progne reveals both to the ever-blind Tereus, and to the shocked reader as well, the plot of the underread. What we as readers tend to miss by focusing our sympathy and interest on the violated Philomena and her ingenious handiwork is the more hidden narrative of the "loving" mother who has herself also been mutilated to the extent that her sexuality, her desire, her subjectivity, and her role in reproduction have been summarily effaced behind the label "mother." Progne's rash action flies in the face of the convention that asserts, as the Old French narrator reminds us, that it is "right and natural for all human beings . . . that a mother not kill or dismember her child" (Si con requiert droiz et nature / De tote humainne creature . . . Que mere ne doit son anfant / Ne ocire ne desmanbrer" vv. 1315–16, 1318–19). Her violent response reveals how what is here termed natural for mothers reflects female sentiment less than it mirrors cultural values that construct what women should feel.

As an answer to Philomena's rape and to her own subjugation in marriage to the ravisher Tereus, Progne's decapitation of Itys corrects this misprision, stating without words that whereas women may not be able to control what enters the vagina by force, they can more readily control what is produced from that female orifice in the form of children. To assert that women are life-givers alone, denying them the ability also to take life away, is to wrest from them the full force and potency of the subjectivity attendant to the life-giving process. If Philomena's tapestry conveys to Progne the message that she is not indeed dead, not finally silenced, not ultimately powerless, that is to say that she refuses the verbal and sexual subjugation imposed by Tereus, that she is in short, *not his*, Progne's meal of human flesh sends Tereus a parallel message: that his child is *not his* alone, but also a product of the woman's body, which thinks and feels and acts in ways which defy the marital and maternal subjugation that tend to view her as *his* vessel for procreation.

It is true that in killing her son, Progne also kills part of himself, and this heroine fully acknowledges the tragedy of such an act: Itys does not deserve death and that death at the hand of the mother is an especially bitter one, "Morir t'estuet de mort amere / a mere," (You must die a bitter death, death from the mother's hand, v. 1301). But in killing Tereus's son Progne also kills the fetishized phallus, redefining the child as hers to both produce and destroy. Thus does she remind Tereus in an especially poignant way of woman's power to create human flesh. As the two sisters work together, mixing with their hands the parts of Itys's body into a palatable stew ("Puis ont la char apareilliee / Antr'eles deus mout bien et tost"; Then they prepared the flesh, working together well and quickly, vv. 1334–35), they prepare to make of Tereus a body, pregnant with child, but one that he cannot deliver into life. When Progne explains finally, in response to Tereus's insistent "ou est Itis?" (v. 1380), that he carries the child within him though it is not whole, "Dedanz toi as ce que tu quiers, / Mes n'i est mie toz antiers. / Partie an as dedanz ton cors / Et partie an as par defors" (You carry everything you want inside you, but it is not whole. You have part of it inside your body and part outside, vv. 1403–6), she implicitly contrasts Tereus's vile state with that of a mother who carries a whole future being within her.

It is significant that Tereus does not fully understand these words, just as he earlier fails to perceive the hidden meaning in Progne's invitation to eat: "Mes cil ne puet aparcevoir / De quel mangier ele li prie" (But he dos not understand which meals she alludes to, vv. 1366–67). It is only when his startled gaze falls on the more tangible image of his son's severed head, tossed in his face by Philomena as a silent reminder of her silenced voice, that Tereus finally knows that he has been tricked:

> Si li a tote ansanglantee
> La teste an mi le vis gitee.
> Tereus voit qu'il est traïz,
> (vv. 1411–13)

(She threw the thoroughly bloody head in his face. Tereus then saw
that he had been betrayed,)

It is at this point, when looking at the visual image of his son's mutilated
body, an image prepared by Progne's savagely sculpting hands, that Tereus
falls silent. In a twisted mimicry of the silence that previously held him
spellbound and speechless when gazing on Philomena's erotically fragmented body, Tereus now cannot say a word:

> S'estut une piece esbaïz
> Qu'il ne se mut ne ne dist mot"
>   (vv. 1414–15)

(He remained stunned a while, not moving or saying a word)

The tables have turned, the revenge is complete. Not so much because
Tereus has shed the role of victimizer to become the victim, but because
the sisters' joint work has redefined the terms of Tereus's sight. The effect
of Progne and Philomena's plot is to refocus the male gaze, transferring it
from the female body beautified through metaphorical dismemberment to
the male body literally dismembered. Rather than constructing the image
he views, the ravisher is now forced to read a message sent to him by
another, by two women who use their hands to communicate in images
rather than words. Much as Progne earlier read the silent message that was
encoded visually in Philomena's tapestry, Tereus now reads the visual representation of his son's death and his own helplessness in restoring the
dismembered body to life. Women's work in this context forces Tereus to
see that no matter how hard he looks at the decapitated head of his innocent son, his eyes cannot recreate what only the woman's body can produce: the male issue needed to inherit his kingdom. He cannot play
Pygmalion with his son.

In taking away her child's life, Progne also significantly gives life to
another, to Philomena, substituting for the natural birth of a male heir the
metaphorical rebirth of a sister she has believed to be dead.[33] The verb *issir*
figures prominently throughout this tale, first marking Philomena's appearance before Tereus as she emerges (*issir*) from an ajoining room to be
"born" into her beautiful static pose in the lengthy portrait that constructs
her femininity: "Atant est d'une chanbre issue / Philomena eschevelee"

(Philomena, disheveled, came out of a room, vv. 124–25). In the revenge scene, immediately following Progne's explanation that Tereus holds his son captive within his own body (vv. 1403–6), Philomena again emerges unexpectedly from an adjoining room, this time holding the bloody head that makes Tereus realize his tragic inability to give birth to the child within him: "Philomena qui s'iert reposte / An une chanbre iluec decoste /S'an issi fors a tot la teste" (Philomena, who had been waiting in an adjacent room, came out of the room with the head, vv. 1407–9). If Tereus created the first Philomena with his desiring gaze, this second "birth" of the heroine results from Progne's concerted efforts to free her sister from the confines of the *maison gastee*, the womblike prison where the ravisher enclosed his captive, denying her nothing but the ability to leave (*issir*):

> Ne ja ne li fust contredite
> Nule chose granz ne petite
> Fors l'issue de la meison
> (vv. 1151–53)

(Nothing was denied her, great or small, except passage out of the house)[34]

As Tereus's prior imprisonment of Philomena is now revisited upon him in the form of an offspring made captive, Progne gives the male child back to Tereus, putting it literally inside his body, and gives birth instead to a female, restoring life to a "murdered" sister.

One haunting detail of the seduction scene leading up to Tereus's fateful meal makes especially clear how the murder of Itys provides a thorough rewriting—not just of Philomena's rape—but of the more pervasive medieval formulation of the heroine's constructed beauty. Amid the details of Progne's careful preparations for the feast—her guiding Tereus to the table and seating him comfortably for a pleasurable meal (vv. 1372–74)—a single, unexpected line referring to the "beautiful white tablecloth" spread out beneath the tyrant's dinner by the mother/murderer carries us back instantly to the initial portrait of Philomena's beauty. There the virgin's forehead, teeth, chin, neck, throat, and chest were all as white as her beautifully static hands; all stilled, killed into a picture of virginal loveliness. The *biaute* established in this image resonated most tellingly in Tereus's direct address to the innocent virgin just before he raped and imprisoned

her. Professing his passion, he calls her not "Philomena" but more anony-
mously "Bele," the Beauty he will devour in the name of love, "Bele, fet il,
or sachiez bien / Que je vos aim et si vos pri / Que de moi façoiz vostre
ami" ("Beauty," he said, "know that I love you and implore you thus to
make me your lover," vv. 766–68).

In the dinner scene, the beauty and whiteness of the eroticized female
body are transferred to a tablecloth spread out by woman's hands as part
of the act of serving food (a cloth perhaps even woven by a woman):

> Cele li a la table mise
> Et la nape fu bele et blanche.
> (vv. 1376–77)

(She set the table. The tablecloth was beautiful and white.)

Although tablesetting is not one of the skills attributed to Philomena in
the initial portrait of her *savoir*, it is something that the women in this
narrative know how to do. The tablecloth detail emblemizes how the
woman's body has shifted in the course of this tale from being beautiful
to being knowledgeable in a way that redefines the very terms of *biaute* and
sagesse. Throughout this gory chronicle of rape, mutilation, decapitation,
and murder, the lovely and silent Philomena has been depicted primarily
as *bele* and only secondarily as *sage*: "Avuec la grant biaute qu'ele ot / Sot
quanque doit savoir pucele," (Along with the great beauty she possessed,
she knew how to do everything a young woman should, vv. 170–71). But
in the final scene Philomena speaks on behalf of every *pucele* whom she
defines first as *sage* and then *cortoise* (v. 1461). Speaking here not as a
woman but as a nightingale who "sings as sweetly as she knows how"
(Chante au plus *doucemant* qu'el set, v. 1466, my emphasis), Philomena
uses a partially restored voice to recast Tereus's prior deceptively sweet
seduction of her, "*doucemant* l'acole et beise" (Sweetly/gently he hugs and
kisses her, v. 749, my emphasis). Her song, composed of a single word,
evokes murder in all the complex ramifications this tale has shown it to
possess.[35] Singing the sweet song of killing, "oci, oci" (killed, killed,
v. 1467) she reminds us how women have worked with their hands
throughout this tale to speak in unconventional ways, thereby "killing" off
traditions that oppress them. Itys has been killed, it is true; Itys the son of
Progne but also Itys heir to his father's brutal violation of virgins and

wives. But what else has come to an end? The unwilling complicity of a mother in propagating and fostering such offspring, Tereus's empowered gaze on Philomena's body, the innocence of the naive virgin who knows nothing of rape and deceit, myths of passionate love and feminine beauty, myths of marriage, maternal love, and paternal protection. What survives is a realignment of the patrilineal configurations that traditionally linked father to son, wife to husband, and father to daughter into an alternative bonding between women. Sisters join together with a mother not their own and with that mother's daughter by using language based on sight, not sound. Their newly defined "voice" issues from a female body that includes the maternal body, the nurturing body, the life-giving and life-destroying body, the silent body that speaks through movement, gesture, and the activities of women's work.

That is the beauty of this female body. Collapsing the dichotomy that typically holds beauty apart from knowledge, these women's bodies know, know how to do things, extraordinary things, like speaking without words. Their hands can talk.

Notes

1. Alice Colby, *The Portrait in Twelfth-Century French Literature*.
2. Ovid, *Metamorphoses*, 242.
3. Hélène Cixous, in *The Newly Born Woman*, 67.
4. Luce Irigaray, *Speculum of the Other Woman*, 115. And in the French edition:

> Belle de corps, parée d'or par lui et pour lui, la femme sera encore réservée, modeste, pudique, quant à son sexe. Discrètement complice de sa dissimulation. Assurant ce double jeu d'exhiber son corps, ses bijoux, pour mieux cacher son sexe. Car si le "corps" de la femme présente quelque "utilité", représente quelque "valeur", c'est à condition d'en masquer le sexe. Ce *rien* à consommer. Fantasme, de plus, comme bouche avide (*Spéculum de l'autre femme*, 143).

5. Denise Riley, *Am I That Name? Feminism and the Category of "Women" in History*, 98.
6. Although *Philomena* has been considered by some to be the first work of the master of twelfth-century French romance, Chrétien de Troyes, others argue, largely on linguistic grounds, that it does not belong to Chrétien's corpus. For a concise summary of the arguments on both sides and an analysis of proverbial expressions within the *Philomena* that lends credence to the view that Chrétien

composed the work, see Elisabeth Schulze-Busacker, "Philomena: Une révision de l'attribution de l'oeuvre."

7. *Philomena*, v. 207. For an English translation, see *Three Ovidian Tales of Love*, ed. and trans. Raymond J. Cormier.

8. This heroine thus becomes very different from the rape victim in the *Histoire d'O*, whose orifices have no linguistic or sexual agency. See Kaja Silverman, "*Histoire d'O*: The Construction of a Female Subject."

9. For an incisive feminist reading of rape in Ovid's "Philomel and Procne" and related myths, see Patricia Klindienst Joplin, "The Voice of the Shuttle is Ours," esp. 43. Other literary accounts of rape and lingual mutilation are found in Shakespeare's *Titus Andronicus*, where Lavinia is raped, her tongue cut out, and her arms cut off to prevent her from writing, though she writes using a stick in her teeth. See Jane Marcus, "Still Practice, A/Wrested Alphabet: Toward a Feminist Aesthetic." On Shakespeare's *The Rape of Lucretia*, see Stephanie Jed, *Chaste Thinking: The Rape of Lucretia and the Birth of Humanism*. For recent feminist work on women weavers, Nancy K. Miller treats Ariadne and Arachne in "Arachnologies: The Woman, the Text, and the Critic." On Penelope see Peggy Kamuf, "Penelope at Work," in *Signature Pieces: On the Institution of Authorship*; and Carolyn Heilbrun, in *Hamlet's Mother and Other Women*. On Helen and Philomela, see Christine Froula, "The Daughter's Seduction: Sexual Violence and Literary History."

10. Miller, "Arachnologies," 274.

11. See especially Joplin, "The Voice of the Shuttle," 45–52.

12. The narrator's voice is especially obvious in the following lines: "Philomena eschevelee / Ne sanbloit pas nonain velee, / Car granz mervoille iert a *retreire* / Son jant cors et son cler vieire" (The disheveled Philomena did not appear as a veiled nun. Her beautiful body and light face were wonders to *describe*, vv. 125–29); "Se je apres ces trois i fail / Et j'i metrai tot mon travail. / Desqu'anpris l'ai n'an quier recroire: / Plus dirai qu'on ne porroit croire" (Though I, like these other three writers, might fail [in describing her], I will work hard at it. Until I have undertaken it, I do not plan to give up. I will say more than one might believe possible, vv. 135–38).

13. "Tel l'ot Deus feite que Nature / Mien esciant i fausist bien / S'ele i vosist comancier rien" (God had fashioned her such that Nature, it seems to me, would do wrong if she attempted to add anything," vv. 142–44); "Car Nature s'an fu penee / Plus que de nule autre rien nee, / Si ot tot mis quanqu'ele pot" (Nature worked harder on her than on any other creature. She put all she had into this, vv. 167–69). For Nature's role in fashioning Enide, see vv. 430–32 of Chrétien de Troyes's *Erec et Enide*. For God's efforts in creating Soredamors, see Chrétien's *Cligès*, v. 800; and on Nature's role vv. 820–21.

14. In "Shakespeare's *Will*: The Temporality of Rape," 35, Joel Fineman highlights Shakespeare's reference to the beautiful female body that speaks like an orator who seduces, but he fails to note the extent to which this body's "voice" results from male fantasy and desire. For a compelling analysis of how the same female beauty that inspires love and heroism in a range of Old French romances also often

authorizes sexual aggression against courtly heroines, see Kathryn Gravdal, *Ravishing Maidens: Writing Rape in Medieval French Literature and Law*.

15. Philomena's ignorance places her in a very different category from the women of Susan Brownmiller's *Against Our Will: Men, Women, and Rape*, which sees rape as a strategy of keeping women in a perpetual state of fear. As the perfectly innocent virgin, Philomena has neither will nor fear.

16. The portraits are evenly balanced in terms of space: 31 lines for beauty (vv. 140–70) and 36 for knowledge (vv. 170–205).

17. Jean Frappier, *Chrétien de Troyes, l'homme et l'oeuvre*, 69. Cf. Frappier's example of dialectic in Philomena's query about women's words.

18. See also vv. 363–66, where Pandion explains that nothing pleases him more than Philomena, that all his pleasures are in his daughter, that he lives by her alone and has no other sustenance: "Mes or n'ai mes rien qui me pleise; / An ma fille sont tuit mi eise, / Par li vif je tant solemant, / Car n'ai autre sostenement," (I have nothing else that pleases me now. All my joys are in my daughter. I live by her alone for I have no other sustenance).

19. "Love" as the source of the trouble is cast as a female because the Old French "Amors" is a feminine noun. She is not "sage" and does not act "wisely" when carrying out her will, "D'on n'est ele pas sage.-/ -Si est. Mes ele a tel corage / Qu'il ne li chaut de nul savoir, / Quant sa volante puet avoir" (Thus is she not wise.—Yes she is. But she has such courage/will that wisdom makes no difference to her when she can have her way, vv. 421–24). The narrator tells us that Tereus would have been sage to avoid this liaison (vv. 449–51). Succumbing to it, he is reduced to the braying and shouting of love's victims (v. 400), becoming quintessentially womanlike as he suffers, temporarily, a complete loss of speech, "Tote a perdue la parole" (He completely lost his speech, v. 390). It is also significant in retrospect that when Philomena refuses to speak to her father on Tereus's behalf, she explains that Tereus should have enough power and *savoir* to get what he wants (vv. 280–86).

20. See also v. 1194.

21. The passage provides a distinct counterpoint to Ariadne's thread that guided Tereus into the labyrinth and out again. For a revealing analysis of the way this text exploits the semantic resonances suggested by the heroine's name: Philomena, *fil, fille, fils, mener*, see Nancy Jones, "The Daughter Text and the Thread of Lineage in the Old French *Philomena*," in manuscript, 14–26.

22. Ovid tells us only that Philomena "Gave it [her tapestry] to one old woman, with signs and gestures / To take it to the queen, so it was taken," 148.

23. This is in fact the major tenet of the widely misunderstood phenomenon of *ecriture féminine*. See Introduction, 7–9.

24. That Progne cooks instead of weaving to tell her story and how that activity relates to women's work in weaving will be discussed below.

25. "Quant ele ot *s'ovraigne* finee / Tel come ele la *sot ovrer*" (When she had finished her work, as she knew how to do it, vv. 1134–35, my emphasis).

26. For an especially cogent reading of the Old French *Philomena* in terms of its feudal context, see Nancy Jones, "The Daughter's Text."

27. After the initial rape, we remember, Tereus returned regularly to the forest hideaway to "take his pleasure" : "Qu'a force tot ses buens feisoit / de li cil qui l'avoit traïe" (He who had betrayed her repeatedly took his pleasure from her by force, vv. 1068–69).

28. Pandion too is said to have been nourished by the sight of his virginal daughter (v. 366).

29. The introduction to the *Philomena* provided by the *Ovide moralisée* in which the text is preserved explains how Pandion gave Progne to Tereus in payment for having saved his lands from invasion by barbarians (vv. 8–20).

30. Progne later explains how Tereus's intervention specifically prevented the sisters from speaking with each other (vv. 1274–75).

31. Toni Morrison, *Beloved*; Adrienne Rich, *Of Woman Born: Motherhood as Experience and Institution*, 24, 256–57.

32. "Ne vangier ne vos sai ne puis / Del felon qui ce vos a fet (I do not know how to avenge you against the traitor who did this to you, vv. 1288–89).

33. Cf. Progne's mourning and burial of her sister, though in the absence of a body (v. 1056).

34. And earlier, "Qu'el n'a ne congie ne leisir / De fors de la meison issir," (She is not at liberty to leave/go out of the house, vv. 1081–82).

35. This birdsong harks back to the raucous bird noises that furnished bad omens during Tereus and Progne's wedding ceremony (vv. 15–36). For an extended discussion on the nightingale's cry, see Wendy Pfeffer, *The Change of Philomel* (New York: Peter Lang, 1985).

4. Rewriting Men's Stories: Enide's Disruptive Mouths

Let us begin our discussion of *Erec et Enide* with a different story, not with the well-known tale told by the master author of twelfth-century French romance, Chrétien de Troyes, but with an alternate version of the classic courtly narrative he made famous. Let us start with a retelling of the traditional Old French adventure story, delivered this time from the mouth of a female protagonist in another text altogether, the *Lai du Lecheor*.[1] This anonymous short narrative from the twelfth century begins by outlining the standard storytelling process for Old French tales of love and adventure as we know it. But the tale soon shifts to a pointed critique of that literary system articulated by one of the courtly ladies figured in the narrative. The narrator of the *Lai du Lecheor* explains first how Breton storytellers gathered typically to recount their amorous and chivalric adventures in the company of well-dressed ladies:

> Soloient granz genz asembler
> Por la feste au saint honorer,
> Les plus nobles et les plus beles
> Du pais, dames et puceles,
> Qui dont estoient el pais
> N'i avoit dame de nul pris
> Qui n'i venist a icel jor;
> Molt estoient de riche ator
> (vv. 3–10)

(Important people used to gather in honor of that saint's day: the country's most noble and most beautiful women,[2] ladies and young ladies from that region. There was not a woman of any value who did not come that day. They were very richly attired)

These well-dressed noble women constitute the audience for courtly narrative along with clerics, knights, and people of other professions: "clers et chevaliers, / Et plusors genz d'autres mestiers; / Dames i ot nobles et beles, / Et meschines et damoiseles" (vv. 43–46). They all come to hear the adventures of knights who fashion their past exploits into orally delivered tales:

> Et la érent conté li fet
> Des amors et des drueries
> Et des nobles chevaleries;
> Ce que l'an estoit avenu
> Tot ert oi et retenu:
> Lor aventure racontoient
> Et li autre les escoutoient
> (vv. 16–22)

(Deeds of love and lovemaking and noble chivlary were recounted there. Everything that had happened was heard and remembered. They [knights] told of their adventures while others listened)

Women do not figure, it seems, among the storytellers recounting chivalric adventures, nor among the harpers or musicians who carry the prize-winning story to distant lands:

> Chascuns a son fet reconté;
> S'aventure disoit chascuns,
> (vv. 50–51)

(Each one recounted his deed and told of his adventure,)

> Car cil qui savoient de note
> En viele, en herpe et en rote
> Fors de la terre le portoient
> Es roiaumes ou il aloient
> (vv. 35–38)[3]

(Those who knew how to play the vielle, the harp, and the rote carried it [the favorite *lai*] away to other lands where they traveled)

While the Old French pronouns *chascuns* and *cil* used in the preceding examples do not preclude the possible existence of women within a group of taletellers or musicians, neither do they suggest female participation in these activities. By contrast, the *Lai du Lecheor* subsequently details one particular storytelling contest in which a female protagonist clearly takes up the role of speaker as eight women break off from the larger group of listeners to speak among themselves. Termed "wise" and "learned," "noble, courtly, and esteemed" (*sages, ensaingnies, franches, cortoises,* and *proisies,* vv. 57–58), these women become the audience for a single female speaker who critiques the way male storytellers have told their tales. She says:

> Molt oi ces chevaliers parler
> De tornoier et de joster,
> D'aventures, de drueries,
> Et de requerre lor amies:
> D'icelui ne tiénent nul plet
> Por qui li grant bien sont tuit fet.
> Par cui sont li bon chevalier?
> Por qoi aimment a tornoier?
> Por qui s'atornent li danzel?
> Por qui se vestent de novel?
> Por qui envoient lor joieaus,
> Lor treceors et lor aneaus?
> Por qui sont franc et debonere?
> Por qoi se gardent de mal fere?
> Por qoi aimment la donoier,
> Et l'acoler et l'embracier?
> Savez i vos nule achoison
> Fors sol por une chose non?
>
> (vv. 65–82)

(I have long heard these knights talk about tournaments and jousting, adventures and lovers, questing for ladies. They make no mention of why all these great deeds are undertaken. Why are knights good? Why do they like to fight in tournaments? For whom do young men dress up? For whom do they wear new clothing? For whom do they send their jewels, treasures, and rings? On whose account are they genteel and generous? On whose account do they refrain from wrongdoing? Why do they like courting, hugging, and kissing? Do you know any reason but one?)

The standard response to this question, in courtly literature and the critical commentary on it, is that knights undertake valiant exploits for the lady, the courtly descendent of the troubadour's *domna*, a woman revered and adored by the chivalric lover, who puts her on a pedestal and keeps her there.[4] The narrative scenario informs many of Chrétien de Troyes's romances. But the female speaker in the *Lai du Lecheor* provides a different answer to her own rhetorical question, suggesting that there is more to courtly romance than meets the eye, and more than we as readers have previously surmised.

Detailing for her female audience the unseen, unstated element that motivates knightly endeavor, this female storyteller alludes cryptically to a thing (*une chose*) that provides the greatest pleasures, "les granz doucors":

> Ja n'avra nus tant donoié
> Ne biau parlé ne biau proié
> Ainz qu'il s'em puisse departir,
> A ce ne veille revertir;
> D'ice viénent les granz douçors
> Por coi sont fetes les honors.
>
> (vv. 83–88)

(Never would anyone [any knight] court so long nor speak so nicely nor plead so sweetly before taking his leave if he did not want to come back to this: from this thing comes the greatest pleasures, the reason why honorable deeds are done.)

Then, with a verbal chutzpah wholly uncharacteristic of courtly heroines, the female speaker in the *Lai du Lecheor* states frankly that what is hidden in the Arthurian adventure story, that coveted *chose* concealed behind the accounts of valiant knights and beautiful ladies, is no less than female genitalia. In a most unladylike fashion, she speaks of *con* (cunt):

> Maint homme i sont si amendé
> Et mis em pris et em bonté,

Qui ne vausissent un bouton
Se par l'entente du con non.
            (vv. 89–92)[5]

(Many men are improved, revived by it, made worthy and good,
men who would be worth nothing if not for the thought-of/desire-
for cunt.)

In this female speaker's view, chivalric prowess is inspired less by
meditation on the elegant beauty of the knight's favorite lady than by the
eroticized female body that that beauty masks. The female speaker in the
Lai du Lecheor thus graphically renders the process we have witnessed
more obliquely in the Old French *Philomena* whereby the putative lover's
interest in the unnamed vagina is concealed behind elaborate descriptions
of the heroine's lovely face. This lady storyteller puts it bluntly: "no woman's face is so beautiful that she could keep her lover if she lost her cunt":

Nule fame n'a si bel vis
Por qu'ele eust le con perdu,
Ja mes eust ami ne dru.
            (vv. 94–96)

We should remember here that this woman's critique is leveled less
against the medieval practices of love and prowess than against the transformation of courtly behavior into tales that leave something out. The
questing knights' stories take no account ("ne tienent nul plet"), she
tells us, of female sexual difference, which remains obscured behind descriptions of the lady's beautiful face. If, in other examples of courtly narrative, the lady's lavish clothing tends to hide her sexual difference, here
the very fabric of the romance narrative itself works to conceal the eroticized anatomy of female protagonists figured within it. Men's stories of
love and adventure are cast in this instance as creating an elaborate detour
around the formidable female *con*, the unknown territory of female sexuality that resists and contests the logic of the same. Chivalric storytellers
talk of love and adventure in order to avoid confronting the female body,
says the lovely lady of the *Lai du Lecheor*. Thus do her crass words de-
bunk the fiction of the role she herself is meant to play, revealing it to be
an amusing literary convention and a wanting cultural construction of
femininity.

The skeptical reader might object here that the words of the out-spoken "Lady" in the *Lai du Lecheor* cannot be taken as representing a "real" woman's voice because they originate with the tale's anonymous author, who was most likely male. Indeed this woman cannot be considered to speak "as a woman," in any totalizing sense, to tell a story utterly her own or wholly distinct from the master narratives already circulating among twelfth-century storytellers. But this is not only because she is a literary character. Our own voices as contemporary women are also constructed in many ways, also conditioned by cultural patterning and inherited literary tradition.[6] Carolyn Heilbrun has cogently explained how women—whether historical women functioning as speakers and writers or their fictional counterparts who tell their stories in literary texts—have no specifically female plots to guide them, no narrative plots of their own.[7] They must rewrite old stories, engaging and recasting stereotypes in order to resist them.[8]

Resistance to the stereotype of the courtly lady is what I hear in the comments of the female voice in the *Lai du Lecheor*. This is not to say that the female speaker of the *Lai* thoroughly repudiates the culturally constructed sexuality represented by the elaborate layers of clothing and adornment that typically construct the courtly lady's beauty and silence. Such a move is impossible, as Judith Butler has cogently explained:

> If sexuality is culturally constructed within existing power relations, then the postulation of a normative sexuality that is "before," "outside," or "beyond" power is a cultural impossibility and a politically impracticable dream, one that postpones the concrete and contemporary task of rethinking subversive possibilities for sexuality and identity within the terms of power itself.[9]

If we agree with Butler that "there is no gender identity behind the expressions of gender; that identity is performatively constituted by the very 'expressions' that are said to be its results" (25), we can read the female speaker in the *Lai du Lecheor* as a character who performs within the given cultural construction of femininity to remake or redo it. At least we can choose to read her inscribed voice that way. We can begin to ask how this woman's constructed voice "does" or "redoes" the gender identity that has been imposed upon her, how she operates within a matrix of power relations, repeating its conventions while also displacing them. Our question then becomes what kind of gender construction is being played out in this purportedly female critique of male storytelling conventions?

When the female speaker in the *Lai du Lecheor* tells her female audience that all men want is *con*, we hear on the one hand the stereotypical reduction of women's anatomy to pleasure-giving genitalia so prevalent in the misogynous registers of Old French farce and fabliau. But we can also see, as in farce and fabliau themselves, how the status of that *con* changes significantly when it speaks, rather than functioning as the object of another's speech. If in asserting that men really want nothing other than *con*, the speaking lady of the *Lai du Lecheor* reiterates the commonplace that men want to possess women as objects, she also reveals that men want what women have, that is to say: the sweet *chose* that women, as subjects, can choose to give or withold. The *con* typically objectified as an isolated body part has here shifted significantly toward (if not into) the subject position as it becomes an integrated part of the speaking female. Delivering her critique of male storytelling within an alternate literary economy of women speaking to women about female anatomy, this talking *con*, by its very existence, calls into question the adventure story's standard objectification of the silenced female body. For even more significant than *having* what men want, this heroine purports also to *know* what men want. She then occupies the subject position to the extent that she knows her object, and says so. With a bawdy flair that rings of the wife's pointed remarks in the "Four Wishes of St. Martin," this courtly lady refashions her assigned role as statuesque beauty to speak as a knowing, thinking, and sexualized body all at the same time.[10] There is no question that this *con* has a head.

If *Erec et Enide* Were "Enide's Romance"

Chrétien de Troyes does not mention *con* in his classic Arthurian tale of love and adventure known by modern readers as *Erec et Enide*. Neither do his female protagonists refer overtly to women's body parts. But I want to take the *Lai du Lecheor* as a point of departure for reading Chrétien's romance because it stages a rivalry between men's stories and women's stories that Chrétien's text works so hard to obscure. By highlighting the love story between his protagonists along with the hero's reputation and chivalric prowess—the very topics addressed by male taletellers in the *Lai du Lecheor* ("Des amors et des drueries / Et des nobles chevaleries," vv. 17–18)—Chrétien diverts our attention away from one of the more difficult questions at the heart of his romance: the status of the woman's voice, her right to speak versus the necessity of keeping her silent.

The issue is not, to my mind, simply one of wifely obedience, nor of love, though the Griselda story lurks barely beneath the surface of this highly complex tale. Whether or not Enide should speak, when and under what conditions she might talk, forms part of a larger narrative problem concerning authorship, or more specifically: "Who's speaking" the Arthurian adventure story? Who's telling the tale we read/hear and how might that tale change with a change in the gender of the speaker? The heroine, Enide, is perhaps best known for parading somnolently throughout the first 2000 lines of Chrétien's text in utter silence before uttering the first in a series of curt, but disruptively uncourtly, statements.[11] These moments of female speech, however corrected and appropriated by the end of the tale, allow us to see how the most fundamental rivalry played out in this text exists between the male adventure story and female retellings of it. In this sense *Erec et Enide* provides a particularly apt medieval case study for addressing the questions posed in the longstanding debate between Nancy K. Miller and Peggy Kamuf over the relative importance of knowing "who's speaking" (male or female) in the literary text and "what difference it makes."[12]

Erec et Enide begins with a description of the author's own literary practice and ends with tales told differently by its male and female protagonists. It is the relation between overt invocations of the storytelling process and the scattered instances of female speech throughout the romance that interests me here, the relation between tales told officially to the courtly world and tales told by female protagonists who, like the eight women of the *Lai du Lecheor*, stand most often apart from the courtly milieu, speaking typically in private or sometimes even in "silent" monologues.

If we read *Erec et Enide* not as a master narrative of Chrétien de Troyes's rhetorical skill but as a tale of female voices speaking against that tradition of storytelling, we get a new picture of love and courtliness, romance and adventure. We begin to see how the objectification of the lovely lady, so crucial to the working of the courtly milieu, where she provides the inspiration for feats of prowess, the audience for chivalric combat, and the supportive listener for tales of adventure, focuses principally on the female body. The heroine's speech more staunchly resists colonization and appropriation; her constructed voice cannot be fetishized as easily as her fictive flesh.

When Chrétien's lovely heroine Enide "wakes up" from her slumber in the land of silence and begins to talk, she, much like the female speaker in the *Lai du Lecheor*, tells unsettling stories. Altering the standard scenario of courtly romance in many ways, she speaks within, but apart from, the master narrative, significantly rewriting the very *conte d'aventure* that creates her as a silent object of the heroic knight's desire. From this perspective Chrétien's romance shows how women, who are essential to the working of the courtly world, can nonetheless make "gender trouble"[13] within it, not only with their bodies but more significantly with the voices that issue from them.

Conjointure: Coupling for/with Pleasure

The pleasure of this text, as is typically the case with Old French romance narratives, resides in the telling of a love story. But whose pleasure is at stake here and what are its parameters? Chrétien warns in the prologue to *Erec et Enide* that the attentive author must be careful not to silence any material that might bring pleasure to his audience. The storyteller's careful craft involves speaking out, giving voice to thoughts and words in order to please the listener:

> car qui con estuide entrelait,
> tot i puet tel chose teisir
> qui molt vandroit puis a pleisir.[14]

> (Whoever neglects his learning may easily silence something that would later give much pleasure.)

The rhyme sounded here between *pleisir* and *teisir* posits a relationship between the author's speech and the pleasure of the text, telling us in essence that to silence literature is to withold pleasure.

Elsewhere in this romance, however, courtly pleasure is defined, in line with the female speaker's observation in the *Lai du Lecheor*, as deriving from enjoyment of the woman's body. This sexual pleasure takes place in private and in the silence of the medieval bedchamber. When Enide, who is cast throughout the tale as the ideal object of desire, valiantly fends off the amorous advances of the *comte vaniteux*, she promises to deliver the carnal union he desires, craftily rhyming *pleisir* with *seisir*:

> Car je ferai vostre pleisir:
> Por vostre me poez seisir.
> (vv. 3357–58)

(I will do your bidding; you can take me as your own.)

Pleisir here connotes the purely physical bliss proffered by the naked woman's body, the kind of pleasure that the comte de Limors also hopes to attain from his proposed liaison with Enide:

> La dame est moie et je sui suens,
> si ferai de li mon pleisir.
> (vv. 4800–4801)

(The lady is mine and I am hers; I will do as I want with her.)

If these two admirers are thwarted in their efforts to woo Enide and seize her body, Erec of course succeeds at this task. And at the end of the forest adventure, when Erec and Enide are reconciled as spouses and reunited as lovers, *pleise* rimes appropriately with *beise*:

> Ansanble jurent an un lit,
> et li uns l'autre acole et beise:
> riens nule n'est qui tant lor pleise.
> (vv. 5200–5202)

(They lay together in bed, hugging and kissing. Nothing could have pleased them so much.)

This scene of erotic reconciliation recalls the incident that sparked the couple's arduous adventure earlier in the romance, the problematic encounter in the bedchamber at Carnant, which is in fact the motor force behind the entire romance. Pleasure, in this case excessive carnal pleasure, is the very reason that Erec and Enide embark on their protracted forest journey. Erec, as we remember, had been so caught up in the actions of *acoler* and *beisier* that he neglected his chivalric duty in favor of love:

> Mes tant l'ama Erec d'amors,
> que d'armes mes ne li chaloit,
> . . . .
> si an fist d'amie et sa drue;
> en li a mise s'antendue,
> en acoler et en beisier
> (vv. 2430–31, 2435–37)

(Erec loved her so much that he neglected armed combat. He made her his lover and sweetheart. He put all his attention into hugging and kissing her)

Within the context of Chrétien's first romance, pleasure then carries two distinct meanings as it derives from two distinct sources: the act of conferring pleasure can come either from the author or his heroine, from the speaking subject, who offers the pleasure of his tale to a listening audience, or from the silent object of desire, who can potentially provide the pleasure of the female body. The polarity thus implied sets male speech against female sexuality, suggesting a rivalry between *boche d'home* and *corps de femme*, between the romance author and his female protagonist.

Chrétien's avowed project, in full, is to transform the standard conte d'avanture into a pleasureable *bele conjointure*. He proposes in the process to weave into his narrative the unspecified *tel chose* generally neglected, he tells us, in the adventure story:

> Li vilains dit an son respit
> que *tel chose* a l'an an despit
> qui molt valt mialz que l'an ne cuide
> (vv. 1–3, my emphasis)

(The peasant says in his proverb that one may hold in contempt *something* that is worth much more than one believes)

But what is at stake in this shift from the grammatically masculine *conte d'avanture* to the feminine *conjointure*? What precisely is this *bele conjoin-*

ture that Chrétien boasts of as his distinctive literary accomplishment? And what is the *tel chose* included or absorbed within it?

The neologism *bele conjointure* has been taken generally to signify a masterful weaving together of diverse narrative elements.[15] Yet if we think of *conjointure* in the sense of coupling, joining, bringing together in amorous liaison or linking in marriage,[16] we see how the romance author has metaphorically transferred the act of coupling with a woman, with her enigmatic *chose*, into the realm of literary creation that is his alone. This is a particularly deft example of colonizing the unknown terrain of the female body by absorbing it into discourse in the way Irigaray describes: "the really urgent task is to ensure the colonization of this new 'field,' to force it, not without splintering, into the productions of the same discourse" (*Spéculum*, 137).[17] In a sense, Chrétien's neologism gives his project away, for we can hear within this ostensibly new literary practice of *conjointure* the *con* that it contains and usurps. The pleasure of the heroine's body has become in this instance the pleasure of the romancer's text. Or at least that is what Chrétien's prologue proposes.

Men's Stories: The *Conte (comte) d'avanture*

The point is driven home even more clearly through a flurry of homophonic resonance that draws on the base sound *con* to outline a process of all-male storytelling. Within the space of four lines, the prologue repeats the word *contes* in various semantic configurations that make it read almost as a verb conjugation, establishing the morphology of the Arthurian adventure story in terms of men who tell tales about valiant men to male listeners:

> d'Erec, le fil Lac, est li *contes*,
> que devant rois et devant *contes*
> depecier et corronpre suelent
> cil qui de *conter* vivre vuelent.
> (vv. 19–22, my emphasis)

(This is a story about Lac's son, Erec, a story often corrupted and deformed when told before audiences of kings and counts by those who attempt to make a living from telling tales.)

Chrétien designates the literary world of the *conte d'avanture* as comprising a tale (*contes*) about a count (*contes*), Erec, identified by his patrilineal descent, a tale told regularly before kings and counts (*contes*) by professional male storytellers (cil qui de *conter* vivre vuelent). Women, typically excluded from playing the key roles of creator or heroic subject in the courtly scenario of literary production, are here also absent as listeners.[18]

But in a telling deviation from the rules for narrative composition set out in Chrétien's prologue, the recipient of, and principal listener for, the first chivalric tale within this tale—Yder's glowing account of Erec's extraordinary valor—is a woman, Guenevere:

> La ou Ydiers vit la reïne,
> jusque devant ses piez ne fine,
> et si salua tot premiers
> le roi et toz ses chevaliers,
> et dist: "Dame, an vostre prison
> m'anvoie ci uns gentix hon,
> uns chevaliers vaillanz et preuz"
> (vv. 1179–85)

(When Yder saw the queen, he went up to her. He greeted the king and his knights first, then said, "Lady, a noble man sent me to your prison, a valiant and worthy knight")

The queen has also performed previously as a teller of tales, but one whose adventure story differs substantially from male accounts of knightly glory. Her report to Arthur's men about Erec's unfortunate encounter with Yder's dwarf paints a picture of embarrassing defeat:

> L'avanture lor a contee
> qu'an la forest avoit trovee
> del chevalier que armé vit
> et del nain felon et petit
> qui de s'escorgiee ot ferue
> sa pucele sor la main nue,
> et ot feru tot ansimant
> Erec el vis molt leidemant.
> (vv. 323–30)

(She told them of the adventure that she had witnessed in the forest, of the armed knight she had seen and the treacherous little dwarf who had hit her maiden on the bare hand with his whip and outrageously struck Erec in the face.)

The Erec of Guenevere's tale could not be more different from the accomplished "chevaliers cortois" portrayed in stories of Erec's incomparable prowess told by his companion knights throughout the narrative.[19] Indeed Guenevere's performance as a romance storyteller in the early moments of Chrétien's text raises the problematic question of woman's place in the courtly world of combat and storytelling. Her tale of Erec's chivalric ineptitude is significantly twice corrected at subsequent moments: first by Yder's prototypical account of Erec's knightly valor and later by Erec's own account of his adventures (v. 6416) told through the voice of the narrator. Yder's account takes up precisely where Guenevere's left off, narrating the beaten Erec's comeback:

> uns gentix hon,
> uns chevaliers vaillanz et preuz,
> cil cui fist hier santir les neuz
> mes nains de la corgiee el vis;
> vaincu m'a d'armes et conquis.
> (vv. 1184–88)

(A noble man, a valiant and strong knight, whose face was made to feel the knots on my dwarf's club yesterday. He vanquished me in combat and conquered me.)

Erec's tale at the end of the romance simply omits the unflattering incident that Guenevere's story so pointedly records. But his *conte* goes further, erasing the presence of this female protagonist altogether, along with many other women who have populated the romance, including the poem's heroine, Enide. Speaking only of his chivalric encounters and omitting his less courtly moments, Erec retells Guenevere's story according to the terms laid out in Chrétien's prologue. He tells a *conte* about men from which women are absent:

si com il lor conta et dist:
des trois chevaliers qu'il conquist,
et puis des cinc, et puis del conte
qui feire li volt si grant honte;
et puis des jaianz dist aprés;
trestot en ordre pres a pres
ses avantures lor conta.

(vv. 6429–35)

(He told them and spoke about the three knights he had conquered,
and then the five, and then about the count who wanted to shame
him so, and then he told about the giants. All in order, one after the
other, he recounted his adventures to them.)[20]

This and preceding tales of knightly *avanture* contained within Chrétien's romance play well to the male-dominated community at Arthur's
court, a place defined by the imposing presence of the king's barons,
whose names are detailed at length in several key scenes (vv. 311–20,
1671–82). But the intense male bonding that links members of this chivalric world is perhaps most evident during the actual scenes of combat,
where a host of reflexive verbs typically joins rival knights in a perfectly
balanced mutual exchange. Even the enemy functions more as a partner
than a rival in the world of codified chivalric coupling, as the following
fight between Erec and Yder attests:

Cil plus d'un arpant s'antr'esloingnent,
por assanbler les chevax poignent;
as fers des lances se requierent,
par si grant vertu s'antre fierent
que li escu piercent et croissent,
les lances esclicent et froissent;
depiecent li arçon derriers,
guerpir lor estuet les estriés;
contre terre amedui se ruient,
li cheval par le chanp s'an fuient.
Cil resont tost an piez sailli,
des lances n'orent pas failli,
les espees des fuerres traient,

felenessemant s'antre essaient
des tranchanz, granz cos s'antre donent;
li hiaume cassent et resonent.
(vv. 865–80)

(They drew well away from each other, spurred their horses to take their places. They sought each other with the blades of their lances. They struck each other so vigorously that their shields broke and crumbled. Their lances shattered and flew apart. The back of their saddles broke open. They had to abandon their stirrups. Both fell to the ground. The horses fled across the field. The two knights jumped to their feet again. They had not missed with their lances. They unsheathed their swords and treacherously tried to deal each other heavy blows with the sharp blades. Their helmets resonated and broke apart.)[21]

Linked through plural verbs bearing a single subject "they," neither combattant acts alone or works against the other. They move in tandem, even falling off their horses *together* ("contre terre amedui se ruinent," v. 873), enacting a synthesis of being that is unequaled in any love scene between Erec and Enide.

Even the moment at Caradigan when the lovers' mutual glance is described does not evoke the extended balletic pleasure of knights joined in combat:

N'an preïssent pas reancon
li uns de l'autre regarder:
molt estoient igal et per
de corteisie et de biauté
et de grant debonereté.
(vv. 1482–86)[22]

(Neither one took ransom from looking at the other. They were equal in courtliness, beauty, and graciousness.)

Verbs indicating symmetrical and symbiotic action do not dominate here. Rather nouns lump the couple together in an immobile unit ("corteisie," "biauté," "debonereté," and further on, "meniere," "mors," "matiere"), while adjectives fight for predominance over one another as we hear that "no one could in truth choose the best one nor the most beautiful nor the wisest" (que nus qui le voir volist dire / n'an poïst le meilleur eslire / ne le plus bel ne le plus sage, vv. 1489–91).

Most telling is the glaring inaccuracy of two lines asserting the lovers to be equally beautiful images:

> onques deus si beles ymages
> n'asanbla lois ne mariages.
> > (vv. 1495–96)

(Never before had the laws of marriage joined two such beautiful images.)

For in what precedes we have witnessed Erec looking at Enide with all the power of Pygmalion to sculpt and form her beautiful body:

> De l'esgarder ne puet preu faire:
> quant plus l'esgarde et plus li plest,
> ne puet müer qu'il ne la best;
> volantiers pres de li se tret,
> en li esgarder se refet;
> molt remire son chief le blont,
> ses ialz rianz et son cler front,
> le nes et la face et la boche,
> don granz dolçors au cuer li toche.
> Tot remire jusqu' a la hanche,
> le manton et la gorge blanche,
> flans et costez et braz et mains
> > (vv. 1466–77)

(He cannot get enough of looking at her. The more he looks, the more it pleases him. He cannot resist desiring/looking at her. Gladly he moves closer to her and continues looking. He looks especially at her blond hair, smiling eyes, and smooth forehead, her nose and face and mouth, which bring joy to his heart. He looks at everything down to the hips—her white chin and neck, thighs and chest and arms and hands)[23]

The heroine's look, which is said to return Erec's gaze, produces no such "bele ymage" of the desirable knight. We hear that she looked at him, with no indication of what she saw:

> mes ne remire mie mains
> la dameisele le vasal
> de boen voel et de cuer leal
> qu'il fesoit li par contançon.
>   (vv. 1478–81)

(The young lady eyed the knight with desire and a loyal heart no less avidly than he had looked at her.)

Thus when we are told that the lovers looked at each other mutually, though we see only what Erec sees, the supposed equality of their "beles ymages" falters. We wonder how the couple could be "so similar, of one character and one substance" (d'une meniere, d'unes mors et d'une matiere, vv. 1487–88), as the text later asserts. In terms of the mechanics of the gaze that constructs subjectivity, it seems rather that Erec is "plus sage"—as he plays the role of knowing subject—while Enide remains clearly "plus bele."[24]

Indeed Enide here becomes beautiful only to the extent that her body is constructed by Erec's gaze upon it. The point is made strikingly in the scene of the couple's first encounter where Erec's description of the beautiful Enide omits certain key features that we as readers see, namely, those traits that mark her inferior social status. The reader/listener thus perceives two Enides: a lower-class young woman in tattered clothing who emerges from a workshop (ovreor, v. 442), stables Erec's horse (v. 451), and later arms him as would a squire (v. 709) and the beautiful, noble creature whose hair rivals that of the courtly Iseut (vv. 411, 422–24). The image of beauty that Erec constructs reflects only those aristocratic qualities that resemble his own: the ovreor where he would never be, the gestures of stabling and arming, the tattered clothes must be left out, as they are later left behind, because they fall beyond the mirror of his courtliness.[25]

The hierarchy implicit in the heterosexual love relation that makes Erec sage while Enide remains bele contrasts sharply with the symbiosis of male combattants whose actions could in fact accurately be characterized as "d'une meniere, d'une mors et d'une matiere" as they "s'antr'esloingnent, se requierent, s'antre fierent, se ruient, s'antre essaient des tranchanz, granz cos s'entre donent" (draw away from each other, seek each other, strike each other, fall down together, try out their blades together, deal each other heavy blows, vv. 865–79). These men give themselves to each other more equally and more completely than the professed lovers ever do. And such coupling gives rise to the stories of male heroism that further cement ties between men in the Arthurian world, where the *conteur* tells a *conte* to an audience of *contes et rois*.[26] But where is the female *con* in all of this? And how might the sexualized woman's body it represents tell the Arthurian tale differently?

Women's Stories: The *conte (con) de femme*

Readers of courtly romance have long defined the Old French *conte d'avanture* as a tale predicated on the unknown, literally on that which has not yet happened, on "ce qui est a venir." It is the unknown dilemma that will befall a knight that gives the hero an occasion to prove his valor and subsequently hear it recorded in stories that bring joy or pleasure to the listener. But what is this unknown that knights are forever conquering? The uncharted territory that they perpetually seek to tame and control echoes hauntingly of "these uncharted territories, these dark continents, these worlds through the looking glass/on the other side of the mirror" that Irigaray evokes to describe man's view of female sexuality (*Speculum*, 136).[27] Could it be that in its affirmation of male subjectivity the *conte d'avanture* relocates onto the field of chivalric combat the unknown field of female sexual difference, temporarily substituting coupling between men (*conbatre*) for heterosexual liaison with a woman (*conjointure*)?

The *con* is precisely, we are told euphemistically, what gets Erec into trouble at Carnant, where his dalliance in the marriage bed through actions of *acoler* and *beisier* causes him to neglect chivalric *conjointure* with men in battle:

> N'avoit mes soing de tornoier:
> a sa fame volt dosnoier.
>
> (vv. 2433–34)

(He no longer took an interest in tournaments but preferred to spar with his wife.)

Erec has neglected, that is, the combat itself and the male hugging and kissing that so often accompany it, as in Erec's encounter with Gauvain, "de joie l'acole et anbrace" (full of joy, he hugs and embraces him, v. 4136) or his combat with Guivret, "Li uns l'autre beise et acole" (they hug and kiss each other, v. 3900). The trouble with Enide in this scene is that she intervenes literally and problematically between men, splitting the bonds of male *conjointure* through the use of her sexualized body.

But that body and the heroine's sexual identity are inextricably linked throughout this romance with the woman's voice.[28] The testing adventure in particular is undertaken for two express reasons. First because Enide has seduced her knight with the pleasure of amorous embraces, drawing him away from public tournament and joust. But secondly, and no less important, because this supposed seductress has exercised her voice, daring to describe her knight's dalliance as "recreantise," or chivalric neglect. The dilemma initiated by the allure of female sexuality in this romance has thus been aggravated by the activity of the companion orifice, the woman's mouth. The avowed purpose of the testing adventure is to bring both offending orifices under control: to curtail Enide's erotic activity, enabling Erec to reestablish his prowess as a knight, and to curb the intrusive woman's voice that first enunciated the charge of *recreantise*. At the end of the forest adventure, Erec makes explicit the link between Enide's erotic misdeed and her speech by pardoning his lover/wife for two related offenses, one sexual and the other linguistic:

> Je vos le pardoing tot et quit
> del forfait et de la parole.
> > (vv. 4892–93)

(I forgive you everything: the words and the deed.)

Nothing intrinsically harmful characterizes the fateful words that Enide utters at Carnant.[29] Lamenting her role in distracting Erec from fulfilling his chivalric obligations, she proclaims only indirectly and very cautiously his own chivalric neglect:

> "Lasse, fet ele, con mar fui!
> de mon païs que ving ça querre?

Bien me doit essorbir la terre,
quant toz li miaudres chevaliers,
li plus hardiz et li plus fiers,
qui onques fust ne cuens ne rois,
li plus lëax, li plus cortois,
a del tot an tot relanquie
por moi tote chevalerie.
              (vv. 2492–2500)

(Wretch, she said, miserable me! Why did I leave my homeland to
come here? The earth should swallow me up since the best knight,
the boldest and bravest, the most loyal and courtly who ever was
either count or king has, because of me, abandoned all chivalry.)

In describing Erec's failed knighthood, Enide initiates no charge of her
own. She simply repeats the laments formerly articulated by Erec's own
companions:

Si conpaignon duel en avoient;
sovant entr'ax se demantoient
de ce que trop l'amoit assez.
              (vv. 2439–41)

(His companions were grieved on account of this. They often
lamented among themselves that he loved her too much.)

She reiterates accusations she has overheard: "Par ceste terre dïent tuit"
(Everyone around here is saying . . . , v. 2540). But words formerly pro-
nounced by honorable knights create a radically different effect when they
issue from the mouth of a woman. If the laments of Erec's companions at
arms express concern, while Enide's concern seems also to condemn, it is
partially because this woman's speech is linked not to public declaration
but to private body functions. We remember that in the scene at Carnant,
Enide speaks from the privacy of the bedchamber and more specifically
from the very bed where she has "pleased" her failed knight.

Although the forest adventure is most famous because throughout
the journey Erec issues injunctions for Enide's silence,[30] the scene also

includes a spate of directives that distance the knight from the troublesome female flesh. Taking Enide along on the forest adventure appears at first to be a gesture of joining together with her, recasting the lovers' previously private and excessive sexual coupling into a more acceptable form of public union:

> mes il lor jure et acreante
> qu'il n'an manra ja conpaignon,
> se sa fame solemant non.
>   (vv. 2688–90)

(But her [Erec] swore and pledged to them that he would take along no companion other than his wife.)

But the verbal combat that ensues between Erec and his female rival, different from those battles that typically bond men together, actually works to hold the heterosexual couple apart. Erec's instructions to Enide throughout the forest trial affects a *disjointure* from the troublesome female body. He first requires Enide to ride alone ahead of him (vv. 2770–71), where she serves as bait to provoke attackers whom he can vanquish.[31] On many occasions, Erec instructs Enide to stay behind as he joins rival knights in battle elsewhere.[32] Because Enide so often rides and sits alone, the largest portion of her speech during the forest trial occurs in the form of monologue, spoken not to Erec but privately to herself (vv. 2829–39, 2962–78, 3100–3112).[33] Yet she does speak. If Erec remains deaf to most of this heroine's pointed words during the testing adventure, we hear them all. What we hear is Enide speaking not from the masculinized "head" that would underwrite chivalric norms but from a female body that actively resists them. We hear, in effect, this heroine rewriting the very adventure story that contains and constructs her, outlining the possibility of other versions that traditionally have gone untold and unrecorded. Her words map out for us the varied ways in which the *conte d'aventure*, when placed in the mouth of a woman, comes out differently.

If the scene at Carnant demonstrates how Enide could damage Erec's reputation as a knight by speaking of his *recreantise*, succeeding scenes reveal how her words could ruin Erec's chivalric identity by voicing stories of his potential failure, his carelessness, or ignorance. When Enide first defends her decision to speak out despite Erec's injunction for silence, she posits the knight's possible defeat, citing her fear that the three attackers might harm him:

> Ci vienent poignant apres vos
> troi chevalier qui molt vos chacent;
> peor ai que mal ne vos facent.
> (vv. 2842–44)

(Here come three knights riding after you in hot pursuit. I am afraid they will harm you.)

Her story not unlike Guenevere's tale of Erec's unchivalric encounter with Yder's dwarf, casts the perfect knight in the role of a loser, one who might be harmed by his opponent, rather than one who effortlessly wins the fray. Enide's second speech paints an equally unchivalric portrait of Erec being struck by one of five rival brigands:

> et li cinquiesmes a vos muet
> tant con chevax porter le puet;
> ne gart l'ore que il vos fiere.
> (vv. 2987–89)

(The fifth one is coming toward you as fast as his horse will carry him. He'll soon strike you.)

When Chrétien counters these "women's stories" with reports of Erec's success against both sets of attackers, the difference between his telling of Erec's adventures and Enide's version becomes all the more apparent. Her narrative directly undermines the essence of the adventure story by substituting for the necessary "unknown" a description of what is about to take place, "three knights are coming," "five knights are waiting to attack." Her comments not only deflate Erec's skill, they replay the troublesome imbalance of Carnant by placing the heroine in a position of knowing more than her knight does. Even though the entire forest escapade is staged by Erec as a test of Enide, he is made to occupy at these key moments a position of apparent inferior knowledge.

Elsewhere Enide justifies her decision to speak by depicting Erec as forgetfully incompetent. During the encounter with Guivret she observes:

> Je voi bien que mes sires pansse
> tant que lui meïsmes oblie;
> donc est bien droiz que je li die.
>
> (vv. 3748–50)

(I see that my lord is deep in thought, so much so that he forgets himself. Thus is it right for me to speak to him.)[34]

When fleeing the *comte vaniteux*, Enide breaks her silence to correct Erec's tactical miscalculation, telling him they must speed up if they are to escape:

> Se nos alons an tel meniere
> ne poez de ci eschaper.
>
> (vv. 3550–51)

(If we continue like this, you won't escape from here.)

At these moments Enide speaks, however hesitatingly, however awkwardly, as the informed subject playing to Erec's less knowledgeable object. Her "women's stories" are emitted piecemeal and quietly, remaining always under the mystifying cover of wifely obedience and courtly love, though they contest the very terms of woman's subservient place in both marital and courtly contracts.

Enide again moves problematically into the subject position when rebuking Guivret for having attacked the wounded Erec. As her pointed words remind this knight of a chivalric code he has apparently forgotten, she alone appears to know how knights should behave:

> Que ja n'an valdroit mialz tes pris,
> se tu avoies morz ou pris
> un chevalier qui n'a pooir
> de relever, ce puez veoir,
> car d'armes a tant cos soferz
> que toz est de plaies coverz.
>
> (vv. 5003–8)

(Your reputation will never be enhanced by capturing or killing
a knight who is unable to get up. You can see this; he has suffered
so many blows that he is covered with wounds.)

Doesn't he realize, she implies, that his reputation is at stake? And we as
reader/listeners overhearing this exchange are made to see how the
knight's hard-earned *pris*, established in battle and disseminated through
tales of glory, can be threatened by the counter-narrative of a woman who
would change that story, calling him a *chevaliers maudit*: "Chevaliers, mau-
diz soies tu" (v. 4991).

With the comte de Limors, Enide condemns outright the feudal trading of women in marriage upon which her own liaison with Erec is based.
Flatly rejecting the count's marriage proposal, though it echoes almost
exactly the objectifying terms of Erec's earlier offer, Enide now asserts that
this commodification of women cannot bring her *joie*:

> Cele respont: "Sire fuiez!
> por Deu merci, lessiez m'ester;
> ne poez ci rien conquester;
> rien qu'an poïst dire ne faire
> ne me poroit a joie atraire."
>   (vv. 4672–76)

(She answers: "Go away, sir! In God's name, leave me alone; you
cannot conquer anything here. Nothing you can say or do will bring
me joy.")

Having initially ignored the count's threats, "Cele ne li vialt mot respondre, / car rien ne prisoit sa menace" (She did not wish to respond
because she did not take his threat seriously, vv. 4786–87), she ends by
openly defying them along with everything else he says:

> Ahi! fet ele, ne me chaut
> que tu me dïes ne ne faces:
> ne criem tes cos ne tes menaces.
>   (vv. 4806–8)

("Ah!" she said, "whatever you say or do means nothing to me. I'm not afraid of your blows or threats.")

Enide could, in theory, have made this statement to Erec as well. She does, after great deliberation, ignore his equally intimidating *menaces*. And if her blanket rejection of the count's speech includes his earlier appraisal of her beauty, we can hear in it an implicit critique of the objectification she suffered from Erec's similarly masterful desire to transform her into something he considers worthwhile. The count offers to fashion Enide, Pygmalion-like, into a countess:

> Vostre biautez, qui tant est fine,
> bone avanture vos destine,
> que je vos recevrai a fame,
> de vos ferai contesse et dame.
> (vv. 4663–66)

(Your fine beauty destines you for good fortune. I will take you as a wife and make you a countess and a lady.)

Erec had proposed with equal authority to make Enide a queen:

> Que je l'an manrai an ma terre,
> se Dex la victoire m'an done;
> la li ferai porter corone
> (vv. 662–64)

(I will lead her to my lands if God grants me victory. There I will have her wear a crown)[35]

Of course Chrétien leads us to believe that Enide responds differently to the two offers because she is in love with the valiant Erec and thoroughly disinterested in the presumptuous count. But the verbal echo between the two incidents helps us to see how both knights' constructions of woman as obedient *fame* or beautiful *amie* deny a place to female subjectivity. Each time Enide breaks her silence we are reminded pointedly of how men's stories in this romance so often elide the speaking, knowing female subject.

The crucial difference introduced when women speak is perhaps most apparent in Enide's manipulative encounter with the comte vaniteux. When she coyly constructs a false tale of future romance and coupling, a love story in which seizing the female body to derive pleasure in sex is paired with taking the prized woman by force from a rival knight:

> Mes, biax sire, or vos apaiez,
> car je ferai vostre pleisir:
> por vostre me poez seisir
> . . . .
> mes demain anvoiez ceanz
> voz chevaliers et voz sergenz,
> si me feites a force prandre.
>   (vv. 3356–58, 3379–81)

(But, good sir, calm yourself; I will do your bidding: you can take me as your own. Tomorrow send your knights and men-at-arms here and take me by force.)

Outlining a chivalric scenario consonant with the courtly exchange of women later codified in the custom of Logres in Chrétien de Troyes's *Chevalier de la charrette*, Enide here describes the standard courtly fight and its resolution: when the attacker attempts to take the lady by force, her defender will fight back fiercely and courageously. The winner gets the woman, to do with as he pleases, for she is now his *amie*:

> si me feites a force prandre;
> mes sires me voldra desfandre,
> qui molt est fiers et corageus.
> Ou soit a certes ou a geus,
> feites le prandre et afoler
> ou de la teste decoler.
> Trop ai menee ceste vie,
> je n'aim mie la conpaignie
> mon seignor, ja n'an quier mantir.

Je vos voldroie ja santir
an un lit certes nu a nu.
                    (vv. 3381–91)

(And take me by force. My lord, who is very bold and brave, will
defend me, in earnest or in jest. Have him captured and wounded or
have his head cut off. I have led this life too long. I have no interest
in my lord's company and do not want to lie about it. I would like
to feel you naked beside me in bed.)

The most significant feature of this "woman's story" is not, to my
mind, that Enide lies to the count in order to protect Erec's life. But that
is the message that the narrator's commentary underscores through
phrases like the following:

Bien sot par parole enivrer
bricon, des qu'ele i met l'antante;
mialz est asez qu'ele li mante,
que ses sires fust depeciez.
                    (vv. 3410–13)

(She knew how to intoxicate a rogue with words as soon as she put
her mind to it. It is better that she lie to him than have her lord cut
to bits.)

But we as reader/listeners can witness in this scene a more important
sleight of hand: that Enide "knows how to confuse, confound, dizzy" the
listener "through her speech" (Bien sot par parole enivrer, v. 3410) because
when she tells the standard tale of Arthurian romance and adventure, it
necessarily comes out differently. Although this female storyteller *knows*
the requisite narrative elements that make a pleasing courtly tale, when she
articulates them from her mouth and body, the story becomes a dream, a
trick, a mirage. In fact in this instance it disappears altogether. For the
narrative Enide recounts will never take place, at least not the way she tells
it here.[36]

When this heroine articulates the basic "men's story," it doesn't work;
something crucial is lost in the transfer. Or perhaps something is added.[37]
But we learn unequivocally from this incident that Enide's story diverges

critically from the chivalric model it proposes. It is as if she states here between the lines: this is not my story. I can tell it; but it will be just a story, a fiction, even a falsehood. Certainly not the kind of story Chrétien boasts of in his prologue as a tale destined to advance the teller's reputation and outlast all others.

Enide's stories, simply put, do not convey the same kind of knowledge (*estuide*, *escience*) as Chrétien's tale. Neither do they simply reverse the terms of the male/female equation, placing a knowledgeable woman at the top of the chivalric hierarchy. Rather they make "gender trouble" within the system, showing how one could tell the chivalric tale differently, thereby exposing what it hides. One could reveal, for example, as Enide does repeatedly, that knights might fall short of the chivalric ideal or that ladies might refuse the commodification and fetishizing that that ideal requires. Enide's words then do not simply posit the woman's story as an antidote or corollary to the chivalric men's story, supplying the "missing half" of a binary equation. Enide's stories in this romance disrupt the most fundamental literary *conjointure* on which male adventure stories are built.[38] They do so by refusing the binary logic governing chivalric practice and substituting in its place a logic that rings of Irigaray's paradoxical "both at once," that position forged from holding one view and its irreconcilable opposite simultaneously. The stance is symptomatic, according to Irigaray, of woman's necessarily indeterminate social positioning. As Diana Fuss explains, "Both at once signifies that a woman is simultaneously singular and double; she is 'already two—but not divisible into one(s),' or, put another way, she is '*neither one nor two*'"[39] This is precisely what Enide herself later says.

Who Is Enide—Where Does She Stand?

Erec has structured the forest trial, by contrast, according to the either/or logic of chivalric exchange in which two knights fight and one *or* the other wins. This means sometimes that one lives and the other dies, or more often that one knight wins the lady and the other goes to court to tell his tale of defeat. But the poles of prescribed conduct cannot be confused any more than a typical knight could be truthful and dishonest or courtly and unchivalrous at the same time.[40] Following this logic, Erec can envision only two options for his wife's participation in the forest journey: either speech or silence, the implication being that her speech should be curtailed and silence imposed. As the narrator explains:

> qu'ele ne set lequel seisir
> ou le parler *ou* le teisir.
>
> (vv. 3713–14)

(She does not know which to choose: speaking *or* silence.)

And yet we have seen all along how this heroine speaks most often during the forest trial to herself, her voice being positioned, as in those fateful moments at Carnant when Erec overhears or only partially hears her words, somewhere *between* silence and full-blown speech. Often speaking only to describe the impossibility of her speech, Enide reveals to us during her moments of imposed silence that—in defiance of courtly logic—she participates fully in *neither* realm Erec has outlined. Rather, she straddles them both. Although she is ostensibly mute during the forest journey, we hear her ask, "will I not dare to speak?" ("Dex! serai je donc si coarde / que dire ne li oserai?" vv. 2836–37), and in a subsequent moment of supposed silence, she asserts, "I cannot not talk," ("ne leirai que je ne li die" v. 2978).

Enide's indeterminate status as a speaking subject emerges most clearly perhaps during the encounter with Guivret. As she hears the rival knight approach but is afraid to break Erec's injunction to silence (vv. 3708–11), the narrator explains:

> Sovant del dire s'aparoille
> si que la leingue se remuet,
> mes la voiz pas issir n'an puet,
> car de peor estraint les danz,
> s'anclost la parole dedanz,
> et si se justise et destraint:
> la boche clot, les danz estraint
> que la parole hors n'an aille.
>
> (vv. 3716–23)

(She often prepared to speak, moving her tongue. But her voice could not come out because, out of fear, she clenched her teeth, closing her words inside. Thus did she govern and restrict herself, her mouth closed and teeth clenched so that speech could not issue forth.)

A long monologue follows during which Enide speaks alone only to question whether or not she should speak at all, underscoring how this heroine often speaks from silence or speaks without speaking, a position unaccounted for by the binary logic that Erec invokes to structure the forest trial. Indeed when Enide speaks up, without necessarily speaking out, on three successive occasions, her voice epitomizes what for Erec is a thoroughly unknown option: the polar extremes of speech and silence might constitute a false binary, there might be terms between the extremes. And here we come to perhaps the most famous of Enide's lines in this romance, spoken when the conte de Limors, who finds her lamenting over Erec's presumably dead body, asks pointedly whether Enide is this knight's wife or his lover:

> Si li comança a enquerre
> del chevalier, qu'ele li die
> s'ele estoit sa fame ou s'amie.
>> (vv. 4648–50)

(He began to inquire about the knight, asking that she tell him whether she was his wife or his lover.)

Thoroughly undercutting the binary construction of this chivalric world view, Enide responds simply, "L'un et l'autre" (v. 4651), meaning "both at the same time" and therefore "neither one alone" or "neither one at all, actually." Similar to those moments cited above where Enide speaks without speaking, she now answers the count's question without answering it on his terms. By conflating the poles of the dichotomy *fame/amie*, Enide suggests in her cocky response first of all that the distinction between *fame* and *amie* is meaningless because the two roles depicted by these terms bear such strong resemblance to one another and secondly that the terms *fame* and *amie* are equally inadequate to describe her current position as a speaking subject.

Indeed earlier scenes of this romance have established what it means to be a *fame* in the world of Arthur's knights. The *fame* played by Enide is a young woman given away by her father, traded as a commodity that can be made into a lady and a queen. This *fame* is properly subservient to her husband and deferentially silent. The role of *amie* is played by ladies vying for the distinction of being tagged "la plus bele," often through winning beauty contests that establish a knight's prowess; all remain appropriately silent. To successfully play the part of either *fame* or *amie* in this romance requires that a woman be as beautiful as she is speechless. The perfect courtly heroine, whether wife or lover, must be seen but not heard.[41]

The full import of this heroine's claim to being both *fame* and *amie* consists, to my mind, in her introduction of a third term into the equation, outlining a position lying between the stereotypical extremes of courtly femininity. For if Enide is literally both Erec's beautiful wife and his lover, through marriage and through sex, she rejects the silence that those categories require. Rather than being fully in the knight's possession, as the Old French possessive adjective would indicate—"sa fame ou s'amie"—Enide suggests through her paradoxical linking of traditionally opposed roles, through the *et* of her "l'un et l'autre," that the heroine of Arthurian romance can endow the terms of wife and lover with new meaning, restructuring their heretofore mutually exclusive relation. Her *conjointure* is not narrative synthesis or stylistic harmony; it is a simultaneously coming together and holding apart of the female flesh and its supposedly antithetical speech. In this *conjointure*, the *con* is not appropriated into literature or tamed into obedience. It talks.

These readings of Enide's speech are not emphasized by the romance narrator. Indeed, Erec's pardon of Enide's verbal and sexual transgressions, couched as it is in the mystification of love, seeks to cover over the seriously disruptive potential of this heroine's speech:

> Et Erec, qui sa fame an porte,
> l'acole et beise et reconforte;
> antre ses braz contre son cuer
> l'estraint; et dit: "Ma dolce suer,
> bien vos ai de tot essaiee.
> Or ne soiez plus esmaiee,
> c'or vos aim plus qu'ainz mes ne fis,
> et je resui certains et fis
> que vos m'amez parfitemant.
> Or voel estre d'or en avant,

ausi con j'estoie devant,
tot a vostre comandemant.
                    (vv. 4879–90)

(Erec, carrying his wife away, hugged, kissed, and comforted her.
He clasped her in his arms against his heart and said, "My sweet
sister, I tested you in every way. Don't worry, for I love you now
more than ever before. And I am certain and convinced that you
love me fully. Now I want to be, as I was before, entirely at your
command.)

Yet when the narrator asserts several pages later that Erec has tested
and proven Enide's worth, "Erec, qui bien l'a esprovee," (v. 5097), we
wonder what exactly he has proven. He was supposedly testing her love,
"bien vos ai de tot essaiee," whereas we know him also to have been testing
his own prowess. He is now assured that she loves him dearly, "et je resui
certains et fis / que vos m'amez parfitemant" (vv. 4886–87), though he is
now equally assured of his own chivalric honor. He will be at her command, he says, "tot a vostre comandemant" (v. 4890), as he supposedly
was before, meaning he will be in command as she follows along.[42]
Through her words, however, Enide has flatly disobeyed her husband's
orders, ignored his threats, refused to underwrite the dichotomy of speaking and silence that structures his world. She has, in short, challenged the
status of her imposed identity as both *fame* and *amie*. Enide's speech has
thus altered the very definition of *avanture* as Erec understands it, revealing that the chivalric system must change if it is to accommodate the
speaking female body. The binary logic that Erec invokes, equating silence
with obedience and speech with disobedience is thus overthrown by the
woman who speaks in spite of directives not to. By using her voice, Enide
has changed the rules of the game that requires sexual and linguistic subservience as guarantors of her husband's authority and his pleasure.

Erec acknowledges none of this. By pardoning Enide's misdeeds and
speech and allowing that she may not in fact have misspoken at all, he
buries the import of her highly problematic words beneath the cover of
kisses. The Old French *parole* now rhymes tellingly with *acole*:

'Et se vos rien m'avez mesdit,
je le vos pardoing tot et quit

del forfet et de la parole.'
Adons la rebeise et acole.
                  (vv. 4891–94)[43]

(And if you spoke ill of me, I pardon you fully: for the deed and the
words. Then he hugged and kissed her.)

Implying that the lady under scrutiny has fulfilled Erec's desires, when in
fact she has carried out none of his commands, this happy resolution ig-
nores the crucial fact so cogently stated by Erec himself during the testing
adventure: he does not know how to stop Enide from speaking. He cannot
make her do what he wants:

Erec respont: Po me prisiez,
quant ma parole despisiez;
je ne vos sai si bel prier
que je vos puisse chastier
                  (vv. 3553–56)

(Erec answered: "You show little respect for me when you disregard
my words. I don't know how to convince you to follow
instructions")

The key words here, "je ne vos sai si bel prier" (I don't know how to
convince you, literally to beg you), summarize the linguistic helplessness
that has characterized Erec's verbal interaction with Enide throughout the
forest adventure. This is the crucial point where his *sagesse* proves weakest.
For if the Arthurian heroine's body can be effectively colonized through
the courtly ideology of Beauty, her speech more staunchly resists the chivalric world's attempts to tame and appropriate it. Even the most chivalric
knight, the *miauldres chevaliers* lauded in tales of adventure at Arthur's
court, here lacks sufficient knowledge and prowess to keep the Beauty quiet.
In stark contrast to her assigned role in courtly narrative, the Arthurian
Beauty here emerges with a mind and a voice that resist appropriation.

La Joie de la Cort: Adventure Redefined by Women

The point is made even more cogently in the famous scene termed enigmatically "the Joie de la Cort."[44] Located at a far remove from the story-

telling arena of Arthur's court, this isolated garden (*cort*)—where the romance's final adventure takes place—offers an alternate economy of love and heterosexual coupling in which women make the rules. Indeed the terms of the relationship between the garden's inhabitants: an unnamed woman, revealed later to be Enide's cousin, and her chivalric *ami*, Maboagrain, have been established by the verbal prowess of a woman's voice. In a radical redefinition of the system that earlier objectified Enide as a gift or *dons* to be traded between men,[45] Enide's cousin now extracts from her knight a verbal *dons* that makes him subject to her superior knowledge. Maboagrain explains:

> Cele pucele, qui la siet,
> m'ama des enfance et je li.
> A l'un et a l'autre abeli
> et l'amors crut et amanda,
> tant que ele me demanda
> *un don*, mes el nel noma mie.
>   (vv. 6002–7, my emphasis)

(The maiden sitting there loved me from childhood, and I loved her. We found each other pleasing, and our love grew and improved until she asked me for a *boon*. But she did not say what it was.)

Enide's cousin succeeds in holding her knight in this garden of delights (v. 6047) because *he did not know* what she would ask: that he not leave the garden until conquered in battle by another knight ("que ja mes de ceanz n'istroie, / tant que chevaliers i venist / qui par armes me conqueïst" vv. 6026–28). Maboagrain has been trapped literally by an unknown meaning hidden within the words of his ladylove.[46] Rather than conquering the unknown on the field of battle, he has encountered the unknown of a woman's voice that he cannot vanquish or master. As if to echo, while changing significantly, the terms of Chrétien's prologue, this woman has used all her *estuide*, *escience*, and *savoir* to bring forth a *tel chose* invisible to others: a promise of love and heterosexual romance, a life of amorous coupling devoid of chivalric *conjointure*.[47] There is no camaraderie here of men joined in combat; no tales of chivalric prowess. Only a single knight paired silently and in isolation with a single woman.

Yet Maboagrain responds to the lady's request by invoking idiosyncratically a code of courtly conduct that belongs to a world he no longer inhabits. His model of behavior reflects the terms of interaction that typically link chivalric partners like Erec and Guivret for whom words must be matched with deeds:

> —Ja plus ne vos quier demander,
> fet Erec, molt m'avez promis;
> mes sire estes et mes amis
> se l'uevre est tex con la parole.
>
> (vv. 3896–99)

(I would never ask you for more than that, said Erec. You have promised me a lot: you are my lord and friend if your deeds match your words.)

In keeping with this logic, Maboagrain feels compelled to fulfill his pledge to Enide's cousin:

> Reisons fu que je remainsisse,
> ainz que ma f'iance mantisse,
> ja ne l'eusse je plevi.
>
> (vv. 6029–31)

(It was right for me to remain [with her] rather than be untrue to my oath. Or I should never have sworn it.)

The very terms of the verbal contract between the unnamed lady and this knight require, however, his removal from the chivalric world into an alternate economy where different rules apply. We have seen in the forest adventure how Enide, for one, does not abide by the convention that conjoins word and deed. Rather she agrees repeatedly to be silent, only to break the promise soon thereafter (vv. 2772, 2918–19). The garden of Maboagrain's *amie* stands similarly beyond the pale of proper Arthurian speech and conduct.[48] This woman is neither a *fame* nor an *amie* in the typical sense of the silent beauty sheltered and protected by an honorable knight. Although she is stereotypically beautiful, stretched out on an elegant bed, where she provides the bait for incoming knights (vv. 5833–36), this heroine also speaks against the conventions of the courtly adventure story. And, like Enide during the forest trial, she speaks from a position of knowing more than her knight.

This unsettling of the gendered hierarchy that typically governs courtly interaction provokes Maboagrain to characterize the lady's speech as verbal trickery (vv. 6040–47). Yet it is only in Maboagrain's account of the couple's encounter that the unnamed woman's voice emerges as devisive. When the female protagonist explains her amorous "adventure" with Maboagrain, she speaks of mutual accord, of their wanting the same thing and voluntarily agreeing to it:

> La feïmes noz covenanz
> antre nos deux, tex con nos sist.
> Einz ne vos rien qu'il ne volsist,
> tant que amer me comanca,
> si me plevi et f'ianca
> que toz jorz mes amis seroit
> et que il ça m'an amanroit;
> moi plot et a lui d'autre part.
> (vv. 6224–31)

(There we exchanged vows, as it suited us both. I wanted nothing that he did not also want. Such that as he began loving me he pledged and promised that he would always be my lover and that he would bring me here. This pleases me and him as well.)

This is her story, her version of the story of past events. It is consonant with her rereading of *joie de la cort* as signifying mutually shared "erotic pleasure in the garden" rather than the more public "joy of the court" that is enshrined by men's stories after Erec liberates Maboagrain. Indeed one important consequence of Maboagrain's captivity is that tales of his prowess have been suppressed while he remained hidden within his lady's erotically charged garden. Although this accomplished knight has regularly fended off rivals in combat and thus could not be charged with the *recreantise* that marked Erec's stay at Carnant,[49] Maboagrain has remained nonetheless utterly unknown:

> Maboagrins sui apelez,
> mes ne sui mes point coneüz,

an leu ou j'aie esté veüz,
par remanbrance de cest non
s'an cest pais solemant non;
car onques tant con vaslez fui,
mon non ne dis ne ne conui.
                    (vv. 6082–88)

(I am called Maboagrain but I am not known at all by that name in
the places I have been seen, but only in this land, because as long as
I have been a knight I have not spoken my name or declared it.)

No stories that boast of Maboagrain's prowess can circulate through
the halls of Arthur's court because all of this knight's opponents have been
silenced through beheading. They can tell no tales of defeat, nor record
their rivals' success:

Onques nus ne vint d'autre terre
la Joie de la Cort requerre
qu'il n'i eüst honte et domage
et n'i leissast la teste an gage.
                    (vv. 5465–68)

(No one has ever come from another land seeking the Joy of the
Court who did not find shame and harm there, leaving his head in
payment.)

In this isolated garden, a woman's words have effectively shortcir-
cuited the chivalric economy based on the knightly encounter and courtly
tale telling that make heroic feats worthwhile. But as a result of Erec's
victory, Maboagrain's prowess will now be known to all. The tales of his
chivalric success will generate the kind of public joy that has characterized
previous heroic incidents at court. As Maboagrain explains to Erec:

Molt avez an grant joie mise
la cort mon oncle et mes amis,
c'or serai hors de ceanz mis;
et por ce que joie an feront
tuit cil qui a la cort vanront,
Joie de la Cort l'apeloient
cil qui la joie an atandoient.
                    (vv. 6068–74)

(You have brought great joy to my uncle and my friends for now I will be released from here. And because all who come to the court will rejoice at this, those who awaited that joy called it the Joy of the Court.)

This courtly *joie* recalls the *joie* experienced by observers of Erec's success at the sparrowhawk contest earlier in the narrative (v. 1241) or the *joie* felt by members of Arthur's retinue who hail Erec's initial arrival at court (v. 1516) or those who witness the subsequent dubbing ceremony of Arthur's men (v. 1963). It is the *joie* produced by men's stories such as the tale of Erec defeating Yder (v. 1158):

Ja li orrons *tel chose* dire
don nos avrons ou joie ou ire
   (vv. 1157–58, my emphasis)

(Now we will hear him tell a tale [literally: such a thing] that will bring us joy or anger)

The unknown *tel chose* recounted by Yder does indeed create *joie* at court, as we have seen, by repairing Guenevere's earlier account of Erec's misstep with the dwarf and establishing beyond doubt his chivalric credentials. The Joie de la Cort furthers the same goal. It is said to be what Erec wants above all else:

La Joie de la Cort demant,
car nule rien tant ne covoit.
     (vv. 5556–57)

(He asked for the Joy of the Court because he wanted nothing as much as this.)

As "the thing he aspired to most of all," (La chose a coi il plus baoit, v. 5723), this *joie* emerges curiously, in a supposed love story, as even more desirable than the knight's lady, Enide. She serves as a means to an end, to this heroic end, in fact, something the knight needed along with armor and weapons in order to win the sparrowhawk contest and launch his play for winning the Joie of the Cort as well. Enide represents "quanque il li estut" (v. 680), what Erec needs in order to win at chivalry, rather than what he most desires (*covoit*, v. 5557). Erec seeks the adventure of the Joie de la Cort partly because it is unknown, "donez la moi, que que ce soit" (give it to me, whatever it may be, v. 5558) and partly because, like all good adventures, it will bring him honor. His host explains, "se vos a joie an esploitiez / conquise avroiz si grant enor / onques hom ne conquist graignor" (If you perform successfully, you will have conquered such a great honor. No man has conquered a greater one, vv. 5616–18).

But this feat of ultimate prowess does not further the joy of Enide's cousin, who has told a different tale of love and amorous coupling. If her *joie* proves *doloreuse* for the hapless knight who falls victim to it, as we are told by King Evrains (v. 5562)—much as Erec's *conjointure* with Enide at Carnant brought displeasure to the chivalric world—the official *joie* inaugurated by Erec causes this heroine pain. For her it means *disjointure*, separation and loss:

> La Joie que ele veoit
> ne li venoit mie a pleisir;
> . . . .
> a cui la Joie enuioit fort,
> por ce qu'il li estoit a vis
> c'or ne seroit mes ses amis
> avoec li tant con il soloit,
> quant il del vergier issir doit.
>   (vv. 6142–43, 6162–66)

(The Joy that she saw did not please her at all. . . . The Joy troubled her greatly because it was obvious to her that now her lover would no longer be with her as he had been, since he was to leave the garden.)

The episode of the Joie de la Cort is especially significant for our purposes because it enacts a breaking away from women reminiscent of Erec's attempt to silence Enide during the forest adventure. And it effects more importantly a curtailment of women's speech that the earlier forest trial did not fully achieve. As Erec triumphs over Maboagrain and escapes being silenced by the loss of his head, he silences another voice: that of Enide's female cousin, whose *don contraignant* is now defunct. Returning to the more standard narrative line of the *conte d'avanture*, we will hear no more from this verbally astute heroine or her cousin Enide, both of whom lapse into silence.

When Enide recounts the tale of her adventures to her cousin during the episode of the Joie de la Cort, her previously resistant voice is absorbed into a narrative that remains properly chivalric. Focusing on Erec's skills and achievements, she tells of love, joy, and marriage (vv. 6242–66) but does not mention the trial in the forest or the sexual and verbal offense that occasioned it. Chrétien here provides an abbreviated version of the story of Erec and Enide that eliminates its noncourtly elements, a story that neatly parallels Erec's own revised version of the tale. This unproblematic story placed in the mouth of the romance's problematic heroine serves as a corrective to her previous verbal faux pas. Her speech here supports and endorses the world of chivalry that it had challenged at Carnant. Despite the romance author's claims that Enide has revealed the entire *avanture* without hiding (*celer*) or neglecting (*entrelais*) anything (vv. 6267–71), her account offers a carefully truncated version of events we have witnessed, a tale rewritten in a more pleasing or more "joyous" vein. Enide's revised tale becomes an exemplum passed from woman to woman as a means of recuperating the aberrant female into the chivalric milieu, as Bossy has astutely observed (34). As Enide's tale teaches her cousin the importance of hierarchy in marriage, he explains, a third woman (unremarked by most readers) conveys the same story of wifely obedience to the noblemen at Arthur's court: "Que qu'eles parolent ansanble, / une dame seule s'an anble, / qui as barons le vet conter / por la Joie croistre et monter" (While they talk together, a lone woman goes to tell the barons in order to increase their joy, vv. 6275–78).

If this incident effectively recuperates the voice of the tale's most outspoken female protagonist, the scene of coronation finds her mute. The act of crowning focuses almost solely on Erec. Absorbed into the role of proper wife and queen, Enide sits silently next to her husband (v. 6772) during a long descriptive passage that devotes only one line to her: "puis ont Enyde coronee" (v. 6825). She is all but absent, except as window dressing for the coronation festivities and, perhaps most significantly, as the potential producer of an heir to the throne. In an earlier scene, when the newly married couple arrived at King Lac's court, Enide prayed at the altar of Nostre Dame, asking Jesus and the Virgin Mary to give the couple an heir:

Devant l'autel de Nostre Dame
menerent dui baron sa fame.
Jesu et la virge Marie
par boene devocion prie
que an lor vie lor donast
oir qui aprés ax heritast.

(vv. 2347–52)[50]

(Two barons led his wife to the altar of Our Lady. She [Enide]
prayed devoutly to Jesus and the Virgin that they might give the
couple an heir during their lifetime.)

Childbirth and the possible production of a male offspring locate
Enide firmly in the domain of the *fame*, distinguishing her irrevocably
from her unmarried cousin. The association with motherhood also facilitates the ultimate absorption of this heroine into the role properly played
by royalty in this romance. During the coronation scene, we are told that
Enide inherits her beauty from her mother, that her mother's function as
a beautiful woman was to produce an equally beautiful daughter:

Bele est Enyde, et bele doit
estre, par reison et par droit,
que bele dame est molt sa mere,
biau chevalier a en son pere.

(vv. 6561–64)

(Enide is beautiful and she should be by reason and by right because
her mother is a very beautiful woman and her father a handsome
knight.)

The artificial creation of beauty in the chivalric world through male combat (*desreisne*) is here again masked by an inference that beauty derives
from heredity (or Nature) alone. This gesture implies that if Enide follows
in the footsteps of her mother and produces a female child, that daughter
will conform unproblematically to the chivalric standards of beauty that
underwrite male identity. If she produces a male child, he will, according
to the same logic, resemble her father, here described as a *biau chevalier*
(v. 6564), the stereotypical knight. As the perfect silent *fame*, Enide's sexuality has been effectively put to the service of perpetuating the chivalric

system and stories about it. As a *dons* to be traded among men, she will give the gift of the heir to chivalry. The female *con*, now absorbed into the official and public *conjointure* of marriage and coronation, poses no threat to the joining of men in chivalry or combat.

But Enide's unmarried cousin cannot so easily be absorbed into the fabric of the adventure story. She remains by her own definition an *amie*, one wielding the *don contraignant* that takes away chivalric potency. As a speaking subject whose body and voice both resist appropriation, this female must be written out of Chrétien's tale if the production of *joie* and *pleisir* are to become the work of the romance author's voice alone. Since there is no place for her as a properly silent and deferential *fame*, this erotic speaking subject must be rejected by the romance author who wants to pirate and market woman's pleasure for his own. She disappears enigmatically from the tale as if having evaporated into thin air.

Indeed, it seems at tale's end that Chrétien has accomplished what Erec could not do, bringing the woman's problematic voice and body under control. He has effectively appropriated the heroine's troublesome voice and excised that of her verbally astute cousin. But in fact this author's avowed mastery over his text remains as incomplete as Erec's desired mastery over his Enide. By his own admission Chrétien is unable to fulfill the directives for successful storytelling that he issued in the prologue to his romance. For even he stops short of revealing all.

At two significant moments in this tale, we hear that *joie* cannot be narrated by *boche d'home*: in the scene of reconciliation between Erec and Enide and at an unusual moment of storytelling after the Joie de la Cort episode.[51] When the narrator describes the reconciliation of Erec and Enide after their prolonged trial in the forest, he confesses the impossibility of recounting their pleasure:

> Li uns ancontre l'autre tance
> comant il li puise pleisir:
> del sorplus me doi bien teisir.
> (vv. 5206–8)

(They vied with each other in finding ways of pleasing. About the rest I must keep silent.)

Returning to the *teisir/pleisir* rhyme of the prologue, which there evoked the author's imperative to tell a pleasing tale, the narrator now repeats the rhyme to different effect: sex is one *pleisir* that cannot adequately be told. In the privacy of the lovers' bedroom, where pleasure is erotic rather than aesthetic, silence prevails over speech. Even the master romancer Chrétien cannot appropriate this *conjointure* into writing. His talent and *boche d'home* cannot, we are advised, match the resources of the female protagonist's pleasurable lips.

Neither it seems can they fully appropriate the function of the woman's public speaking lips. After the Joie de la Cort episode, Chrétien offers modestly to give a quick summary of the *joie* that resulted from Erec's heroic feat, a joy—reminiscent of the pleasure predicted to result from Chrétien's own narrative—that merits boasting. In a literary gesture recalling the opening lines of the *Lai du Lecheor*, Chrétien now tells how the courtly crowd gathered:

> Puis n'i ot nule retenue
> que tuit ne venissent a cort;
> de toz sanz li pueples i cort
> qu'a pié que a cheval batant,
> que li uns l'autre n'i atant.
> (vv. 6126–30)

(Then there was no preventing all the people from coming to court. They came running from all directions, some on foot, some rapidly on horseback. No one waited for anyone else.)

He then outlines two storytelling processes. The men who gathered in the garden to disarm Erec sing a song of joy together:

> Et cil qui el vergier estoient
> d'Erec desarmer s'aprestoient,
> et chantoient par contançon,
> *tuit* de la joie une chançon.
> (vv. 6131–34, my emphasis)

(Those [men] who were in the orchard prepared to remove Erec's armor, and they all tried to outdo one another as they sang together a song about the joy.)

The *tuit* (all of them together), reminiscent of the *tuit* that bound Arthur's men together in a tight *confrerie* when they departed for the hunt early in the tale (v. 64), here evokes once again a coupling among storytelling men. One can imagine how the song of knights united in removing armor from the victorious Erec will inaugurate the kind of public chivalric *joie* that has characterized the telling of men's stories throughout this romance. We have heard that narrative before.

But another tale of *joie* is composed by the ladies, seemingly a different tale, distinct in authorship and perhaps also in content from that told by the knights, even though these women storytellers also choose to call their narrative "le Lai de Joie":

> et les dames un lai troverent
> que le Lai de Joie apelerent.
> (vv. 6135–36)

(The ladies composed a song/tale that they called the song/tale of Joy.)

This tale is predictably little known: "mes n'est gueres li lais sauz," presumably in contrast to the more standard tale of *joie* composed by knights.

Chrétien never tells us what these women say, what their version of *joie* might include. But perhaps we have heard their tale already, in different form, couched in stories told by the resistant voices of Guenevere, Enide, and her cousin, Maboagrain's *amie*. The narrator's brief allusion at the end of Chrétien's romance to a song of joy composed by women sends us back to other women's stories we have heard throughout this narrative, tales that invoke in different ways an alternate, nonchivalric *joie*. One wonders, for example, whether the ladies composing this *lai* will comment, as did the women storytellers in the *Lai du Lecheor*, on the glaring absence of female sexuality from the *conte d'avanture*. Perhaps they will redefine *joie* in the sense of the private coupling with the woman's body preferred by Enide's cousin. We can only imagine what their tale might include: a recasting of the adventure story to make a place for female sexuality and woman's speech, an unsettling of the binary oppositions governing the chivalric code of conduct so as to acknowledge sexual difference rather than subsuming the female within the male. Perhaps they will reject the pat categories of both *fame* and *amie*, allowing instead that lovers might also be wives and that both might be simultaneously erotic and endowed with speech. Or perhaps they will explore ways that the female subject might speak from the locus of *savoir*. This "Lai de la joie," told ostensibly by women, not overtly by Chrétien or his male protagonists, might then reveal something like what the female storyteller of the *Lai du Lecheor* asserts in a different context: what is left out of the *conte d'avanture* as men tell it—what is most neglected or silenced in these narratives—is the female speaking subject. That subject is represented fleetingly by Enide and her cousin. But Chrétien de Troyes does not give us their story intact. We have to read it between the lines, indeed write it ourselves, much as the female protagonists discussed by Carolyn Heilbrun rewrite available plots both to engage and to resist them.

If Chrétien's *Erec et Enide* shows us, on the one hand, how there is no place for the female subject in tales of adventure, how the romance narrative successfully appropriates the woman's body to its own ends, it also shows how women's speech cannot as effectively be colonized by these tales of love and adventure. Although the beautiful bodies of female protagonists are readily made to conform to and underwrite the tenets of chivalry in courtly romance, their voices more thoroughly resist such appropriation. For when courtly heroines speak, as we have seen, they often rewrite the very story that contains them. Their bodytalk exposes what is hidden within the *conte d'avanture*, what is covered up by the homophony of *contes*, *comte*, *conter* that links men together as storytellers and listeners in Chrétien's prologue. Revealing how the female *con* has been appropriated by the *conte d'avanture*, these women's words also show us how the fictionalized bodies bearing that *con* can tell the story differently. When they talk, it matters whose body is speaking.

Notes

1. Gaston Paris, "Lais inédits."
2. "Les plus nobles" could also mean the "most noble men" or "the most noble men and women," though the subsequent description of women suggests that they alone are the subjects of this passage.
3. For the quote in context:

Tote la meillor retenoient
Et recordoient et disoient;
Sovent ert dite et racontée,

Tant que de touz estoit loée;
Un lai en fesoient entr'eus,
Ce fu la costume d'iceus;
Cil a qui l'aventure estoit
Son non meismes i metoit;
Après lui ert li lais nomez,
Sachoiz ce est la veritez;
Puis estoit li lais maintenuz
Tant que partout estoit seuz;
Car cil qui savoient de note
En viele, en herpe et en rote
Fors de la terre le portoient
Es roiaumes ou il aloient.
(vv. 23–38)

4. For a critique of this standard interpretation, see E. Jane Burns and Roberta L. Krueger, Introduction to *Courtly Ideology and Woman's Place in Old French Literature*.

5. In his introductory remarks to the *Lai du Lecheor*, Gaston Paris reads this passage as a joke, assuming that courtly ladies would neither speak this way nor approve of such uncourtly sentiment. The poet, he contends, places these words in the mouth of a courtly lady to provoke a refined laugh among his listeners, who would ostensibly dismiss this woman's speech as improbable and hence insignificant (64). I think her words deserve more serious consideration.

6. See Denise Riley, *Am I That Name?* 98–114; and Diana Fuss, *Essentially Speaking*, 23–37.

7. Carolyn Heilbrun, *Hamlet's Mother and Other Women*, 103–12.

8. Or alternately, as Nancy Miller has argued, women's fiction repeatedly chafes against the "unsatisfactory reality" contained within the maxims of male-defined plots and plausibilities, "Emphasis Added: Plots and Plausibilities in Women's Fiction," in her *Subject to Change*, 25–46.

9. Judith Butler, *Gender Trouble: Feminism and the Subversion of Identity*, 30–31.

10. These seemingly independent female voices are absorbed in the end into the larger frame of male storytelling, however, when the narrator explains how everyone attending the festivities gathered around the ladies composing their *lai* and joined with them in making a *lai* that brought joy to clerks and knights (vv. 109–18).

11. Other characters speak *to* Enide during the early portion of the romance—her father and Erec each pronounce a series of commands that she dutifully fulfills without responding to them (pp. 14, 15, 26, 29). And characters speak *about* her in her presence—Erec and her father discuss the sparrowhawk contest and later plan the couple's marriage (pp. 16, 17, 40, 41). But Enide plays no part in these conversations. Even her best-known "speeches," including the troublesome comments about Erec's failed knighthood, are interior monologues (vv. 2585–2606, 2772–90, 2829–39). With the exception of a few brief instances of reported speech (vv. 1385,

1622), Enide remains throughout the opening scenes of the tale *tote coie* (v. 684). She reverts to this position at tale's end, saying nothing at all during the final coronation.

12. *Diacritics* (Summer 1982), 42–53.

13. I borrow the phrase from Judith Butler's book by the same title.

14. Chrétien de Troyes, *Erec et Enide*, vv. 6–8. English translations are mine.

15. On *conjointure* see especially Douglas Kelly. "The Source and Meaning of *Conjointure* in Chrétien's *Erec*," and his *Sens et conjointure in the* Chevalier de la charrette. Also Michelle Freeman, *The Poetics of Translatio studii and Conjointure: Chrétien de Troyes's* Cligès.

16. See "conjoindre, conjointure" in A. J. Greimas, *Dictionnaire de l'ancien français*.

17. "Le plus urgent est d'assurer la colonisation de ce nouveau 'champ,' de le faire entrer, non sans coups de force ni éclats, dans la production du discours (du) même," (Luce Irigaray, *Spéculum*, 170).

18. But they are present in abundance in the Arthurian court that Chrétien depicts on the following page of our printed text. No fewer than 500 "demoiseles de hauz paraiges / filles de rois gentes et saiges" (ladies of high birth, daughters of noble and wise kings) are said to populate this courtly milieu.

19. See, for example, how the words of the squire who reports Erec's courtly perfection to the *comte vaniteux*, "Li chevaliers est molt cortois, / tant bel home onques mes ne vi" ("The knight is very courtly. I have never seen such a perfect man," vv. 3218–19), are reinforced when the defeated count himself later explains to his men, "Onques ne fu de mere nez / miaudres chevaliers de cestui" ("Never was there born of woman a better knight than this one," vv. 3642–43). Erec later explains to the fallen Guivret the necessity of acknowledging an opponent's victory, "Quant tu me prïes, / oltreemant vuel que tu dïes / que tu es oltrez et conquis;" (When you beg my mercy I want you to say that you are outdone and conquered, vv. 3827–29). Such acknowledgment is often reported to King Arthur at court, thereby publicly establishing a knight's reputation, as Erec explains to Cadoc: "et gardez ne li celez ja / de quel poinne je ai mis hors / et vostre amie et vostre cors. / Je sui a la cort molt amez: / se de par moi vos reclamez, / servise et enor me feroiz" (And be sure not to hide from him [Arthur] what trouble I helped you and your lady out of. If you credit me with this you will do me a great service and further my honor, vv. 4500–4505). A prime example is provided by Yder's accolades of the victorious Erec after the sparrowhawk contest, vv. 1184–88.

20. Women remain typically ancillary in these tales of chivalric success, figuring most commonly as part of a chivalric couple such as the knight *and* his lady helped by Erec in the example cited above or Erec *and* the *pucele* he will bring "ansanble o lui" (v. 1197) to Arthur's court, as Yder reports. They form a necessary backdrop, a kind of windowdressing much like the 500 demoiselles at Arthur's court, who are defined similarly in relation to men as "filles de rois" or "amies de chevaliers" (vv. 52–54).

21. See also how defeated knights often become part of the company (*mesniee*)

of their victor as do Yder (v. 1234) and Guivret (v. 3831), sometimes joining their "rivals" as friends who kiss and hug (vv. 3896–3900).

22. For a detailed study of the function of the gaze in *Erec et Enide* using contemporary film theory, see Sarah Stanbury, "Feminist Film Theory: Seeing Chrétien's *Enide*."

23. Most critics have seriously underestimated the objectification of Enide, especially in scenes describing her alleged beauty and dress, taking these attributes to be an official recognition of her inner merit. Typical of this view, Sara Sturm-Maddox and Donald Maddox explain that "Enide is the perfect harmonization of unadorned beauty, given her by Nature, her creator (vv. 411–41), and the synecdochic vestimentary beauty provided by the Queen, her benefactor and sponsor" ("Description in Medieval Narrative: Vestimentary Coherence in Chrétien's *Erec et Enide*," 56). This is indeed the reading that Chrétien's narrator encourages us to give, but what is the significance of assigning these roles to Enide? What does it mean that Chrétien and Erec construct Enide as a heroine whose beauty is at once supposedly innate but also obviously created, and created specifically, on many occasions, by the male gaze? For a wonderful analysis of how the masculine economy of exchange in the scenes of the hunt and sparrowhawk recuperates the resistant economy of female sexuality, leaving a residue that cannot finally be co-opted, see Laurie Finke, "Towards a Cultural Poetics of Romance."

24. Other scenes also assert the equality of these lovers only to undercut the claim. At Carnant the love shared equally between them, "De l'amor qui est antr'ax deus" (v. 2048 and earlier vv. 2037–47), becomes painfully unequal when Enide must be "plus hardie" to suffer the pain of deflowering (vv. 2049–54). Erec incurs no equal pain. Similarly, with the comte de Limors, the line expressing mutually reciprocal sentiment is followed by an assertion of his dominance: "La dame est moie et je sui suens, / si ferai de li mon pleisir" (The lady is mine and I am hers; thus I will do as I please with her, vv. 4800–01). When Erec's beauty is described, he becomes a spectacle as a "chevalier si loé" (such an esteemed knight, v. 86), a mounted knight, a galloping man of action; his dress contributes to this image of accomplished chivalry. He can be "biax" and "bel" (vv. 87–89) while remaining a subject. See also vv. 5450 ff.

25. On several other occasions the romance charts how Enide's beauty derives less from Nature or heredity than from the desiring look of the male viewer of her body. See especially vv. 422–23: "De ceste tesmoingne Nature / c'onques si bele criature / ne fu *veüe* an tot le monde" (Nature bears witness that such a beautiful creature had never been *seen*, vv. 1707–14, my emphasis). While rereading the criticism of *Erec et Enide*, I was especially struck by how consistently readers of the poem have missed this point, accepting unproblematically the ideology of chivalry, love, and marriage that Chrétien invents. Enide becomes then, in a wide range of readings, the vehicle for a higher good. For Glyn Burgess she is the means of transcendence allowing monarchy and chivalry to be functionally united ("The Theme of Beauty in Chrétien's *Philomena* and *Erec et Enide*"); for Donald Maddox, Enide represents the mythic force enabling monarchy and chivalry to be reconciled (*Structure and Sacring*, 187); for Eugene Vance, she facilitates twelfth-century humanism's harmonizing of Aristotelian rationalism and Neoplatonic mysticism

(*From Topic to Tale: Logic and Narrativity in the Middle Ages*, 40); for Sally Musseter, she represents the *trivium* whose goal is John of Salisbury's "truth" that
guarantees the welfare of society ("The Education of Enide"); for Winthrop Wetherbee, Enide serves as the helpmate for the Platonic philosopher-king (*Platonism
and Poetry in the Twelfth Century: The Literary Influence of the School of Chartres*,
239); Denyse Delcourt sees her as an instrument of transformation (*L'Éthique du
changement dans le roman français du 12e siècle*); and Lee Patterson casts her in the
role of the guide leading Erec to establish the "new society" envisioned in the
poem's conclusion ("Virgil and the Historical Consciousness of the Twelfth Century: The *Roman d'Enéas* and *Erec et Enide*," 194). Although Patterson argues
forcefully for Enide's subjectivity as a guide for the hero's development, the importance he accords to the newly established monarchy at poem's end leads him to
accept, along with others less cognizant of Enide's problematic status in the narrative, her thorough effacement within the "higher good" figured here as the "new
society," elsewhere as feudal monarchy, cosmological unity, spiritual *sapientia*,
Chartrain truth, Platonic kingship. Historically, these systems have excluded or
marginalized women.

26. Jacques Lacan recognized in the early seventies that courtly love is an
affair between men (*Séminaire XX, Encore*).

27. "Mais comment aménager ces territoires obscurs, ces continents noirs, ces
au-delà du miroir?" (Irigaray, *Spéculum*, 168).

28. For a sensitive and careful reading of *Erec et Enide* that pays special
attention to Enide's speech, see Michel André Bossy, "The Elaboration of Female
Narrative Functions in *Erec et Enide*."

29. For another example of the inexact repetition inaugurated by a female
voice, see Caren Greenberg's analysis of how Echo "abducts" the first person pronoun ("Reading Reading: Echo's Abduction of Language").

30. Erec directs Enide not to speak at the following moments: vv. 2764–69,
2912–17, 3074–76, 3511–13, 4956–57. He also curtails her hearing (v. 3538) and sight
(v. 3004). His insistence on her deference occurs in vv. 2297, 2846, 3553. These
passages have raised a protracted debate regarding Erec's possible motivations,
aptly summarized by Norris J. Lacy, "Narrative Point of View and the Problem of
Erec's Motivation." Lacy argues convincingly that the issue is moot because Chrétien's narrative technique deftly witholds from the reader/listener any clue as to
character motivation.

31. Erec here places Enide in a position of possible rape as Bossy points out,
("Elaboration," 28).

32. When Erec fights the first attackers, Enide "waits elsewhere" (v. 2911);
after battling the five brigands, Erec brings their horses back to where Enide
waits (vv. 3069–72); Erec rides off into the forest to engage the *comte vaniteux*
(vv. 3608–11); when battling the two giants, Erec instructs Enide to "wait for me
here" (vv. 4296–97) and later returns to her (vv. 4543–44, 4558); Enide also waits
apart while Erec fights with Maboagrain at the Joie de la Cort (vv. 5814–15).

33. See Bossy's comments that Enide holds forth most vociferously when Erec
is unconscious ("Elaboration," 33).

34. John Plummer reads Enide on the model of a feudal counselor whose

advice to her lord echoes the tenets of *bien dire* and *bien aprandre* set out in Chrétien's prologue: one who has an obligation to speak the truth and teach the right that will lead eventually to "joy" for the court (*"Bien dire* et *Bien aprandre* in Chrétien de Troyes's *Erec et Enide"*). In this reading Enide once again serves the "higher good" of teaching proper conduct as she is absorbed and effaced by Chrétien's strategy of appropriation.

35. The *comte vaniteux* proclaims in the same vein, "Je feroie de vos m'amie" (I will make you my lover, v. 3316). These claims are borne out most completely in the costuming scene at Caradignan when Erec instructs Guenevere to dress the newly arrived maiden (vv. 1575–1660). Two *puceles* carry out the task of beautifying the heroine by covering her body with lavish clothing in a procedure that extends over 85 lines. They then cryptically attribute the resultant beauty to the work of Nature, erasing their own and Erec's substantial contribution to it (vv. 1648–52).

36. Chrétien subsequently narrates instead a fight between Erec and the count in which Erec wins the female prize (vv. 3561–3652).

37. The chivalric narrative Enide provides here differs most obviously from its Arthurian counterparts because of the string of imperative verbs that construct it. Telling the count how to proceed, Enide sets the stage for, and orchestrates the plot of, his future action in a mode uncharacteristic of the interaction between knights and ladies.

38. Later in the romance, however—during the Joie de la cort episode—Chrétien absorbs this resistant voice by having Enide recount her past adventures to a long-lost cousin. The narrative remains properly chivalric, focusing on Erec's skills and achievements.

39. Irigaray, *This Sex*, 24, 26, cited by Fuss in *Essentially Speaking*, 58.

40. The great exception to the rule is of course Chrétien's Lancelot. See Matilda T. Bruckner, "An Interpreter's Dilemma: Why Are There So Many Interpretations of Chrétien's *Chevalier de la Charrette?"*

41. My reading diverges in this regard from that of Barbara Nelson Sargent-Baur, who argues that Enide plays the roles of both *fame* and *amie* but not simultaneously because the two cannot be reconciled ("Erec's Enide, 'sa fame ou s'amie'?"); and from that of Joan Brumlik, who claims that Erec wants to kill the outspoken real *fame* and remake Enide as the more pliant and metaphoric *amie* ("Chrétien's Enide: Wife, Mistress, and Metaphor"). To my mind, the two roles are equally constructed, equally problematic, and more similar than we have previously acknowledged.

42. Fanni Bogdanov demonstrates how the reconciliation speech reiterates troubadour lyric conventions, making Erec's claim that he will be henceforth at Enide's command a mere figure of speech ("The Tradition of the Troubadour Lyrics and the Treatment of the Love Theme in Chrétien de Troyes's *Erec et Enide*," 82, 89).

43. The mystification of love surfaces intermittently to obscure crucial differences between Erec et Enide. See, for example, vv. 4825, 4885, 4897, 5098, 5198. Scholars have long noted that Erec and Enide seem to communicate best without speech. See, for example, W.T.H. Jackson, "Problems of Communication in the Romances of Chrétien de Troyes," 41; Joan Ferrante, *Woman as Image in Medieval*

Literature, 80–81; Barbara Nelson Sargent-Baur, "Erec's Enide," 384–85. On the effects of the mystification of love in Chrétien's *Yvain ou le Chevalier au Lion*, see Roberta L. Krueger, "Love, Honor, and the Exchange of Women in *Yvain*."

44. For a study of critical commentaries on the Joie de la Cort episode, see Terence Scully's "The *Sen* of Chrétien de Troyes's *Joie de la Cort*."

45. See the initial terms of Erec's acquisition of Enide (vv. 631–32, 1317–30) and the subsequent conversation between Erec and the count of Caridigan (vv. 1263–71).

46. Earlier in the tale, Enide has extracted a similar vow from the *conte vaniteux* that he will do as she wishes (vv. 3397–3404). But this, we soon learn, facilitates her plan to trick him.

47. Jean Frappier has traced the widespread use of the *don contraignant* in all of Chrétien's romances and the Old French matter of Britain, where it can be used alternately by male or female speakers. Indeed the motif's first appearance in *Erec et Enide* occurs when Erec asks the vavasor for a *don* (Enide) to be repaid by a *guerredon* (marriage gift). But this trading of women as *don* is significantly recast when Enide's cousin later deploys the *don contraignant* to very different effect. Frappier reacts quizically that the cousin's *don contraignant* seems unnecessary since Maboagrain is already twice imprisoned: by his love and his word as a knight. Yet the full force of the latter *don* resides precisely, it seems to me, in the way it carefully rewrites the use of *don* in the marriage scene. The female protagonist whose body was initially objectified as the marriage gift now occupies the position of a subject endowed with the problematic gift of speech ("Le Motif du 'don contraignant' dans la littérature du Moyen Âge").

48. See especially Laurie Finke's reading of the garden as "the unrepresentable locus of female genitalia" ("Towards a Cultural Poetics of the Romance," 147).

49. As Maboagrain himself explains, "onques mes d'armes ne fui las, / ne de combatre recreüz" (vv. 6056–57). He has combat with other knights but no *conjointure* in the sense of camaraderie or companionship.

50. These lines form part of a 28-line passage that occurs only in the Guiot manuscript. See Carleton Carrell's translation of *Erec et Enide*, 320–21.

51. The inexpressibility topos occurs as well during the coronation scene but only as an instance of the narrator's subtle boasting. After issuing the disclaimer, the narrator proceeds to tell the tale at great length, flaunting the masterful poetic skill that Chrétien claims to possess in the prologue. He can make a memorable tale, we are told, a tale to be proud of, because his mouth and tongue have the power that other men lack:

> Des or comancerai l'estoire
> qui toz jorz mes iert an mimoire
> tant con durra crestïantez;
> de ce s'est Crestïens vantez.
>
> (vv. 23–26)

(Now I will begin the story that will be remembered henceforth as long as Christianity endures. Chrétien boasts of this.)

5. Why Beauty Laughs: Iseut's Enormous Thighs

> "She's beautiful and she is laughing."
> —Hélène Cixous, "The Laugh of the Medusa"

The wise and wizened hag named La Vieille in Jean de Meun's *Roman de la Rose* advises her inscribed female listeners that the successfully seductive woman should laugh with her mouth closed:

> Fame doit rire a bouche close,
> car ce n'est mie bele chose
> quant el rit a guele estandue.[1]

(A woman should laugh with mouth closed, because it is not a pretty sight when she laughs with her mouth wide open.)

Keeping the lips together has a practical implication: it will hide the woman's unseemly teeth:

> Et s'el n'a denz bien ordenes
> Mes [tres] laiz et sans ordre nes,
> Se les mousrtoit par sa risee
> Mains en porroit estre prisee.
> (vv. 13363–66)

(If she does not have straight teeth, but ugly and crooked ones, showing them when she laughs would make her less attractive.)

But La Vieille offers another rationale for her remarks, one that echoes strongly the logic used to construct female anatomy in those Old French fabliaux that link female lips to genital labia.[2] Women who laugh with their mouth open, she explains, will seem too wide and split apart: "trop sanble estre large et fandue" (v. 13362).[3] The Old French past participle *fandue*, meaning literally split or broken open, derives from the verb *fandre* (*fendre*), which also produces the noun form, *fendace*, denoting more specifically female genitalia.[4] So the lady listeners of La Vieille's speech, who are advised in accompanying lines of this text to dress up their bodies, make up their faces, remove unwanted pimples, and conceal bad breath, are here also told in one highly suggestive phrase to keep their mouths closed and their legs together. La Vieille suggests pointedly that to laugh with a gaping mouth means in some sense to split apart the lower body and open the lower, genital mouth as well. Neither gesture becomes the elegantly attired and properly attractive medieval lady.

Yet the stereotypically beautiful queen, Iseut, the coveted object of Tristan's desiring gaze in Béroul's *Roman de Tristan*, flagrantly breaks both rules. The romance begins with scenes featuring Iseut as a masterful dissembler, the lavishly dressed courtly consort who keeps her benevolent husband guessing; under the influence of the queen's carefully crafted speech, King Marc is unable to pin down the precise facts of his wife's alleged adulterous liaison with his own nephew, Tristan. But Iseut's dissembling does more than simply hoodwink a gullible spouse. By the time her case comes to trial, the sinous speech of this exemplary medieval beauty has broken into laughter and her elegantly concealed body has literally "split open" publicly for all to see. The result of this process is not however to denigrate the female mouth by equating it with the lower and more corporeal labia, as the fabliaux so often suggest. Iseut remains the heroine of this very popular Old French romance, despite her patently uncourtly gestures. They are her bodytalk, the laughing mouth and open thighs that boldly redefine the very terms of medieval beauty.

Beauty as a Liar

Béroul's version of *Le Roman de Tristan* features two scenes of consummate lying and playacting, each directed by the astute and able Queen Iseut. In the opening scene under the pine tree and in the prolonged trial that concludes the romance,[5] this highly atypical medieval "beauty" deftly plans and orchestrates the course of events, instructing her lover, Tristan, to play his part accordingly. It is she who glimpses her husband, King Marc, hidden in the pine tree above the lovers' trysting place and signals to Tristan, through exaggerated claims of innocence, that he must hide his amorous desire in order not to be trapped by the suspicious husband. It is also Iseut who instructs Tristan to come dressed as a leper to the site where she will be tried for adultery, so that his disguise might enable her calculatedly false oath to appear true.[6] Both scenes produce official declarations of Iseut's innocence despite her amorous involvement with Tristan. In this context, the courtly Beauty appears above all to be a liar.

But Iseut's lying is of a peculiar sort. For what this queen's deceptive statements hide, they also cunningly reveal. To the attentive reader/listener, Iseut's bold and crafty assertions of marital fidelity to King Marc clearly belie her adulterous liaison with the king's nephew. Repeatedly she defines her relationship to the king specifically in terms of her relationship to Tristan. In the scene under the pine, Iseut obliquely blurs the roles of lover and husband when telling Tristan in Marc's hearing:

> Li rois pense que par folie,
> Sire Tristan, vos aie amé;
> Mais Dex plevis ma loiauté,
> Qui sor mon cors mete flaele,
> S'onques fors cil qui m'ot pucele
> Out m'amistié encor nul jor!
>
> (vv. 20–25)

(Lord Tristan, the king thinks that I have loved you sinfully; but I affirm my fidelity before God, and may He punish me if anyone except the man who took my virginity ever had my love!)[7]

The privileged reader is, of course, in on the joke. We know that it was in fact Tristan who took Iseut's virginity. But the gullible king remains ignorant of this fact. And the queen's equivocal statement deftly makes both men the referent for a single crucial act.

During the trial, husband and rival lover are paired more overtly as equals in sexual practice when the queen swears her innocence by stating:

> Qu'entre mes cuises n'entra home,
> Fors le ladre qui fist soi some,
> Qui me porta outre les guez,
> Et li rois Marc mes esposez.
>
> (vv. 4205–8)

(No man has ever been between my thighs, except the leper who made himself a beast of burden and carried me over the ford and my husband King Mark.)

At stake in both instances is Iseut's body—her potentially culpable *cors* in the first example and her eroticized *cuises* in the second. Indeed, throughout Béroul's narrative, Iseut functions corporeally, as an object of exchange between men. She was imported, we remember, from her native Ireland to become King Marc's bride. But before arriving in Cornwall, she inadvertently drank a potion that made her fall hopelessly in love with Tristan. The balance of the tale documents the struggle between uncle and nephew over who rightly should possess the queen. Elaborate scenarios of spying, attempts at entrapment, and the final prolonged trial at the Mal Pas are deployed in an effort to categorize and position the queen's physical being. Does her body belong unequivocally to her rightful husband, King Marc, as medieval law would contend, or has its wandering into the illicit realm of adulterous liaison transformed this body, to some extent at least, into Tristan's possession as well? These are the issues debated by the tale's male protagonists: King Marc, the trouble-making dwarf, and the barons who want to put a just end to the king's cuckoldry and Tristan, who attempts repeatedly to prove the couple's innocence so that he can have Iseut for his own. The efforts of both sides are joined in the binary logic they share: each camp attempts to establish the guilt or innocence of the lovers, to prove that Iseut is *either* Marc's wife *or* Tristan's mistress.

The Queen's Two Bodies

But most interesting for our purposes is the extent to which the female body that serves literally as the commodified subject of this romance functions also and extensively as a speaking subject. When Iseut wishes that God bring a pestilence on her body if anyone has ever *had* her love (*out* m'amistie) other than the man who *had* her as a virgin (*m'ot* pucele), she seems at first to echo exactly King Marc's view of the sexual economy in which women's bodies are either possessed and passed between men or destroyed by a higher male authority. Later in the scene, Iseut attributes to herself the vulnerability and helplessness of an objectified body when she asserts to Tristan in the king's hearing: "if the king heard a word of our encounter, my body would be thoroughly dismembered" (*S'or en sa-voit li rois un mot, / Mon cors seret desmembre tot*, vv. 65–66). She describes subsequently how her *body* trembles for fear that the king might hear of their meeting and burn her at the stake:

> S'un mot en puet li rois oïr
> Que nos fuson ça asenblé,
> Il me feroit ardoir en ré.
> Ne seret pas mervelle grant.
> Mis cors trenble, poor ai grant.
> (vv. 190–94)

(If the king heard even a hint that we were together here, he would have me burned on a pyre, and that would come as no surprise. I am trembling; I am terribly afraid.)

She would prefer, she claims, that that body be reduced to scattered ashes than to make love to anyone but her lord:

> Mex voudroie que je fuse arse,
> Aval le vent la poudre esparse,
> Jor que je vive que amor
> Aie o home qu'o mon seignor.
> (vv. 35–38)

(I would rather be burned alive and have my ashes scattered in the wind than ever in my life love any man except my lord.)

And yet the equivocal *seignor* in this passage can refer, conveniently, either to Marc or to Tristan, much as the man who "had" Iseut as a virgin could potentially be her husband or her lover. Or perhaps neither one in the traditional sense of male possession and female submission. For as this heroine mimics the patriarchal voice that defines women as bodies, she also effectively rewrites it.

While speaking of her body as an object to be possessed by Marc or Tristan, invoking punishments of dismemberment that seem to underwrite the reduction of women to body parts,[8] Iseut enacts that objectification ironically by speaking—the very process that defines subjectivity, not objectivity. Even when reiterating the most reductive definition of femaleness—as a body to be punished—Iseut speaks as a subject that cannily knows its object. Performing for Marc's benefit, saying precisely what he wants to hear, this "subject" plays out the stereotype of the female body as typically constructed by the rhetoric of medieval law and courtly practice. But when Iseut articulates what is conventionally said about the medieval beauty—that her body defines her identity as either faithful or adulterous, as wife or lover—her words tell that tired story differently.

This heroine's speech provides a particularly striking example of the complex process of female mimesis that Irigaray has defined as follows:

> To play with mimesis is thus, for a woman, to try to recover the place of her exploitation by discourse, without allowing herself to be simply reduced to it. It means to resubmit herself—inasmuch as she is on the side of the "perceptible," of "matter"—to "ideas," in particular to ideas about herself, that are elaborated in/by a masculine logic, but so as to make "visible" by an effect of playful repetition, what was supposed to remain invisible: the cover-up of a possible operation of the feminine in language. It also means "to unveil" the fact that, if women are such good mimics, it is because they are not simply resorbed in this function. *They also remain elsewhere.*[9]

"La bele Yseut" in Béroul's romance speaks from that "elsewhere" in a specifically medieval context, defining herself within the masculinized traditions of chivalry, courtliness, and feudal jurisprudence that construct it, while also remaining significantly outside them.[10] When Iseut stands "between men," often bedecked in the lavish clothing typical of medieval heroines, her beauty provides a visible icon of legal and social structures that reduce women to lovely, commodified objects of exchange. Yet when the queen's body speaks, her voice restructures that relation of commodification, repositioning the female body beyond the binary logic that underwrites the value of the visible, the male gaze on female anatomy, and the attendant exclusivity of heterosexual coupling in love. Moving from a position "between men" to one where men fall "between her thighs," Iseut effectively redefines the legal and sexual codes that typically govern courtly romance as she carves out an alternate place for the female heroine's speaking body. At stake in her dissembling is not merely a coverup of the truth, but a thorough redefinition of the terms by which truth is established. As her carefully chosen words mimic but change, through playful repetition, the master discourses that typically construct the beautiful bodies of medieval heroines, this beauty speaks disruptively from another place.

Either/Or Logic Inscribed on Iseut's Body

Ideologies of marriage, queenship, and courtliness impose, in various ways, a logic of either/or choices on the body of Béroul's heroine. Efforts to prove the lovers' guilt or innocence in accordance with the tenets of medieval jurisprudence seek to establish whether Iseut is actually a ruling queen or an outlawed adulteress, a courtly lady who merits legal defense by valiant knights or an oversexed woman who should be led away to live and sleep with lecherous lepers.[11] These options reflect the medieval system of immanent justice that determined truth on the basis of what was seen. Whether in trial by combat, where guilt fell on the slain party, or trial by ordeal, where exoneration resulted when the accused could place his or her hand in the fire without being burned, feudal jurisprudence relied on visible evidence. Since God alone judged the proceedings, the trial was designed to make his divine truth evident by establishing a clear distinction between opposing parties. The first step in the process was the swearing of oaths: after the accuser alleged criminal activity through an officially formulated statement, the defendant swore his or her innocence by rejecting the accusation word for word. Proof of these verbal assertions was then established through the single combat or ordeal that made God's will manifest. Every case emerged as a simple either/or proposition: if innocent of the charges, the accused would win the fight or withdraw the hand unburned. If guilty, the accused would be *shown tangibly* to be a perjuror.[12]

Although this is the legal system at work in many French courtly romances, it is particularly well attested in Béroul's version of the Tristan story.[13] Accused of adultery, both lovers in the tale present their defense in line with the conviction that truth resides in the visible. Tristan offers to perform an *escondit* (in this case trial by combat) through which those who contest his declarations of innocence will be proved wrong by their death. Iseut's *deraisne*, or exculpatory oath, is accompanied by no such physical ordeal in Béroul's version.[14] It serves nevertheless to establish a visual truth and is described characteristically as being seen as well as heard:

Rois, la deraisne avon veüe
Et bien oïe et entendue.

(vv. 4235–40)

(King, we have witnessed [seen] the defense, and listened to it and heard it well.)

Even the possible punishments discussed for Iseut's alleged transgression in Béroul's tale focus decidedly on the visible. And here clothing plays a key role. After Iseut has been caught with Tristan in the king's bedroom and Marc prepares to burn his adulterous wife at the stake, a leper named Yvein offers the alternate possibility of sending the queen to live with the ragtag band of sexually charged lepers:

Yseut nos done, s'ert conmune.
Paior fin dame n'ot mais une.
Sire, en nos a si grant ardor
Soz ciel n'a dame qui un jor
Peüst soufrir nostre convers:
Li drap nos sont au cors aers.
O toi soloit estre a honor,
O vair, o gris et o baudor;
Les buens vins i avoit apris
Es granz soliers de marbre bis.
Se la donez a nos meseaus,
Qant el verra nos bas bordeaus
Et eslira l'escouellier
Et l'estovra a nos couchier
(Sire, en leu de tes beaus mengiers
Avra de pieces, de quartiers
Que l'en nos envoi'a ces hus),
Por cel seignor qui maint lasus,
Qant or verra la nostre cort,
Adonc verra si desconfort.
Donc voudroit miex morir que vivre.

(vv. 1193–1213)

(Give us Iseut to be our common property. No lady ever had a worse fate: Sir, our lust is so strong! No lady in the world could tolerate a single day of relations with us! Our ragged clothes stick to our bodies; with you she was accustomed to luxury, to beautiful furs and pleasures; she learned about fine wines in your great halls of dark marble. If you give her to us lepers, when she sees our squalid hovels and shares our dishes and has to sleep with us, and when, instead of your fine food, sir, she has only the scraps and crumbs that are given to us at the gates —by the Lord in heaven, when she sees our "court" and all its discomforts, she will rather be dead than alive.)

Life with these lascivious men would provide a more appropriate punishment for the adulterous queen than death at the stake, Yvein implies, because Iseut's debauched sexual coupling with Tristan, formerly covered up by the elegant raiment of King Marc's court, will finally be revealed for the putrid sexual congress that it is. The *vair* and *gris* and *baudor* that have graced the queen's body in her role as a royal wife and courtly consort, the very vair and gris that also emblematize Tristan's status as a courtly knight (vv. 2168–69), will be replaced by clothing that delineates members of what Yvein terms the lepers' *cort*. In this court, clothes stick to the ulcerated bodies of men too passionate for women to bear. Thus two courts, one feudal, the other antifeudal, distinctly represented by opposing styles of clothing—one lavish the other impoverished—here delineate two legal options for positioning the heroine's body: placing her either innocently with her husband or guiltily with Tristan.

If "Yseut la bele" is found innocent of the charge of adultery, she will continue to live in honor and royal splendor in Marc's lavish court, as a wife won in battle by the valiant Tristan and handed over to Marc as a gift. Iseut will reside, as Tristan reminds her in the forest interlude, "En tes chanbres, o ton seignor" (In your chambers with your lord, v. 2258),[15] a locus elegantly bedecked with silk drapery:

> et si peüst estre
> En beles chanbres, o son estre,
> Portendues de dras de soie.
> (vv. 2181–83)

(when she could be in beautiful rooms decorated with silk.)

The innocent Iseut could live, that is, in the world of courtliness typified later in this romance by the combined elegance of King Arthur and King Marc, whose retinues are richly arrayed even when camping in tents:

> Ly rois Artus, aprés mengier,
> Au tref roi Marc vait cointoier,
> Sa privee maisnie maine.
> La ot petit de dras de laine,
> Tuit li plusor furent de soie.
> Des vesteüres que diroie?
> De laine i out, ce fu en graine,
> Escarlate cel drap de laine;
> Mot i ot gent de riche ator,
> Nus ne vit deus plus riches corz.
> (vv. 4093–4102)

(After eating, King Arthur went to visit King Mark in his tent, and he took his closest associates with him. Very few of them were wearing woolen clothes; most were dressed in silk. What can I say about their clothing? What wool there was had been dyed a rich scarlet color. There were many finely dressed people there. Never had anyone seen two richer courts.)

King Arthur's elegant attire symbolizes his position to the less plentifully endowed, emblematized at the trial by the contrastingly downdressed Tristan:

> Tu es vestu de beaus grisens
> De Renebors, si con je pens.
> Desoz la toile rencïene
> La toue char est blanche et plaine.
> Tes janbes voi de riche paile
> Chaucies et o verte maile.
> Et les sorchauz d'une escarlate.
> Rois Artus, voiz con je me grate?
> J'ai les granz froiz, qui qu'ait les chauz.
> Por Deu me donne ces sorchauz.
> (vv. 3721–30)

(You are dressed in fine gray cloth, from Regensburg, I believe, and underneath the Reims linen, your skin is white and smooth. I see your legs covered with rich brocade and green net and leggings of scarlet. King Arthur, do you see how I scratch myself? I have chills even when others are hot. In God's name, give me your leggings!)

Living in the courtly world where "every knight has his lady" (Maint chevalier i out sa drue" v. 4086)[16] and defends her honor and her body properly, as Arthur's knights promise to defend Iseut,[17] the queen would fulfill her role as an honored daughter of royalty, parading publicly as "la bele Iseut," whose very body possesses incomparable value. As Tristan explains:

> Ha! roïne franche, honoree,
> En qel terre sera mais nee
> Fille de roi qui ton cors valle?
> (vv. 837–39)

(Oh, noble and honored queen, in what land will there ever be born a princess whose body is worth yours?)

But if found guilty, Iseut would be reduced to a body without adornment and stripped of value, "Qu'ele vive et que ne valle" (she can live and yet want to die [be of no worth] v. 1182) as King Marc puts it; or "Qu'ele vivroit, et sanz valoir" in Yvein's terms (she will live on in disgrace [without value] v. 1176), a pitiful *cors* with arms bound tightly as she is led away to live in that other "court" among the minimal *drap* of lepers. The irony of placing beauty among these beasts is rendered most poignantly when Tristan *sees* his lady led away by Yvein and remarks in astonishment, "quel aventure! / Ahi! Yseut, bele figure" (vv. 1237–38). Beauty could not be more out of place than among the disfigured, leprous bodies. But the either/or logic that opposes beauty to beastliness, wife to adulteress, courtly life to the squalor of a leper's hut does not hold in this romance. It is summarily undone by the effect of Iseut's voice.

Iseut Between Men

The queen consistently refuses to define her position between Marc and Tristan in terms that would establish her clearly as either a faithful wife or an adulterous lover. For her, it is rather a question of reconciling the irreconcilable; of having both husband and lover, of being both wife and mistress. As Iseut's scheming undermines the legal system of guilt and innocence based on the visible, her dissembling also rewrites the hetero-sexual contract that subtends it. As a result of the plotting that makes it possible for her to have both Marc as a husband and Tristan as a lover, she draws the two men together in significant and unexpected ways. Iseut's shrewd linguistic formulations that tie Marc and Tristan together while asserting their separateness reveal a significant, if uncanny, aspect of the love triangle in Béroul's romance: the bond uniting Marc and his queen in marriage depends to a large extent on another bond uniting Marc and Tristan in friendship and kinship. Her astute remarks reveal the extent to which courtly interaction uses women to cement bonds between men. In fact, as Marc and Tristan vie for Iseut's affection, they seem often to function more as mutual accomplices than competitors.

Eve K. Sedgwick has cogently explained the phenomenon of homo-social bonding, whereby the traditional marriage bond uniting a man and a woman can also serve to join two men or groups of men. Woman's role in the marriage contract then becomes less that of a partner than an object of exchange and conduit between men. In this view, homosocial bonding—defined as relations of male mentorship, comradeship, the transmission of culture and power—does not necessarily include genital homosexuality, although it may. Sedgwick's point is that male-centered literary texts are as likely to be about homosocial or homosexual as heterosexual object choices.[18]

In the medieval context, Christiane Marchello-Nizia has shown how homosexual bonding becomes particularly explicit in the thirteenth-century *Prose Tristan* and *Prose Lancelot*. The love between Lancelot and Guenevere is made possible through a male intermediary, Galehot, who is erotically attracted to Lancelot; and Tristan's interest in Iseut in the prose version of the tale is kindled in response to Palamedes's prior love for her. In Marchello-Nizia's analysis, male bonding delineates above all a relation of power. Desire by the knight for the woman in these instances is not desire for just any woman but, as in a chessgame, for the queen—that is to say, for the power that she represents as the king's wife and consort. By courting her, the lover indirectly courts the king's favor. Here again, as in Sedgwick's analysis, erotic union with the female masks a homosocial union between men.

Béroul's text contains ample evidence of strong homosocial bonding between Marc and Tristan accompanied by a curious lack of jealousy over Iseut. Marc's distrust of the lovers and his suspicion of their adultery focuses almost exclusively on the defection of his nephew-turned-rival, not on the loss of his beautiful wife. Explaining how Marc's marriage with Iseut has caused him much suffering (v. 126), Tristan laments during the scene under the pine the king's loss of affection for him: "Bien sai que mot me het li rois" (I know very well that the king hates me, v. 203). He asks the queen to intercede on his behalf, to reestablish the bond of male friendship that has previously united them, "tenez-moi bien a mon ami" ("Reconcile me with my friend," v. 160). Marc later tells Iseut how he felt extreme sympathy for his nephew while listening to Tristan recount his success against the Morholt and his suffering after being wounded by the dragon:

> Et qant je vos oï retraire
> Le mal q'en mer li estut traire
> De la serpent dont le garistes,
> . . . .
> Pitié m'en prist an l'arbre sus.
> (vv. 483–85, 491)

(And when I heard him recount to you the suffering he endured at sea, because of the dragon's wound from which you cured him, . . . I felt great pity up there in the tree.)

Curiously, however, the reconciliation between Marc and Tristan that results from Iseut's careful speech under the pine tree leads also to a reconciliation of the threatened lovers. Henceforth, Tristan will be both on good terms with the king and at his leisure to enter the queen's bedroom:

> D'or en avant avra loisir
> D'estre o Yseut a son plaisir.
> . . . .
> Accordez est Tristan au roi.
> Li rois li a doné congié
> D'estre a la chanbre; es le vos lié
> (vv. 533–34, 568–70)

(From then on he would be able[19] to be with Iseut whenever he
wished. . . . Tristan was reconciled with the king, and the king gave
him permission to be in the royal chamber. Now he was happy!)

As Iseut's own equivocal words repeatedly suggest, the heterosexual
link between Tristan and Iseut and the homosocial bond between Tristan
and Marc are interdependent relationships. Yseut's most duplicitous statements routinely call attention to this fact, detailing how her liaisons with
Tristan and with Marc both disrupt and cement the bond between the two
men. The queen says twice to Tristan in the king's hearing that she loved
him only because of his familial link to Marc:

> Que por lui par vos aie ameit:
> Por ce qu'eres du parenté
> Vos avoie je en cherté
> . . . .
> Sire, mot t'ai por lui ame
> Et j'en ai tot perdu son gre
> (vv. 70–72, 79–80)

(That he himself is the reason that I loved you: Because you were his
relative, I held you very dear. . . . Sir, I loved you for his sake, and I
have thereby lost his favor)

Contending that she owes Tristan something because it was thanks
to him that she became Marc's queen, Iseut defines the complementary
roles of the two men on either side of her in a particularly apt sentence
that places her *je* neatly between the codependent *lui* and *vos*:

> mais je li dui
> Anor faire non trop frarine.
> Par *lui* sui je de *vos* roïne
> (vv. 418–20, my emphasis)

(but I owed it to him not to treat him dishonorably: It is because of
him that I am your queen)

The pattern repeats when the lovers plan to leave the forest. Proclaiming his affection for the king who loved him dearly, Tristan laments his exile from court in terms of his emotional separation from Marc:

Dex! tant m'amast mes oncles chiers,
Se tant ne fuse a lui mesfez!
. . . .
Tristran s'apuie sor son arc,
Sovent regrete le roi Marc,
Son oncle, qui a fait tel tort
                    (vv. 2170−71, 2195−97)

(God! My uncle would have loved me so if I had not betrayed him! . . . Tristan leaned on his bow, regretting the wrong he had done to King Mark, his uncle)

Tristan's plan, however, is twofold: to affect a new reconciliation with Marc, "Gel serviroie a grant honor, / Conme mon oncle et mon seignor" (I would serve him with honor as my uncle and my lord, vv. 2239−40), and to maintain his amorous rapport with Iseut, "Roïne franche, ou que je soie, / Vostre toz jors me clameroie" (Noble queen, wherever I will be, I will always be yours, vv. 2249−50). Tristan hopes to reestablish the love triangle that has been temporarily disrupted by the purely heterosexual coupling of the forest interlude.

Marc does visit the forest hideaway, and in a scene now famous for its ambiguous and highly charged treatment of linguistic and iconographic signs, he redefines his relationship with the lovers in a way that brings him symbolically closer to Tristan. Attributing particular significance to the space that separates the sleeping couple, "Qu'entre eus deus avoit devise" (that there was a space between them, v. 1996), a space occupied by the sword that Tristan used to kill the Morholt, Marc proclaims the lovers' innocence. It is as if he views that space between Tristan and Iseut as a place held open for him in the triangular love relationship; he could be between them, lying next to them both. In response to this realization, Marc removes Tristan's famous sword and replaces it with his own, thus exchanging tokens of male prowess, identity, and sexuality:

L'espee qui entre eus deus est
Souef oste, la soue i met.
                (vv. 2049–50)

(He gently removed the sword that was between them and placed
his own there.)

The king's gestures toward Iseut, however, suggest the dissolving of a relationship. Whereas the exchange of swords with Tristan signals the establishment of a bond between men, the apparent "exchange" of rings with
Iseut undoes a bond previously established. Marc returns to her a ring that
she has given him and takes back the wedding ring that he had offered her
(vv. 1812–13, 2027–31). These gestures can be interpreted in many ways.
Marc claims that they are designed to communicate his sympathy for the
lovers (v. 2024). Tristan, conversely, is sure that they suggest malice on the
king's part (vv. 2093–2100). Whatever their significance, Marc's signals to
the lovers ultimately call Tristan back to court; they prefigure Marc's actual
call to Tristan in the darkness of night when his nephew delivers the message of reconciliation, "Por Deu, beaus niés, ton oncle atent! (In God's
name, dear nephew, wait for your uncle! v. 2473). Elsewhere we are told
outright that Tristan does not simply want to leave the forest and return
to court. His express desire is to reestablish the love bond between Iseut
and Marc, to make her once again the queen of her lord (vv. 2256–58). But
Tristan also wants to reinstate his own privileged status with the king. The
return of Iseut will enable the banished knight to reenter the service of his
feudal lord, Marc, as he explains to him:

Mais, s'or estoit vostre plesir
A prendere Yseut o le cler vis,
N'avroit baron en cest païs
Plus vos servist que je feroie.
                (vv. 2604–7)

(But if it should now be your wish to take back the fair Iseut, you
would have no baron in the country who would serve you better
than I.)

By returning the queen to her husband's bedchamber, Tristan will once
again reestablish the triangle that makes of adultery and marriage odd
bedfellows.

If surprisingly little jealousy divides Marc from his nephew-rival in this scenario, considerable overt jealousy pits Tristan against Marc's barons elsewhere. We know from earlier portions of the Tristan story (reconstructed from other versions of the tale) that Tristan himself has upset the homosocial balance that once linked Marc to his "men." It was the barons, we remember, who, distressed by Marc's favoritism for his valiant and accomplished nephew, encouraged the king to marry. Their hope was to replace Tristan as the object of Marc's affection with a new bride, expecting that this woman would cement male ties of friendship, honor, and prowess. But the plot failed. Iseut outlines the parameters of the resultant scenario during the second part of her speech under the pine:

> Se li felon de cest'enor,
> Por qui jadis vos conbatistes
> O le Morhout, quant l'oceïstes,
> Li font acroire (ce me senble)
> Que nos amors jostent ensenble.
> (vv. 26–30)

(Even though the slanderous barons of this land, for whose sake you once fought with the Morholt and killed him, have obviously convinced the king that we are united in love.)

Tristan is particularly despised, as the passage suggests, because he stole the honor that the barons felt was rightfully theirs. By successfully killing the Morholt, a fierce enemy who had long exacted a yearly tribute from Marc's subjects, Tristan established his own prowess and revealed thereby the barons' weakness and inadequacy. Stripped of chivalric valor, these *felons*—as the text repeatedly calls the barons—resort to guileful speech, calumny, and malicious chatter in an attempt to sever the bond that still firmly links Tristan to Marc. The barons are said to have "misled" the king (*desveier* v. 89), "made him believe things that were not true" ("lui font acroire / de nos tel chose qui n'est voire," vv. 83–84). Through their envious counsel (vv. 1061–62), they succeed finally in making Marc banish his nephew, as the king explains:

> Par lor parler, par lor mentir
> Ai mon nevo de moi chacié.
> (vv. 3194–95)

(Because of their words, their lies, I sent my nephew away from me.)

The barons are in fact a perfect match for the linguistically shrewd Iseut, the difference being that their claims of adultery are grounded in fact, whereas Iseut's declarations of innocence are, at best, only partially true.

Thus the traditional love triangle that places Iseut between Marc and Tristan is accompanied in this tale of dissembling by a second triangle of equal importance: that which pits the barons with their subversive talk against the verbally astute lovers. Both parties vie for Marc's attention and approval as he vacillates undecidedly between condemning the lovers according to the barons' advice or banishing the barons as calumniators who wrongly accuse the innocent couple. Rivalry in this case is not based on love, or the exchange of women that inevitably subtends it in courtly romance, but on storytelling, on the ability to deceive, persuade, or seduce with words. And Iseut's role in this scenario is predicated less on her body than on the voice that repositions that body outside of the expected subject/object dichotomy.

Beauty in Name Only

Despite the leper Yvein's assertion that Iseut at Arthur's court enjoyed the "luxury of fine furs and pleasures," we rarely see, or hear of, the queen's lavishly dressed body in the course of Béroul's romance, at least not in the parts of the text that have survived. Indeed, one wonders why "la bele Iseut," evoked throughout medieval French literature as a paragon of feminine beauty, never emerges in Béroul's text as the object of lengthy physical description. The lavish portrait of Enide's beauty and elegant dress in Chrétien de Troyes's *Erec et Enide* establishes that heroine's extraordinary physical attractiveness by stating explicitly that she was "more beautiful than Iseut":

> c'onques si bele criature
> ne fu veüe an tot le monde.
> Por voir vos di qu'Isolz la blonde
> n'ot les crins tant sors ne luisanz
> (vv. 422–25)

(Never had a more beautiful creature been seen. I tell you truly that even Blonde Iseut did not have hair as light or shiny)

Yet the paradigm of Iseut's extraordinary beauty appears in Béroul's romance only comically, through a wry comment addressed to King Marc by Tristan, disguised as a leper. "There is only one woman more beautiful than my lover," Tristan asserts, "la bele Yseut." Rounding out the stereotypical portrait that links feminine beauty and elegant clothing in courtly romance, Tristan contends that his unnamed ladylove dresses as Iseut does.

> Mais plus bele ne fu que une.
> —Qui est ele?—La bele Yseut:
> Einsi se vest con cele seut.
> > (vv. 3774–76)

("But there is only one woman more beautiful than she." "Who is that?" "The beautiful Iseut! She even dresses as the other one did.")

The joke of course is that this leper's lover *is* la bele Iseut, wife of King Marc, and that she not only dresses like her, but in the same clothing. All of which suggests that clothing makes the woman, in this romance as in so many other courtly narratives where the female body is fetishized under layers of silk that make its sexual specificity disappear.[20] But such is not the case, it turns out, with "la bele Yseut," whose body, dress, and beauty appear only sporadically and fleetingly in Béroul's version of the Tristan story. Nowhere do we find a lengthy portrait of Iseut's face, hands, and white skin like those extensive catalogues of body parts used to evoke the beauty of Philomena or Enide. Even Iseut's fine clothes receive only limited mention.

The narrator first describes Iseut's clothes in complete isolation from her body, as a kind of shopping list of fabrics purchased by the hermit in preparation for the queen's return from the forest to join her husband, King Marc. Only the final line of this inventory links the clothes, almost incidentally, with the queen who is said to wear them:

> Li hermites en vet au Mont,
> Por les richeces qui la sont.
> Assés achate ver et gris,
> Dras de soie et de porpre bis,
> Escarlates et blanc chainsil,
> Asez plus blanc que flor de lil,

> Et palefroi soeuf anblant,
> Bien atornez d'or flanboiant.
> Ogrins l'ermite tant achate
> Et tant acroit et tant barate
> Pailes, vairs et gris et hermine
> Que richement vest la roïne.
>
> (vv. 2733–44)

(The hermit went to the Mount [St. Michael's Mount in Cornwall], because of the rich market held there. He bought gray and white furs, silk and rich purple fabrics, fine wool and linen far whiter than lilies; and he bought a gentle riding horse with a harness of brightest gold. The hermit Ogrin bought and bartered and acquired by credit enough precious cloth and gray furs and ermine *to dress the queen richly*. My emphasis)

On her return to court, Iseut's clothes are evoked in a brief eight-line segment that leads us to a remarkably terse description of her body, eyes, and hair. As Dinas removes her cape, we hear:

> Du col li a osté la chape,
> Qui ert d'escarlate mot riche.
> Ele out vestu une tunique
> Desus un grant bliaut de soie.
> De son mantel que vos diroie?
> Ainz l'ermite, qui l'achata,
> Le riche fuer ne regreta.
> Riche ert la robe et gent le cors:
> Les eulz out vers, les cheveus sors.
>
> (vv. 2880–88)

(He removed her rich scarlet cape from her shoulders. She was wearing a tunic over a silk chemise. What can I tell you of her mantle? The hermit who bought it never regretted the great cost. The robe was rich and Iseut was beautiful [literally, "of noble body"]. Her eyes were green, her hair golden.)

A final allusion to the "porpre d'inde" Iseut wears upon entering the church (v. 2980) completes the highly fragmented portrait of a body whose features are scattered intermittently across 100 lines of text, and a body whose beauty here goes entirely unmentioned. This stately return of Iseut to King Marc is said to provoke in the courtly spectators a sentiment of reverence for their queen paralleled only by the honor they bestowed upon her on her wedding day:

> Mot l'ont le jor tuit honoree:
> Ainz le jor que fu esposee
> Ne li fist hom si grant honor
> Con l'on li a fait icel jor.
> (vv. 3003–6)

(Everyone honored her greatly that day: never, since the day she was married, had she received as much honor as they bestowed on her that day.)

This "marriage" procession, however, lacks the clear focus on female beauty that dominated, for example, Enide's lavish wedding. Iseut's raiments are present and remarked almost incidentally, absorbed within the larger decorative framework of an entire town bedecked with drapery to celebrate the occasion:

> Quar, ce saciez, ainz n'i ot rue
> Ne fust de paile portendue:
> Cil qui n'out paile mist cortine.
> Par la ou aloit la roïne
> Est la rue mot bien jonchie.
> (vv. 2967–71)

(And imagine this: every street was hung with brocaded cloths, and those who did not have brocade hung tapestries. Wherever the queen went, the streets were strewn with flowers.)

The epithet "la bele" that rings in the ears of many readers familiar with the Tristan material as synonymous with "Iseut" actually appears with frequency only in the latter fourth of Béroul's text, figuring most prominently in scenes that feature King Arthur and his courtly milieu.[21]

There, "la bele Yseut" evokes predictably the lovely and revered lady who merits protection from able knights willing to defend her in battle.

Despite the recurrent epithet attesting to this heroine's beauty in the tale's last segment, we never really see Iseut in the kind of detail that outlines the facial and corporeal features of Philomena or Enide. No one looks longingly at Iseut from near or far. In the scene of the forest hideaway when King Marc comes upon the sleeping lovers and lingers fondly over the image of what he perceives to be their innocent embrace, one might expect a description of the queen's delicate beauty or of a body that incites desire in the viewer. Instead we find a rather clinical account of what the king *sees* as the verb *veoir* is repeatedly followed by direct objects understood by Marc to desexualize the lovers' encounter. He *sees*, as proof of the lovers' innocence, Iseut wearing her chemise and Tristan his breeches, he *sees* also the two lovers separated by a physical space (*devise*) that precludes direct contact between their bodies or mouths:

> Quant vit qu'ele avoit sa chemise
> Et qu'entre eus deus avoit devise,
> La bouche o l'autre n'ert jostee,
> Et qant il vit la nue espee
> Qui entre eus deus les desevrot,
> Vit les braies que Tristran out.
>   (vv. 1995–2000)

(When he saw that she was wearing her chemise and saw that there was a space between them and that their mouths were not touching, and when he saw the naked sword which was separating them and saw the breeches that Tristan wore. . . .)

Marc then *sees* on the queen's finger a ring he had given her and on her face, a ray of sunlight:

> Ge voi el doi a la reïne
> L'anel o pierre esmeraudine;
> . . . .
> Le rai qui sor la face brande
>   (vv. 2027–28, 2034)

(I see on the queen's finger her fine emerald ring; . . . the ray of sunlight falling on her face)

He *sees* in short the two lovers sleeping together as bodies significantly separate while united: "Vit ensenble les deus dormanz" (He looked at the two sleeping together, v. 2040). But he does not see in Iseut a sexualized object of desire. The emphasis in this depiction of "la bele Yseut o cler vis" could not be more removed from the lascivious gaze that Tereus cast on the beautiful Philomena or the approving male eyes that construct Enide's beauty in the wedding procession of *Erec et Enide*. If Iseut sleeps silently in the forest interlude beneath the watchful eye of King Marc, she is not the classic "sleeping beauty" whose body is coveted and fetishized in courtly romance.

"La bele Yseut" makes a final appearance at the trial scene on the Blanche Lande, where we hear again briefly of her clothes, of the silks, ermine, and gold that adorn her shoulders and head:

> A tant es vos Yseut la bele.
> . . . .
> La roïne out de soie dras:
> Aporté furent de Baudas,
> Forré furent de blanc hermine.
> Mantel, bliaut, tot li traïne.
> Sor ses espaules sont si crin,
> Bendé a ligne sor or fin.
> Un cercle d'or out sor son chief,
> Qui empare de chief en chief,
> Color rosine, fresche et blanche.
>   (vv. 3824, 3903–11)

(And then the fair [beautiful] Iseut arrived. . . . The queen was wearing garments of silk brought from Baghdad; they were trimmed in white ermine. Her mantle and tunic formed a train behind her. Her hair fell to her shoulders and was tied in linen ribbons over a fine gold net. She wore on her head a golden band that encircled it entirely, and her face was rosy, fresh, and fair.)

This evocation of the queen's lavish clothing recedes, however, into the background behind two surrounding actions that downplay its importance as they radically redefine the status of "Yseut le bele." Iseut's elegantly dressed body appears here before an audience of courtly players who will soon become the onlookers at her trial by ordeal. As they watch, she deftly ties the stirrups around the saddle horn and holding her dress in one hand, swats the horse so that he will pass through the muddy marsh alone (vv. 3885–98). The esteemed King Arthur, King Marc, and all the others watch the queen in reverent amazement:

> La roïne out mot grant esgart
> De ceus qui sont de l'autre part
> Li roi prisié s'en esbahirent,
> Et tuit li autre qui le virent.
> (vv. 3899–3902)

(The queen had been watched closely by those on the other side. The great kings marveled at her, as did all the others who saw her.)

The accomplished skill and authority imbued in this gesture echoes in the equally imposing command Iseut subsequently gives to Tristan: "Ge vueil avoir a toi afere" (I have a proposition for you [we have some business to conduct], v. 3913). The "beauty" of this heroine is shown in both instances not to reside solely in the garments that drape her shoulders and head. Indeed, this "bele" stands in relation to the largely male spectators of her acts as a being fully cognizant of the gaze that falls upon her:

> Oiez d'Yseut com ele fu sage!
> Bien savoit que cil l'esgardoient
> Qui outre le Mal Pas estoient.
> (vv. 3882–84)

(Now hear how crafty Iseut was! She knew that those who were on the other bank of Mal Pas were watching her.)

Iseut's wisdom (*sagesse*) lies not in being a body, but in speaking from the female body. Tristan's response to the queen's ambiguous command, "I don't know what you mean" (Mais je ne sai que tu veus dire, v. 3916), neatly conveys the crux of this beautiful body's position. Nobody knows quite what Iseut means, or where she stands, either here, under the pine, or in any number of other scenes where her body speaks astutely almost despite its beauty. We are told specifically on several occasions that this beautiful heroine knows how to speak, carefully witholding and giving information as suits her purpose: "mot bel a le roi aresnié" (She spoke cleverly to the king, v. 3180) and shortly thereafter, "La bele Yseut, qui parler sot / Tot sinplement a dit au roi" (The fair [beautiful] Iseut who knew how to choose her words, asked the king directly, vv. 3208–9).

Indeed from the beginning of the romance as we now have it, Iseut emerges as more of a voice than a body. In the initial scene under the pine, lines 5 to 92 belong to her alone, with the exception of two lines spoken by Tristan (vv. 82–84). Her voice dominates the trial scene, where she devises her own exculpatory oath (*deraisne*) that dovetails with prior verbal instructions detailing how Tristan should disguise himself as a leper and wait for her at the Mal Pas. In the trial scene in particular, emphasis falls on how the beautiful female body uses her voice to clothe her lover. She does so not in the fashion of Pygmalion, who sculpts and dresses up a perfectly silent statue, but as a beautiful woman who dresses down a man's body—from knight to leper—so it can speak aloud what previously has been hidden. The dynamics of this shift are crucial. And it is Iseut's voice that tellingly restructures the paradigm. Her words recast the familiar scenario of the male lover/onlooker or narrator/creator who dresses, if only metaphorically, the beautiful object of desire. We now witness instead a drama in which a female beauty, who stands outside the subject/object dichotomy, orchestrates the dressing of a man.

The Tale Told Differently

To establish her innocence during the trial at the Mal Pas, Iseut must assert specifically that her flesh has not mingled with Tristan's, that she never had *amor conmune* with the king's nephew (v. 4163)—that is to say, that a social space separates the two lovers. Iseut finesses the task by articulating an unconventional verbal *deraisne* of her own devising:

> Se Damledeu mon cors seceure,
> Escondit mais ne lor ferai,
> Fors un que je deviserai.
> > (vv. 3232–34)

(May God help me, I will offer no defense except one of my own choosing [devising].)

Her legally acceptable oath recasts that crucial space which separated the lovers in the forest hideaway, as the unequivocal *devise* between them ("q'entre eus deus avoit devise" v. 1996) becomes the queen's *deviserai* (I will devise/order/arrange). The clearly perceptible space that earlier allowed Marc to presume the couple's innocence because, as he reasoned, if they had been lovers their bodies would have been positioned differently, "Autrement fust cest'asenblee" (They would be together in quite a different way! v. 2010),[22] now shifts to the less certain verbal space of Iseut's devising. As Iseut invents a verbal formula that makes precise visual separation hazy, the lovers stand on either side of a murky marsh that becomes a metaphor for concealing, not revealing, the true terms of their liaison.

And as a result of Iseut's invented oath, the definition of being "between" changes radically as well. The narrator's declarative "between them was a space" (Et *qu'entre* eus deus avoit devise) differs sharply from the queen's duplicitous "between my thighs . . . there entered no one except the leper who made himself a beast of burden and carried me over the ford and my husband, King Mark" (*Qu'entre* mes cuises n'entra home, / Fors le ladre qui fist soi some, / Qui me porta outre les guez, / Et li rois Marc mes esposez, vv. 4205–8).

Substantially altering the legal value and status that a space "in between two things" might carry, Iseut's words subvert at its core the either/or logic governing the whole of Béroul's romance. The crucial *devise* in the forest hideaway that, in Marc's visual reasoning, marked Iseut's body as belonging to her husband and not to her lover has now become a space big enough to accommodate both men at once. Iseut's oath lumps husband and lover together as men who have come between her thighs:

Ces deus ost de mon soirement,
Ge n'en ost plus de tote gent.
De deus ne me pus escondire:
Du ladre, du roi Marc, mon sire.
(vv. 4209–12)

(I exclude these two from my oath, but I except no one else. I cannot swear it about those two: the leper and my lord, King Mark.)

The female body articulating this claim is neither the "bele Yseut" of courtly renown, nor the repudiated potential prisoner of the leper colony.

Her anatomy, now sexualized by her own definition, by her own devising, can include *both* husband *and* leper, as the categories used previously to distinguish them break down. The leper in this scene is the leper/lover/ knight that the disguised Tristan plays; the husband is the naive cuckold falsely represented by this trial as a potent king and proper spouse. As the space between Iseut's thighs expands in her definition to include *both* lover *and* husband, her body becomes a map for a new legal coding and the site for a redefinition of heterosexual and homosocial bonding.

When "Yseut la Bele" mounts Tristan's back, as a squire mounts a horse, one leg on either side (vv. 3931; 3940), and rides him across the muddy marsh, she enacts visibly and for all to see ("tuit les gardent" v. 3934) what has previously only occurred in private. This public reenact- ment of the adulterous coupling that the lovers have carried on in secret enables the queen to tell openly of her liaison with Tristan while also con- cealing it: "Li ladres fu entre mes janbes" (The leper was between my legs, vv. 4209–13). This line, referring overtly to the moment when the leper carried Iseut legally across the ford and covertly to earlier instances when Tristan came between the queen's thighs illegally and in secret, establishes the female body as a place where binarism dissolves. It is at the site of this speaking body that acknowledgement of guilt can prove innocence and that an outcast leper can also be a courtly knight.[23] It is only in the space "between" Iseut's thighs that husband and lover can be joined as meta- phorical lepers who legitimately love the same woman.

We have heard earlier Tristan's sly quip to Marc explaining that he contracted leprosy when sleeping with his *amie* whose husband was *me- seaus* (leprous, v. 3771). If Tristan is a leper by virtue of the disguise he wears, Marc is leprous only in name and by inference. But the very fact that characters in this romance can be fake lepers, that the appearance and name of leper can apply to persons other than those afflicted with the disfiguring disease, suggests a further erosion of the system of feudal jus- tice that establishes truth on visible evidence. Under medieval law lepers were officially outlaws, outsiders whose mutilated bodies alerted others to their status as criminals duly punished by God. Medieval medical texts, ecclesiastical documents, and folk belief all characterize lepers specifically by their appearance, citing their physical deformity as a mark of moral decay and emphasizing the necessity of standardized dress to ensure im- mediate recognition of them.[24] In Béroul's romance, the distinct identities of King Marc and his nephew Tristan coalesce as fellow "lepers" to the extent that they are both lovers of the queen. That is to say, their status as lepers results, as Tristan's telling remark explains, from their physical contact with the queen, from "coming between her thighs." Her paradoxically eroticized and speaking body provides a place where courtliness and its antithesis can merge.

Once Marc and Tristan come together between Iseut's thighs, she no longer occupies the position "between men." And the options open to all three protagonists change considerably. Because of Iseut's clever words at the trial, Marc does not have to choose *between* having Tristan as his vassal *or* Iseut as his wife. He does not have to give up Tristan to have Iseut, as the barons contend. Tristan, similarly, does not have to choose *between* loving Iseut and maintaining allegiance to the king. The essential conflict in this tale appears then not to exist between Marc and Tristan, for their bond endures, although it is defined in a new way. When Tristan kills the barons one by one in a gesture of personal vengeance, he also serves Marc's purpose, eliminating the power-hungry counselors who have beleaguered and harassed him. As the barons die, so too does their insistence on demonstrable proof and referential language. Against their assertions that Marc must establish the lovers' guilt *or* innocence, and prove himself thereby *either* virile *or* cuckolded, Iseut's convincing lies provide the alternative of a nuanced truth that escapes the logic of binary opposition. The oath Iseut swears on her body refigures the very meaning of the word *between*, which functioned formerly to indicate a space separating two bodies, holding them apart, at a significant distance. "Coming between" Iseut's thighs signifies a way that Marc and Tristan can come together rather than stand apart. Cast initially in this romance as rivals fighting over possession of the woman's body, they emerge in Iseut's redefinition of the courtly world as co-lovers surrounded by and joined within that seemingly enormous female body where opposites dissolve.

But Iseut's oath only succeeds because of Tristan's disguise: because the beautiful woman, object of everyone's gaze at the Mal Pas and the subsequent trial, has performed the crucial operation of dressing her man.

Dressing the Male Body

Horrified earlier at the prospect of having to couple with the repugnant leper Yvein as punishment for her adultery, Iseut ends the tale by coupling quite openly and willingly, if only metaphorically, with another leper, Tristan.[25] But like Iseut's oath, this leper is of the queen's own devising. And it is through him that her words at the trial effectively rewrite the earlier scene where Iseut's body was nearly given over in silence to lecherous lepers. Now her directives "order" things differently, staging a drama that undoes, while seeming to underwrite, the courtly and legal codes that trade women between men.

Having sent word to Tristan via messenger before the trial, the queen instructs Tristan to arrive at the Mal Pas wearing a leper's garb and carrying a staff, his face covered with bumps. After collecting alms in a leper's cup, he is to rendezvous with the queen in private, *en chanbre coie*, as her remarks to the messenger specify:

> Gart moi l'argent, tant que le voie
> Priveement, en chanbre coie.
> $\qquad$ (vv. 3311–12)

(He is to keep the money for me, until I see him alone in a private room.)

Iseut's public declarations of innocence will lead, then, immediately and unproblematically to a secret meeting with a man we know to be her guilty partner. The effect of the disguised leper, the quintessential creation of Iseut's powerful voice, will be to make distinctions between right and wrong literally impossible. As François Rigolot has noted, the *dras de ladres* that Iseut designates as appropriate trappings for her lover/knight effectively recast the function of the incriminating bedsheets, also called *dras*, that nearly sealed the lovers' fate in the scene of the flour on the floor.[26] Those bloodstained *dras du lit* served as the visual proof (*veraie enseigne*, v. 778) of the lovers' adultery, legally establishing Iseut's sullied reputation and condemning her to be burned at the stake. The blood from Tristan's wounds had stained the white sheets during a midnight rendezvous and tainted the queen's reputation, as the narrator informs us:

> Li rois choisi el lit le sanc:
> Vermel en furent li drap blanc.
> $\qquad$ (vv. 767–68)

(The king noticed the blood on the bed; the white sheets were red.)

Tristan's more ambiguous *dras de ladres* will now come into play at another site where it seems the lovers have also met secretly. The queen contends in her message that Tristan will remember the designated meeting place as a spot where she once soiled her own *dras*, her skirts:

Di li qu'il set bien un marchés,
Au chief des planches, au Mal Pas:
G'i sollé ja un poi mes dras.
(vv. 3294–96)

(Tell him that he is familiar with a marsh at the approach to the bridge, at Mal Pas, where I once soiled the hem of my dress [soiled my clothing a little].)

Although we are not told the purpose of this prior meeting, Iseut's allusion to having "soiled her clothing" (*dras*) at this site harks back to the earlier scene of amorous coupling in the bedchamber and suggests that the lovers may have also used the Mal Pas as a trysting place. If this is so, the trial orchestrated by Iseut's wily voice will actually take place at the scene of the crime, or at least the scene of one instance of the lovers' secret liaisons. Iseut's words would then transform the very locale where the lovers joined together previously into the site for proving that they were not together at all.

The queen's reputation, once allegedly sullied by the tainted bed sheets, will now be restored through an elaborate procession of characters soiling their own clothes as they traipse through the mud. Although "li passeor sollent lor dras" (Those who crossed soiled their clothes, v. 3698) Iseut's dress remains untouched. Because of the queen's devising, her having arranged for Tristan's clothing as carefully as she arranges the words of her oath, witnesses to the trial ride horses muddied up to their haunches, "Li cheval entrent jusq'as flans," (v. 3672), while Iseut's unsoiled *cuisses* come out legally clean. The mud that metaphorically clouds the clear vision necessary for establishing guilt or innocence, according to the medieval system of immanent justice, physically blurs distinctions of dress so necessary to establishing social class and status. Stuck in the mud of

Iseut's devising, the dirtied barons are forced to undress, leaving behind the garments that signal their nobility:

Voiant le pueple, se despollent,
Li dras laisent, autres racuellent.
                (vv. 3863–64)

(In front of everyone, they undressed, left their clothes, and put on others.)

Before the trial, the leprous Tristan collects many *fins dras* (v. 3738), along with money, acquiring aristocratic clothing that jars with his apparently impoverished identity while also subtly suggesting his hidden courtliness. As King Arthur donates his boots and King Marc his hood, the knight-turned-leper begins to look more like the knight he is. The uncertain identities of male characters—Tristan balanced between the roles of leper and knight, the barons hovering between courtliness and poverty, and the kings alternating between elegance and squalor—result from the carefully chosen words of a woman whose own clothing (*dras*) will be proven by this trial to be soiled and clean at the same time. The stain of adultery on the bedsheets ultimately leaves no mark on the heroine's outer garments. Telling signs of her liaison with Tristan, which would have been aptly emblematized under the system of immanent justice by the minimal clothing worn by inhabitants of the leper colony, have been transferred significantly from Iseut's body to Tristan's. She stands elsewhere: positioned within the paradox of the innocent adulteress.

When Beauty Laughs and Winks

When she arrives at the Mal Pas, "Yseut la bele" stands literally "alone" (v. 3881) as a beauty who sees, who looks at the men she has arranged strategically apart from her on the other side of the ford. The men stand in a mirror image of their expected relation to one another. Iseut's directives have produced an exact inversion of the hierarchy that normally privileges King Marc's aristocratic court over the "court" of Yvein's lepers. Her words have placed the noble barons in the mud and given the high ground to the leper (Tristan):

> El taier vit ses ainemis,
> Sor la mote sist ses amis.
>> (vv. 3825−26)

(She saw her enemies in the mud while her friend sat on the hill.)

But she herself occupies a third place, standing at a considerable distance from both courtly and uncourtly actors in the scenario she has created. Positioning her body outside of the binary logic that structures much of this romance, Iseut now stands visibly "elsewhere," beyond distinctions between truth and falsehood, guilt and innocence, and beyond the dichotomy that pits female beauty against woman's speech.

The portrait now offered of this heroine aptly registers the shift in her positioning, by detailing scattered facial features not at all reminiscent of the typical romance beauty. Instead of the lovely poised lips and neatly paired eyes of Philomena or Enide, Yseut's face shatters the expected repose and symmetry of medieval female beauty. She displays for the listener an ironic laugh and for the viewer a telling wink. When arriving at the scene of the trial she has so carefully prepared, the stately queen and courtly beauty responds by laughing:

> Atant es vos Yseut la bele.
> El taier vit ses ainemis,
> Sor la mote sist ses amis.
> Joie en a grant, rit et envoise.
>> (vv. 3824−27)

(And then the fair [beautiful] Iseut arrived! She saw her enemies in the mud while her friend sat on the hill. That made her happy, and she laughed and rejoiced.)

Iseut laughs again when the concerned Dinas wonders how this lovely lady will be able to cross the muddy marsh without soiling her own clothes:

> "Cist garez est plain de rouiz:
> Marriz en sui, forment m'en poise,

Se a vos dras point en adoise."
Yseut rist, qui n'ert pas coarde.
                    (vv. 3870—73)

(This marsh is full of filth and I would be most distressed if any of it got on your clothes. Iseut laughed, for she was not afraid.)

And she winks: "De l'uel li guigne, sí l'esgarde" (She winked and looked at him, v. 3874). This is how Beauty speaks to her interlocutor: with a nonverbal sound rather than words, and with her eyes rather than her mouth.[27] Through these unconventional gestures, Iseut conveys her thought, the sagesse that spawned her well-laid plans, her knowledge of what is to come, her utter control of the situation in which she is ostensibly the defendant, the object under everyone's scrutinizing gaze. Can we not hear a similar laugh and see a similar wink in the queen's earlier remarks about her pitiful and helpless *cors* torn between rival men?

Iseut's actual wink at the Mal Pas enables Dinas to understand the thinking behind the queen's visible facade: "Le penser sout a la roïne" (v. 3875). He looks at her not as a beautiful object of desire but as a being who looks back at him, with one eye closed, with a wink accompanied by a laugh: "Yseut rist, qui n'est pas coarde / De l'uel li guigne, si l'esgarde" (Iseut, who is not bashful, looks at him and winks as she looks, vv. 3873–74). Governal had earlier instructed Tristan to look at Iseut in a similar manner, watching for the most subtle sign that she might produce:

Prenez garde de la roïne,
Qu'el n'en fera semblant et signe.
                    (vv. 3581–82)

(Pay close attention to the queen, for she will make no [obvious] sign to you.)

When the beautiful blonde Iseut parades by, "Qant or verra passer s'amie" (v. 3694), Tristan is not to look at her but to look for her look or listen for the meaning hidden within her dissembling speech.

This *bele*, dressed up, but not fetishized by the look of others, looks back through one eye only; the other conceals her planning and devising. In stark opposition to the system of immanent justice based on seeing clearly and completely the full picture of truth, this heroine's wink suggests partial sight, reminiscent of the partial truths she tells that defy the possibility of ever perceiving all there is to see. Having redefined the male gaze that typically constructs female beauty in courtly romance along with the looking necessary to establish guilt or innocence in feudal jurisprudence, this heroine's body sees more through one eye than others see through two.

And her laugh is deadly serious. Far from representing the aimless humor of women, inevitably recuperated by the logic of men,[28] this laugh subverts the legal and linguistic codes previously written on the female body. Now that body, no longer silent or obedient, constructs the world differently. Destroying the binary opposition between comedy and tragedy, Iseut's laugh heralds a mimicry of established legal procedure that turns to subtle mockery. Making the trial funny is not a laughing matter for this heroine. It saves her life. If Iseut's laugh does not record the ineffectual humor of the oppressed, neither does it echo the Bergsonian laugh that signals a position of cultural and strategic superiority. Hers is the laugh (and the wink) of the mimic who recovers "the place of her exploitation by discourse, without allowing herself to be simply reduced to it" (Irigaray, *This Sex*, 76). Submitting to ideas about herself that have been elaborated by masculine logic, Iseut here playfully repeats them—ideas that, from the time of the church fathers, construct woman as the dangerously sexualized Eve or others that, from the time of Ovid, cast woman as the threateningly erotic Medusa.[29] But she replays these notions on a stage of her own devising, rewriting the theatrical scenario to different effect. While mapping out on her own body—through remarks about her potentially guilty *cors*—the legal distinctions that establish wife and mistress as the rightful possession of either husband or lover, she also repositions that very body, literally placing her enlarged *cuisses* around those opposing categories of thought. Stationing herself elsewhere, outside the binary logic that locates women between men, this heroine speaks from a third position, one standing between marriage and adultery, truth and falsehood.

Especially symptomatic of this doubled positioning is Iseut's curious response to Tristan's professed ignorance of her motives at the ford, "Mais je ne sai que tu veus dire," (v. 3916). Iseut answers ambiguously: "Ne vuel mes dras enpalüer" (v. 3917). The sentence means literally "I don't want to get my skirts dirty" and implies a physical dirtying that might take place as she crosses the marsh. But since we know that her skirts are already dirty metaphorically, these words seem also to convey to Tristan the opposite message: "I *do* want to get my skirts dirty, in adultery," and this act of keeping them visibly clean will legally ensure that possibility. The crafty devising of this winking voice has here destroyed the distinction between seeing and not seeing, wanting and not wanting, because it speaks from a third place where the beautiful woman is neither the object of desire and observation nor a female Pygmalion that fetishizes its own lovely object. This heroine is beautiful even with one eye closed and with her mouth cracked open. As she casts her formative gaze on the knights Dinas and Tristan and on the two talismans of courtly conduct, King Marc and King Arthur, she also looks indirectly at us. And she is laughing.

Notes

1. Jean de Meun, *Le Roman de la Rose*, vv. 13359–62. La Vieille's remarks could refer to "smiling" as well as "laughing"; see Philippe Ménard, *Le Rire et le sourire dans le roman courtois en France au Moyen Âge*.

2. See Chapter One above.

3. The line may be translated as either (1) her mouth will seem too wide and split open or (2) she will seem too wide and split open.

4. A. J. Greimas, *Dictionnaire de l'ancien français*, 282.

5. Twelfth-century versions of the Old French *Romance of Tristan* have survived only in fragments. Béroul's text provides a relatively long version of the narrative, though both beginning and end are missing. For a concise statement of the considerable difficulties that confront us in deciphering the single manuscript that survives of Béroul's text and for a summary of episodes left out of this version, see Norris J. Lacy, ed. and trans., *The Romance of Tristan*, xvii–xix. One could add to Lacy's list of textual commentators the recent work of Stewart Gregory, "Further Notes on the Text of Béroul's Tristan." Although scholars generally class Béroul's *Tristan* as a romance, it holds key elements in common with other genres. See Sarah Kay, "The Tristan Story as Chivalric Romance, Feudal Epic, and Fabliau"; Barbara Nelson Sargent-Baur, "Between Fabliau and Romance: Love and Rivalry in Béroul's *Tristan*"; Nancy Regalado, "Tristan and Renart: Two Tricksters."

6. Pierre Jonin has amply demonstrated how Iseut, in the texts of Béroul, Thomas, and the two *Folies*, differs from heroines of the earlier *romans antiques* in her dominance over Tristan and the uncanny control she exercises over her own actions as well as those of others, *Les Personnages féminins dans les romans français de Tristan*, 162–67, 172–73, 203–5. Jean Frappier has attenuated this picture of Iseut's forcefulness, in Béroul's text at least, by charting radical shifts in the heroine's psychological state as she alternates between moments of courage and fear, energy and depression ("La Reine Iseut dans le *Tristan* de Béroul"). See also in this regard Gerald Brault, "Isolt and Guenevere." My remarks will focus neither on Iseut's actions nor on her state of mind, but more specifically on her speech and

its relation to her body. Other feminist readings of the Tristan material include Roberta L. Krueger, "Loyalty and Betrayal: Iseut and Brangien in the *Tristan* Romances of Béroul and Thomas"; Leslie Rabine, "The Establishment of Patriarchy in *Tristan and Isolde*"; and most recently Toril Moi, "She Died Because She Came Too Late: Knowledge, Doubles and Death in Thomas's *Tristan*."

7. Line references are from Béroul, *Le Roman de Tristan*. Translations for the most part are from Lacy's text cited above. Occasionally I have offered alternate translations in brackets.

8. For a Renaissance example of this phenomenon, see Nancy J. Vickers, "Diana Described: Scattered Woman and Scattered Rhyme," which demonstrates how Petrarch's rewriting of Ovid fetishizes Diana's body and silences her by scattering parts of her body in scattered rhyme.

9. Luce Irigaray, *This Sex Which is Not One*, 76.

10. For a discussion of this alternate positioning as a strategy of feminist analysis used by Luce Irigaray and Sarah Kofman, see Elizabeth Berg, "The Third Woman."

11. The narrator repeatedly sides with the adulterous lovers, making the tale less about moral choice or righteousness than about the deployment of various legal and linguistic strategies for proving innocence, as many scholars have shown. See especially Alberto Várvaro, *Béroul's "Romance of Tristan"*; Jean Charles Payen, "Lancelot contre Tristan: La Conjuration d'un mythe subversif"; Norris J. Lacy, "Deception and Distance in Béroul's *Tristan*: A Reconsideration"; Barbara Nelson Sargent-Baur, "La Dimension morale dans le *Roman de Tristan* de Béroul"; E. Jane Burns, "How Lovers Lie Together: Infidelity and Fictive Discourse in the *Roman de Tristan*."

12. See Henry Charles Lea, *The Ordeal*; A. Esmein, *Cours élémentaire du droit français*; Otto Gierke, *Political Theories of the Middle Ages*; Fritz Kern, *Kingship and Law in the Middle Ages*.

13. See R. Howard Bloch, *Medieval French Literature and Law* and "From Grail Quest to Inquest: The Death of King Arthur and the Birth of France"; Pierre Jonin, *Les Personnages féminins*.

14. The version by the Anglo-Norman Thomas includes the ordeal by hot iron.

15. The rhetoric of commodification continues with references to how Marc will not *take* Iseut back again (v. 2604) as he *took* her previously in marriage (v. 2604). Tristan *returns* the queen to Marc (v. 2851).

16. According to Jean Batany, the line has been emended from the manuscript, which reads: "Maint chevalier ont vestu" ("Le manuscrit de Béroul: Un texte difficile et un univers mental qui nous dérange"). The original simply underscores the emphasis on courtly dress we have been discussing. A few lines later, however, we find similar reference to the requisite lady accompanying these well-dressed knights: "N'out chevalier en tot le reigne / Qui n'ait o soi a cort sa feme" (There was not a knight in the realm who did not have his lady at court with him, vv. 4123–24).

17. See especially pp. 106–8 and Iseut's prior plan to request protection from King Arthur: "Et li mien cors est toz seürs, / Des que verra li roi Artus / Mon

mesage, qu'il vendra ça" (And my body will be safe as soon as King Arthur receives my message requesting that he come here, vv. 3273–75).

18. Eve K. Sedgwick, *Between Men: English Literature and Male Homosocial Desire*.

19. This portion, verse 533, is missing from Lacy's base text and translation.

20. See preceding chapters on Enide and Philomena.

21. Two earlier references to Iseut's beauty include Tristan's astonishment when he sees the queen in the company of the leper Yvein: "Ahi! Yseut, bele figure" (v. 1238) and Marc's lament over Tristan's abduction of "Yseut la bele o le cler vis" (v. 1947).

22. Marc also demurs because of the clothes that keep the lovers' bodies safely apart from one another (v. 2008). By contrast, Tristan's leper's costume at the trial facilitates close, adulterous contact between the lovers.

23. We hear repeatedly of Tristan's double identity as leper and knight. The narrator describes Tristan as a leper, but with a sword around his hips (v. 3575). Even as he departs with the leper's *henap* and *puiot*, Tristan plans a tournament where he will hang Iseut's pennant on his lance (vv. 3601–4). We are told that although onlookers see a *ladres*, the body beneath Tristan's cape remains fat and healthy (vv. 3624, 3929). Although the leper describes himself as weak and helpless (vv. 3847–52), Dinas recognizes beneath the cape a strong Tristan (vv. 3853–55).

24. Peter Richards, *The Medieval Leper and His Northern Heirs*; Saul Nathaniel Brody, *The Disease of the Soul: Leprosy in Medieval Literature*; Pierre Jonin, *Les Personnages féminins*, 109–38; Paul Remy, "La Lèpre, thème littéraire au Moyen Âge: Commentaire d'un passage du roman provençal de *Jaufré*"; Laurence Wright, "Burning and Leprosy in Old French Literature."

25. In lines 3913–69 sexual innuendos dominate the verbal exchange between Tristan and Iseut, as Norris Lacy points out. Iseut's "I have a matter to discuss with you" can be taken as "I have a job for you to do," or more explicitly, "I want you." Lacy continues: "In 3928 she [Iseut] leans frequently against his staff (crutch) and exclaims, 'How large you are!' Lines 3965–66 have the queen comment that she has felt what Tristan has beneath his cape, and her remarks that 'his pouch is far from empty' (3566) and that she has felt all the food and money he has in his purse" (*sac*, 3969) may well play on a traditional equivalence in erotic literature: purse-scrotum" (235).

26. My remarks on dress in Béroul's *Tristan* were inspired initially by a wonderful article in which François Rigolot traces the complex function of the multi-valent *dras* as they attest, in varied circumstances, to the lovers' guilt or innocence ("Valeur figurative du vêtement dans le *Tristan* de Béroul"). My effort here is to show more specifically how the narrator's manipulation of the iconographic *dras* relates to Iseut's speech.

27. Barbara Nelson Sargent-Baur has argued, following Philippe Ménard, that since the highly ambiguous function of the verb "rire" in Old French often conveys smiling rather than laughing aloud, Iseut may simply be smiling in line 3827. If so, the smile would express, as Sargent-Baur contends, relief from the anxiety of not knowing how the trial will proceed ("Medieval *Rire, Ridere*: A

Laughing Matter?" 124). I take this instance of *rit*, however, to be a more emphatic and forceful expression on Iseut's part than, for example, the delicate smile of Philomena, whose *boche riant* (v. 153) expresses no irony, authority, or subjectivity whatsoever. Especially in light of the second reference to Iseut's *rire*, which is paired with a knowing wink in vv. 3871–73, and the more general medieval association of female laughter and sexuality—the very subject of Iseut's trial—I think we can reasonably hear Iseut laughing in this sequence. Indeed the suggestive link between Iseut's laughing mouth and her avowedly "open thighs" in this scene is difficult to ignore. On laughing and smiling generally, see Philippe Ménard, *Le Rire et le sourire dans le roman courtois en France au Moyen Âge*.

28. Hélène Cixous, "Castration or Decapitation," 42–43.

29. For an analysis of how medieval interpreters consistently viewed the figure of Medusa as representing the dangerous power of feminine eros, see Sylvia Huot, "The Medusa Interpolation in the *Romance of the Rose*: Mythographic Program and Ovidian Intertext," esp. 874.

Conclusion: Bodies at Stake

I would like to return, in conclusion, to some issues raised at the outset of this study, looking once again at the intersection between our position as feminist medievalists working within the academy and that of the female heroines we read and listen to in canonical medieval texts. And I want to consider, more generally, what Old French texts might contribute to contemporary feminist theory.

The preceding pages have traced varied ways in which medieval heroines can be heard to engage in what I have chosen to call "bodytalk," that is to say, speech issuing from the female body that resists and restructures the social and rhetorical conventions used to figure femininity in select French literary works from the twelfth through the fifteenth centuries. Bodytalk, as I have explained above, is not something that authors make their characters do. It is a reading strategy that enables us, as contemporary feminists, to acknowledge the difference that the rhetorical woman's body might make in our potential readings of fictive women's speech. By listening for bodytalk in the foregoing analyses, we have heard how female characters in the fabliau along with the Old French theatrical Eve can restructure, at key moments, the varied strategies for reducing female identity to the body alone that the French Middle Ages inherited from its Platonic, Aristotelian, and patristic forebears. Representing, on the one hand, the medieval commonplace that figures women as headless bodies— woman as the irrational, pleasure-seeking, oversexed, and wholly corporeal counterpart to the more logical, thinking male—these female protagonists also challenge, through their speech, that very image of the philosophically silenced and metaphorically decapitated woman. Bawdy fabliau women and the vernacular Eve can be heard to assert through their humorous and sometimes racy remarks that female characters in these works indeed have two mouths, not one, insisting in different ways that a public and visible mouth, articulating thoughts from the brain, accompanies the woman's private and hidden genital lips. In making this claim, medieval heroines refigure the terms by which men typically claim to "know" women in some of the most misogynous Old French texts, thus destabilizing the monologism of phallocentric discourses that value male-gendered knowledge over female pleasure. With the benefit of two mouths, female protagonists in a range of Old French texts offer ways of knowing differently. They tell of a female body unknown to the all-knowing male subject, a female body that engages in the carnal activities of sex and childbirth while also thinking and speaking.

Listening for the bodytalk of romance heroines, we have heard Philomena, Enide, and Iseut recast, in varied ways, the less overtly antifeminist paradigm of men desiring women in courtly love. We have heard how their words revise the Ovidian model of male suitors who construct and then covet, Pygmalion-like, the fetishized and silenced female beauty. Even as the lavishly dressed bodies of these lovely ladies, along with their perfectly symmetrical faces, reinforce the reduction of women to fragmented and desexualized body parts, their voices refigure the dominant paradigm of voyeur and object-of-the-gaze that denies subjectivity to women in the romance genre. Telling the story of courtly romance differently, Philomena and her sister Progne refocus the male gaze from the metaphorically dismembered female body to a literally dismembered male one, inaugurating an economy of seeing and knowing based on woman's silent gesture rather than her speech. Enide rewrites the male adventure story, exposing what it carefully hides: heroic knights could be unchivalric, courtly ladies might refuse to behave, and the codes of courtly conduct structuring the adventure story allow no adequate place for the female speaking subject. Iseut's wink and laugh, which destroy the balanced symmetry of the beautiful lady's face, shift the courtly lady's status as an object of exchange between men into that of a subject speaking literally from a different place.

The speech of these heroines, along with their counterparts in farce and fabliau, is significant for contemporary practitioners of feminist theory because it reveals a variety of instances where the female body represented as a site of patriarchy's most reductive definitions of woman can also be a site for possible revision. As the heroines in Old French farce, fabliau, paraliturgical theater, and courtly romance play out the paradox of the speaking female subject that the texts containing them enshrine, we can begin to see the terms of a new female subjectivity emerge, a subjectivity in which the body makes a crucial difference.[1] In listening for the bodytalk of female protagonists, I have not attempted to read for an essential "feminine" in Old French texts. Rather, I have tried in the foregoing analyses to see how the speech of female protagonists, not unlike our own, often occupies simultaneously the conflicting positions of being both male-constructed and specifically female. What Old French narratives can show us, clearly and repeatedly, is how the fictive woman's body that conditions a possible misogynous reading of female identity on the one hand, also opens the possibility for constructing female subjectivity on other terms. The lesson is articulated tellingly by a heroine appropriately named Silence in the thirteenth-century *Roman de Silence*.[2]

Early in the plot of cross-dressed identity that structures the *Roman de Silence*, the tale's young heroine enters into a debate with the allegorical figure Nature regarding the justification for concealing her body, the most lovely body that Nature ever fashioned, beneath men's clothing. Silence's transvestism has been motivated by a royal decree banning all female children from inheriting wealth or title. The child's parents decided at her birth to name their newborn daughter Silentius, using the Latin masculine ending "-us" rather than the feminine "-a" that would give "Silentia." And they had her raised as a boy in the forest, far from the court. When the girl/boy is grown, she/he learns the reason for her unconventional upbringing and defends her continued cross-dressing to Nature, insisting that it cannot be otherwise:

> Donc sui jo Scilentius,
> Cho m'est avis, u jo sui nus
> (vv. 2537–38)[3]

The lines have at least two meanings: I am silent about my female identity; that is, I am cross-dressed as a male and thus socially acceptable as a speaking subject, or else I am no one (*nus*). Or, taking the second sense of *nus*, one can read alternately: I am silent about my female identity (a male in appearance) or else I am nude (revealed to be the actual female body hidden beneath the masculine veneer). The female body is here shown to be a nobody, a nonperson, and further an unknowing body. Perhaps better put: as a woman, Silence is reduced to body alone, to being just a body, a body without the powers of speech and thought or social recognition that are reserved in this stereotypically medieval scenario of femininity for the male, whose body also bears a head.

The heroine Silentius here asserts pointedly what is at stake in the either/or logic of male/female opposition that structures this text through a series of binary struggles between Nurture (environment) and Nature—social equality and sexual difference, inclusion and marginalization, speech and silence. What is at stake for the female attempting to accede to subjecthood, according to this heroine's voice, is the female body itself.[4]

I do not offer this example from the *Roman de Silence* to stage an essentialist argument. Indeed I agree with Teresa de Lauretis that we must get beyond the "red herring" of essentialism that necessarily polarizes the feminist debate by pitting so-called essentialists against poststructuralists.[5] De Lauretis has argued persuasively that if feminist theory is about an essential difference, an irreducible difference, it does not concern a difference between woman and man, "nor a difference inherent in 'woman's nature' (in woman as nature), but a difference in the feminist conception of woman, women and the world" (255). In referring to the importance that Silence accords to the female body in the lines quoted above, I do not take that body to be a pure biological entity. Instead, I prefer to think of woman as a process "coming from the body," thereby taking into account the significance of the body in constructing female subjectivity without reducing identity to anatomy.[6]

The body that Silence describes is not an anatomical reality but, more like the bodies of contemporary women, a site of interface between the biological and the social. For Silence, being the nude nobody means possessing a female anatomy that has a specific and extended history. This heroine's specificity as a woman, not unlike our own, results from a mapping onto the female body of selected cultural and historical factors. As Rosi Braidotti, following Irigaray, has explained, "It's on the woman's body—on her absence, her silence, her disqualification—that phallocentric discourse rests. This sort of 'metaphysical cannibalism,' which Ti-Grace Atkinson analyzed in terms of uterus-envy, positions the woman as the silent groundwork for male subjectivity."[7] Indeed Silence's protracted attempts at playing the man in the *Roman de Silence*, though they enable her to become an accomplished minstrel and successful knight, end with a anticlimactic reinstatement of the status quo based on the heroine's true "nature": she marries King Ebains, the monarch who earlier had issued the ban on female inheritance, and assumes the position of the perfectly silent and subservient royal wife.

Yet the midsection of the romance, which includes Silence's remarks about being cross-dressed as a male or being a female nobody, reveals to the attentive reader the limits and insufficiencies of the system that these comments describe.[8] While characterizing her position as that of a subject trapped in the female body, Silence's words also suggest that there might be a way of reconstructing gender beyond the either/or of nature and culture. Like Philomena's loaded question, "what could woman's words be worth?" which asserts a potential authority for female speech while simultaneously denying its existence, Silence's assertion that woman's nature is biologically determined also intimates that gender roles could be constructed differently, refigured by women who are not in fact silent but who speak from that nude and obviously female body.

What Silence needs, to begin this process of refiguration, is a third term between the dyadic pairs that structure her existence as either present or absent, speaking or silent, male mind or female body. She needs a way to be a subject without playing at being a male subject, a way to move from subjection to subjecthood without the transvestism that her story enacts.[9] It is in this sense that the heroine of the *Roman de Silence* stages one of the key dilemmas facing feminists in the academy today: how can we acknowledge the difference of our biological femaleness and have it make a positive difference in the institution? In Elizabeth Weed's terms: "how can we construct a female subject in order to obtain for women a better, and in many cases less oppressive and literally safer place in the social field, while at the same time always displacing boundaries, always shifting positions to work against the erection of the same old phallocratic structures in the name of identity and the unifying subject?"[10] Where is the third path? Or variations thereof?

The answers to this question will be a long time in coming. But some tentative scenarios are sketched out by the voices of medieval heroines examined in this study. We have heard bourgeois women and noble ladies alike articulate ways of refiguring female subjectivity outside of the inexorable either/or choices that the narratives containing them so often propose. Speaking from a position precariously between the standard misogynous representations of gender and what those representations leave out, the heroines we have discussed can be heard to invoke a nonbinary logic of "both/and." When the wife in the "Four Wishes of St. Martin" insists that "one prick alone is not enough for me," she speaks both as a stereotypically lascivious object of desire and a demanding subject who requires more choices, specifically more than the monolithic phallocentrism of Old French fabliaux will allow. When Eve asks "what knowledge tastes like" in the vernacular *Jeu d'Adam*, her words erode the knowledge/pleasure dichotomy used to distinguish men from women in the Genesis narrative, carving out a conceptual space in which knowledge and pleasure might coexist. Progne's assertion in the *Philomena* that the ravisher Tereus, who has eaten a stew made of his son's flesh, "carries everything he wants inside him" also follows this logic. While she speaks as the subservient and obedient wife who claims to have served Tereus everything he wants for dinner, her words also reveal how that gesture of giving has taken away precisely what Tereus wants most. Playing both object and subject, suppliant wife and empowered murderer, to Tereus's disbelief and horror, Progne heralds Enide, who refuses more overtly to be characterized as either Erec's *fame* or his *amie*. The pat gender roles available to this romance heroine do not fit because, like the adventure story itself, they fail to allocate a place for the female speaking subject. Enide suggests instead a view from "elsewhere,"[11] outside the medieval paradigms that figure women as married or not, taken or ready for the taking, both of which require female silence. And Iseut stands literally "elsewhere" when she pronounces her hybrid truth: "No one has come between my legs except this leper and my husband Marc," repositioning woman beyond the either/or of chivalric possession, as wife or adulteress. Iseut's verbal acrobatics inaugurate the possibility of being truthfully and legally both wife and mistress at once.

These are moments of bodytalk in which the doubled discourse of medieval heroines heralds the ambiguous, paradoxical position of the contemporary female speaking subject as Teresa de Lauretis has defined it: a subject whose identity is "multiple, shifting and often self- contradictory . . . a subject that is not divided in, but rather at odds with, language."[12] The heroines of the medieval texts we have examined can be read as subjects in two senses of the term: both subjected to social constraint and yet also subject in the active sense of maker as well as user of culture. They speak as female subjects who, while constructed by social convention and tradition, also participate in altering and dismantling those constructions of woman.

In charting a third path toward redefining female subjectivity in the texts they inhabit, these heroines do not relinquish, transcend, deny, or repress the body that has been used systematically to define and delimit their identity. Rather, their pointed remarks delivered both from and about that female body reveal a crucial blindspot in Western traditions of figuring femininity. The bodytalk of medieval heroines we have been discussing demonstrates, in varied ways, how Old French literature's emphasis on the female body, its insistent equation of female nature with corporeality, actually leaves the body out. The reduction of women to "headless ass" or lovely silent face, while focusing exclusively on the female body, also obscures that body's complex existence. When Iseut talks about the space between her thighs, when Enide retells the adventure story to include the female body it traditionally obscures, when Philomena and Progne redefine female speech as bodily gesture, each emphasizes the importance of the body in defining female identity. But that identity is figured anew, outside the either/or paradigms that make the body second in importance to the mind.

That the female body as a site of misogynous constructions of female identity could also become a locus for revisioning or rethinking female subjectivity has been argued most forcefully by Luce Irigaray in *Éthique de la différence sexuelle*.[13] Positing sexual difference as the big question that has not been recognized in our time, Irigaray calls for a reinterpretation of relations between the subject and discourse, the subject and the world, such that the feminine might be lived as a space, but not the space of the abyss or the dark continent. Acknowledging that the female body has traditionally been figured as one pole in a gendered dyad that sets the engulfing female anatomy in opposition to the male other that it threatens to engulf (19), we might begin to rethink this gender opposition, Irigaray suggests, by maintaining the interval *between* subject and object. The link joining masculine and feminine would then not be a hierarchical relation. Instead it would be *both* horizontal *and* vertical, Irigaray contends, like the doubled pair of woman's lips (23). And here we return to the very lips that Old French fabliau, farce, and romance genres try so hard to co-opt and suppress.

When Irigaray imagines the female body as a site of possible revision "beyond the classic oppositions of love and hate, of absolute fluidity and ice—a threshold always half-open" (24, my translation), she figures that threshold in terms of woman's lips that know nothing of dichotomous oppositions. These lips do not assimilate, reduce, or engulf; according to Irigaray, "they are the prototype of the intersection 'between.' Those [the lips] of the mouth and those of the vagina do not have the same direction. They are in a sense positioned conversely to what one would expect: the lower ones are vertical" (24, my translation).

This is the unsettling surprise of the female body refigured. It is not what we would expect; certainly not according to the logic of the same that structures woman as a mirror image of man. The surprise of the doubled female mouth unsettles the conventional subject/object relations that would normally move one to wonder, for example, which of these two mouths will dominate? The upper (and horizontal) or the vertical, lower one? Which will play subject to the other's object? Such distinctions make little sense within Irigaray's new map of female anatomy, which eschews by its complex figuration the binary poles of dominance and subservience, speech and silence. Such distinctions make little sense as well in the world of medieval heroines who speak paradoxically from the body in Old French literary texts.

As their voices subtly reshuffle the specifically medieval hierarchies of mind over matter and knowledge over pleasure that consistently privilege the male head over the female body, they show us ways to recast the basic paradigm of Western thought without rejecting the body as a key element for structuring female subjectivity. The moments when bodytalk can be heard most clearly are moments when medieval heroines take themselves, their subjectivity, their body, as an object of study and knowledge: when Silence defines her body as a nobody, when fabliau women discourse on female anatomy, when Enide proclaims her distance from the roles of both *fame* and *amie*, or when Philomena questions the value of her own speech. It is not by denying the body, but by embracing and remaking it that the heroines in Old French fabliau and romance manage to get around the misogynous paradigms used for centuries to structure female nature. Indeed one can never thoroughly repudiate one's culturally constructed gender, as Judith Butler has reminded us.[14] But in rethinking ways to position, define, and understand the female body within the conceptual framework of Western culture, these heroines remind us of the importance of our own embodied identities, our own paradoxical position as speaking bodies in a culture that has no ready place for them.

If one result of feminist theory is to break down the nonambiguous relation between subject and object of knowledge such that knowledge becomes to a large extent self-knowledge, derived from self-scrutiny, the heroines engaging in bodytalk in Old French literary texts remind us that the call for change in the social, economic, and political order is not just disruptive of institutions, of the status quo, of structures of authority and mastery—but that a call for such change is self-disruptive too.[15] To put it more succinctly, the doubled discourse of female protagonists in Old French literature encourages us to remember that in theorizing the body, in insisting that it is metaphorical and socially constructed, we also have to live with it: its history, its experience as semiotically and historically conditioned.[16]

This means that for women practicing feminist studies, readings of literary texts that focus on the metaphorization of women, readings that take no account of the existence of historical women in the Middle Ages, readings that distance the object of study—women—from the female observer/listener all tend to meet resistance, admittedly to varying degrees, in the body of the woman critic. While theorizing the body, we also have to live with it. But like the heroines of Old French texts who engage in bodytalk, we can redefine that body, outline its complexities outside the reductive categories of either/or. Recognizing the historical and rhetorical specificities of the female body, we can begin to redo the gender configurations we find ourselves in.

Notes

1. I do not mean to argue here, or elsewhere in this study, that all women's speech in Old French narrative can be characterized as "bodytalk." Certainly one can find many examples of female characters who speak largely within the established codes of their genre, reinforcing patriarchal views of femininity. Most medieval heroines alternate between reinforcing stereotypes of female sexuality and identity and speaking in ways that erode those views. I am most concerned with moments of doubled discourse where we can hear female protagonists speak in both registers at once.

2. *Le Roman de Silence: A Thirteenth-Century Arthurian Verse-Romance by Heldris de Cornuaille*, ed. Lewis Thorpe.

3. These lines provide the point of departure for a very different reading of the *Roman de Silence* offered by Kate Cooper, "Elle and L: Sexualized Textuality in *Le Roman de Silence*." Other critics who, like Cooper, read the romance's discussions of sexual politics as metaphors for poetic practice and linguistic difference include R. Howard Bloch, "Silence and Holes: The *Roman de Silence* and the Art of the Trouvère"; and Peter L. Allen, "The Ambiguity of Silence: Gender, Writing, and the *Roman de Silence*." On the complexities of cross-dressing in the *Roman de Silence* and other Old French romances, see Michèle Perret, "Travesties et transsexuelles: Yde, Silence, Grisandole, Blanchandine."

4. Kaja Silverman has shown similarly for the *Histoire d'O* how female subjectivity begins not with the female protagonist's entry into language but with the organization of her body ("*Histoire d'O*: The Construction of a Female Subject," 325).

5. Teresa de Lauretis, "Upping the Anti(sic) in Feminist Theory," 256.

6. See, for example, Mary Jacobus, "Is There a Woman in This Text?"

7. Rosi Braidotti, "Envy: or With Your Brains and My Looks," 235.

8. Simon Gaunt has argued convincingly that Heldris de Cornuaille, the tale's author, reveals his fascination with the possibility that gender might be socially constructed, while asserting forcefully that biology determines gender ("The Significance of Silence").

9. Marjorie Garber has explained how even male transvestism reenshrines male subjectivity as the phallus remains the primary index of the male transvestite's identity ("Spare Parts: The Surgical Construction of Gender"). See also her *Vested Interests*.

10. Elizabeth Weed, "A Man's Place," 75.

11. Teresa de Lauretis, *Technologies of Gender*, 26.

12. Teresa de Lauretis, "Feminist Studies/Critical Studies: Issues, Terms, and Contexts," 9.

13. Luce Irigaray, "La Différence sexuelle"; see especially pages 13–25.

14. Judith Butler, *Gender Trouble: Feminism and the Subversion of Identity*, 31.

15. Maria C. Lugones and Elizabeth V. Spelman, "Have We Got a Theory For You! Feminist Theory, Cultural Imperialism, and the Demand for 'the Woman's Voice'."

16. Teresa de Lauretis, *Technologies of Gender*, 18.

Works Cited

Accarie, Maurice. "Féminisme et antiféminisme dans le *Jeu d'Adam*." *Le Moyen Âge* 87, 2 (1981): 207–26.

Allen, Peter L. "The Ambiguity of Silence: Gender, Writing, and the *Roman de Silence*." In *Sign, Sentence, and Discourse: Language in Medieval Thought and Literature*, ed. Julian N. Wasserman and Lois Y. Roney. Syracuse: Syracuse University Press, 1989.

Allen, Prudence. *The Concept of Woman: The Aristotelian Revolution 750 B.C. –A.D. 1250*. Montreal: Eden Press, 1985.

———. "Hildegard of Bingen's Philosophy of Sex Identity." *Thought* (September 1989): 231–41.

Allen, Robert C. *Horrible Prettiness: Burlesque and American Culture*. Chapel Hill: University of North Carolina Press, 1991.

Aquinas, Thomas. *Summa Theologiae*. Trans. Edmund Hill, O.P. Vol. 13. New York: Blackfriars and McGraw-Hill, 1964.

Aristotle. *De generatione animalium*, trans. J. A. Smith, vol. 5. *De partibus animalium*, trans. Wm. Ogle. *De motu* et *De incessu animalium, De generatione animalium*, trans. Arthur Platt. In *The Works of Aristotle*. Oxford: Clarendon Press, 1972.

Auerbach, Nina. "Engorging the Patriarchy." In *Feminist Issues in Literary Scholarship*, ed. Shari Benstock. Bloomington: Indiana University Press, 1987.

———. *Woman and the Demon: The Life of a Victorian Myth*. Cambridge, Mass.: Harvard University Press, 1982.

Augustine. *Concerning the City of God Against the Pagans*. Trans. Henry Bettenson. Harmondsworth, Middlesex: Penguin Books, 1972.

———. *The Confessions of Saint Augustine*. Translated with an introduction and notes by John K. Ryan. Garden City, N.Y.: Image Books, 1960.

———. *De Trinitate*. Ed. J. P. Migne, *Patrologiae Cursus Completus Series Latina*. Vol. 42.

———. "Julian of Eclanum to Florus (in Augustine, *Opus imperfectum contra Julianum*), trans. Elizabeth Clark. In *Ascetic Behavior in Greco-Roman Antiquity: A Sourcebook*, ed. Vincent L. Wimbush. Minneapolis: Fortress Press, 1990.

———. *Letters*. New York: Fathers of the Church, 1951.

———. *The Literal Meaning of Genesis*. Trans. John H. Taylor. New York: Newman Press, 1982.

———. *Oeuvres de Saint Augustin*. Paris: Bibliothèque Augustienienne, 1959.

Bal, Mieke. "Sexuality, Sin, and Sorrow: The Emergence of the Female Character (A Reading of Genesis 1–3)." *Poetics Today* 6, 1–2 (1985): 21–42.

Batany, Jean. "Le Manuscrit de Béroul: Un texte difficile et un univers mental qui nous dérange." In *La Légende de Tristan au Moyen Âge*, ed. Danielle Buschinger. Université de Picardie, Centre d'études médiévale, Göppingen: Kümmerle Verlag, 1982.

Beck, Jonathan. "Genesis, Sexual Antagonism, and the Defective Couple of the Twelfth-Century *Jeu d'Adam*." *Representations* 29 (Winter 1990): 124–44.

Bédier, Joseph. *Les Fabliaux: Études de littérature populaire et d'histoire littéraire du Moyen Âge*. Paris: É Bouillon, 1893. 6th ed. reprint Geneva: Slatkine, 1982.

Belsey, Catherine. *The Subject of Tragedy: Identity and Difference in Renaissance Drama*. London: Methuen, 1985.

Berg, Elizabeth. "The Third Woman." *Diacritics* (Summer 1982): 11–20.

Béroul. *Le Roman de Tristan*. Ed. Ernest Muret. Paris: Firmin Didiot, 1903. Reprint. Paris: Honoré Champion, 1962.

———. *The Romance of Tristan*. Ed. and trans. Norris J. Lacy. New York: Garland, 1989.

Bloch, R. Howard. "From Grail Quest to Inquest: The Death of King Arthur and the Birth of France." *Modern Language Review* 69 (1974): 40–55.

———. *Medieval French Literature and Law*. Berkeley: University of California Press, 1977.

———. "Medieval Misogyny." *Representations* 20 (Fall 1987): 1–24.

———. *Medieval Misogyny and the Invention of Western Romantic Love*. Chicago: University of Chicago Press, 1991.

———. "New Philology and Old French." *Speculum* 65 (1990): 47–58.

———. *The Scandal of the Fabliaux*. Chicago: University of Chicago Press, 1986.

———. "Silence and Holes: The *Roman de Silence* and the Art of the Trouvère." *Yale French Studies* 70 (1986): 81–99.

Blumenfeld-Kosinski, Renate. *Not of Woman Born: Representations of Caesarean Birth in Medieval and Renaissance Culture*. Ithaca, N.Y.: Cornell University Press, 1990.

Bogdanov, Fanni. "The Tradition of the Troubadour Lyrics and the Treatment of the Love Theme in Chrétien de Troyes's *Erec et Enide*." In *Court and Poet: Selected Proceedings of the Third Congress of the International Courtly Literature Society, Liverpool, 1980*, ed. Glyn Burgess. Liverpool: Francis Cairns, 1981.

Bogin, Meg. *The Women Troubadours*. New York: Norton, 1980.

Bossy, Michel André. "The Elaboration of Female Narrative Functions in *Erec et Enide*." In *Courtly Literature: Culture and Context: Selected Papers from the 5th Triennial Congress of the International Courtly Literature Society, Dalfsen, the Netherlands*, ed. Keith Busby and Eric Cooper. Amsterdam/Philadelphia: John Benjamins, 1990.

Bowen, Barbara. *Les Caractéristiques essentielles de la farce française*. Urbana: University of Illinois Press, 1964.

Braidotti, Rosi. "Envy: Or With Your Brains and My Looks." In *Men in Feminism*, ed. Alice Jardine and Paul Smith. New York: Methuen, 1987.

———. "The Politics of Ontological Difference." In *Between Feminism and Psychoanalysis*, ed. Teresa Brennan. London/New York: Routledge, 1989.

Brault, Gerald. "Isolt and Guenevere." In *The Role of Woman in the Middle Ages: Papers of the Sixth Annual Conference of the Center for Medieval and Early*

Renaissance Studies, State University of New York at Binghamton, ed. Rosemarie Morewedge. Albany: State University of New York Press, 1975.

Brody, Saul Nathaniel. *The Disease of the Soul: Leprosy in Medieval Literature*. Ithaca, N.Y.: Cornell University Press, 1974.

Brooke-Rose, Christine. "Woman as a Semiotic Object." *Poetics Today* 6, 1–2 (1985): 9–20.

Brown, Peter R. L. *The Body and Society. Men, Women, and Sexual Renunciation in Early Christianity*. New York: Columbia University Press, 1988.

Brownlee, Kevin. "Discourse and Process in *Aucassin et Nicolette*." *Yale French Studies* 70 (1986): 167–82.

Brownmiller, Susan. *Against Our Will: Men, Women, and Rape*. New York: Simon and Schuster, 1975.

Bruckner, Matilda T. "Na Castelloza, *Trobairitz*, and Troubadour Lyric." *Romance Notes* 25, 3 (Spring 1985): 239–53.

———. "An Interpreter's Dilemma: Why Are There So Many Interpretations of Chrétien's *Chevalier de la Charrette?*" *Romance Philology* 40, 2 (1986): 159–80.

Brumlik, Joan. "Chrétien's Enide: Wife, Mistress, and Metaphor." *Romance Quarterly* 35, 4 (November 1988): 401–14.

Brundage, James A. *Law, Sex, and Christian Society in Medieval Europe*. Chicago: University of Chicago Press, 1987.

Bullough, Vern. "Medieval Medical and Scientific Views of Women." *Viator* 4 (1973): 485–501.

Burgess, Glyn. *Marie de France: An Analytical Bibliography*. London: Grant and Cutler, 1977.

———. "The Theme of Beauty in Chrétien's *Philomena* and *Erec et Enide*." In *An Arthurian Tapestry: Essays in Memory of Lewis Thorpe*, ed. Kenneth Varty. Glasgow: University of Glasgow Press, 1981.

Burns, E. Jane. *Arthurian Fictions: Rereading the Vulgate Cycle*. Columbus: Ohio State University Press, 1985.

———. "How Lovers Lie Together: Infidelity and Fictive Discourse in the *Roman de Tristan*." *Tristania* 8, 2 (Spring, 1983): 15–30.

———. "The Man Behind the Lady in Troubadour Lyric." *Romance Notes* 25, 3 (Spring 1985): 254–70.

———. "Knowing Women: Female Orifices in the Old French Farce and Fabliau." *Exemplaria* 4, 1 (Spring 1992): 81–104.

———. "This Prick Which Is Not One: How Women Talk Back in Old French Fabliaux." In *Feminist Approaches to the Body in Medieval Literature*, ed. Linda Lomperis and Sarah Stanbury. Philadelphia: University of Pennsylvania Press, 1992.

Burns, E. Jane and Roberta L. Krueger. Introduction to "Courtly Ideology and Woman's Place in Medieval French Literature." *Romance Notes* 25, 3 (Spring 1985): 205–19.

Burns, E. Jane, Sarah Kay, Roberta L. Krueger, and Helen Solterer. "Feminism and the Discipline of Old French Studies: *Une Bele Disjointure*." In *Medievalism and the Modern Temper: The Discipline of Medieval Studies*, ed. Stephen G. Nichols and R. Howard Bloch. Stanford, Ca.: Stanford University Press, forthcoming.

Butler, Judith. *Gender Trouble: Feminism and the Subversion of Identity*. New York and London: Routledge, 1990.

Cerquiglini, Bernard. *Éloge de la variante: Histoire critique de la philologie*. Paris, 1989.

Chrétien de Troyes. *Cligès*. Ed. Alexander Micha. Paris: Champion, 1957.

———. *Erec et Enide*. Ed. Mario Roques. Paris: Champion, 1976.

———. *Erec et Enide*. Ed. and trans. Carleton Carrell. New York: Garland, 1987.

———. *Philomena*. Ed. C. de Boer. Paris: Éditions Paul Geuthner, 1909.

Cixous, Hélène. "Castration or Decapitation?" Trans. Annette Kuhn. *Signs* 7, 1 (1981): 41–55.

———. "The Laugh of the Medusa." In *New French Feminisms: An Anthology*, ed. Elaine Marks and Isabelle de Courtivron. Amherst: University of Massachusetts Press, 1980.

Cixous, Hélène and Catherine Clément. *The Newly Born Woman*. Trans. Betsy Wing. Minneapolis: University of Minnesota Press, 1986.

Clark, Elizabeth. "Adam's Only Companion: Augustine and the Early Christian Debate on Marriage." *Recherches Augustiniennes* 21 (1986): 139–62.

———. "Vitiated Seeds and Holy Vessels: Augustine's Manichean Past." In *Ascetic Piety and Women's Faith: Essays on Late Ancient Christianity*. Lewiston, N.Y.: Edwin Mellen Press, 1986.

Cohen, Gustave. *Histoire de la mise en scène dans le théâtre religieux du Moyen Âge*. Paris: Champion, 1926.

———, ed. *Recueil de farces françaises inédites du 15e siècle*. Cambridge, Mass.: Medieval Academy of America, 1949.

Colby, Alice. *The Portrait in Twelfth-Century French Literature*. Geneva: Droz, 1965.

Cooper, Kate. "Elle et L: Sexualized Textuality in *Le Roman de Silence*." *Romance Notes* 25, 3 (Spring 1985): 341–60.

Cormier, Raymond J., ed. and trans. *Three Ovidian Tales of Love*. New York: Garland, 1986.

Cornuaille, Heldris de. *Le Roman de Silence: A Thirteenth-Century Arthurian Verse-Romance by Heldris de Cornuaille*. Ed. Lewis Thorpe. Cambridge: W. Heffer and Sons, 1972.

Crist, Larry. "*Le Jeu d'Adam* et l'exégèse de la chute." In *Études de civilisation médiévale, IXe–XIIIe siècles: Mélanges offerts à Edmond-René Labande*. Poitiers: C.É.S.C.M., 1975.

Culler, Jonathan. "Reading as a Woman." In *On Deconstruction: Theory and Criticism After Structuralism*. Ithaca, N.Y.: Cornell University Press, 1982.

Dane, Joseph. "Clerical Propaganda in the Anglo-Norman *Representacio Ade (Mystère d'Adam)*." *Philological Quarterly* 62 (1983): 241–51.

Delcourt, Denyse. *L'Ethique du changement dans le roman français du 12e siècle*. Geneva: Droz, 1990.

Dragonetti, Roger. *La Vie de la lettre au Moyen Âge: Le conte du Graal*. Paris: Éditions de Seuil, 1980.

Dronke, Peter. *Women Writers of the Middle Ages: A Critical Study of Texts from Perpetua (c. 203) to Marguerete Porete (c. 1310)*. Cambridge: Cambridge University Press, 1984.

du Bois, Page. *Sowing the Body: Psychoanalysis and Ancient Representations of Women*. Chicago: University of Chicago Press, 1988.

Esmein, A. *Cours élémentaire du droit français*. Paris: Sirey, 1930.

Faust, Diana M. "Women Narrators in the *Lais* of Marie de France." *Stanford French and Italian Studies* 58 (1988): 17–28.

Felman, Shoshana. "Women and Madness: The Critical Phallacy." *Diacritics* 5, 4 (Winter 1975): 2–16.

Ferrante, Joan. "Male Fantasy and Female Reality in Courtly Literature." *Women's Studies* 11 (1984): 67–97.

———. *Woman as Image in Medieval Literature: From the Twelfth Century to Dante*. New York: Columbia University Press, 1975. Reprint. Labyrinth, 1985.

Fetterly, Judith. *The Resisting Reader: A Feminist Approach to American Fiction*. Bloomington: Indiana University Press, 1978.

Fineman, Joel. "Shakespeare's *Will*: The Temporality of Rape." *Representations* 20 (Fall 1987): 25–76.

Finke, Laurie. "Towards a Cultural Poetics of Romance." *Genre* 22 (Summer 1989): 109–27.

Fisher, Sheila and Janet E. Halley, eds. *Seeking the Woman in Late Medieval and Renaissance Writings: Essays in Feminist Contextual Criticism*. Knoxville: University of Tennessee Press, 1988.

Flax, Jane. "Political Philosophy and the Patriarchal Unconscious: A Psychoanalytic Perspective on Epistemology and Metaphysics." In *Discovering Reality: Feminist Perspectives on Epistemology, Metaphysics, Methodology, and Philosophy of Science*, ed. Sandra Harding and Merrill B. Hintikka. Dordecht: D. Reidel, 1983.

Frappier, Jean. *Chrétien de Troyes, l'homme et l'oeuvre*. Paris: Hâtier-Boivins, 1957.

———. "Le Motif du 'don contraignant' dans la littérature du Moyen Âge." *Travaux de linguistique et de littérature* 7, 2 (1969): 7–46.

———. "La Reine Iseut dans le *Tristan* de Béroul." *Romance Philology* 26, 2 (1972): 215–28.

Freeman, Michelle. "Dual Natures and Subverted Glosses: Marie de France's 'Bisclavret.'" *Romance Notes* 25, 3 (Spring 1985): 288–301.

———. "Marie de France's Poetics of Silence: Implications for a Feminist *Translatio*." *PMLA* 99 (1984): 860–83.

———. *The Poetics of Translatio studii and Conjointure: Chrétien de Troyes's "Cligès."* Lexington, Ky.: French Forum Publishers, 1979.

Froula, Christine. "The Daughter's Seduction: Sexual Violence and Literary History." *Signs* (Summer 1986): 621–44.

Fuss, Diana. *Essentially Speaking: Feminism, Nature, and Difference*. London/New York: Routledge, 1989.

Gallop, Jane. "The Father's Seduction." In *The Daughter's Seduction: Feminism and Psychoanalysis*. Ithaca, N.Y.: Cornell University Press, 1982; London: Macmillan, 1989.

———. "Snatches of Conversation." In *Women and Language in Literature and Society*, ed. Sally McConnell-Ginet, Ruth Borker, and Nelly Furman. New York: Praeger, 1980.

———. *Thinking Through the Body*. New York: Columbia University Press, 1988.

————. "*Writing and Sexual Difference*: The Difference Within." *Critical Inquiry* 8, 4 (1982): 797–805.

Garber, Marjorie. "Spare Parts: The Surgical Construction of Gender." *Differences* 1, 3 (1989): 137–59.

————. *Vested Interests: Cross-Dressing and Cultural Anxiety*. London/New York: Routledge, 1992.

Gaunt, Simon. "The Significance of Silence." *Paragraph* 13 (1990): 202–16.

Gierke, Otto. *Political Theories of the Middle Age*. Trans. Frederic W. Maitland. Cambridge: University Press, 1900. Reprint Cambridge/New York: Cambridge University Press, 1987.

Gilbert, Sandra and Susan Gubar. *The Madwoman in the Attic: The Woman Writer and the Nineteenth Century Imagination*. New Haven, Conn.: Yale University Press, 1979.

Goldin, Frederick. *The Mirror of Narcissus and the Courtly Love Lyric*. Ithaca, N.Y.: Cornell University Press, 1967.

Gravdal, Kathryn. "Camouflaging Rape: The Rhetoric of Sexual Violence in the Medieval Pastourelle." *Romanic Review* 76, 4 (1985): 361–73.

————. *Ravishing Maidens: Writing Rape in Medieval French Literature and Law*. Philadelphia: University of Pennsylvania Press, 1991.

Greenberg, Caren. "Rereading Reading: Echo's Abduction of Language." In *Women and Language in Literature and Society*, ed. Sally McConnell-Ginet, Ruth Borker, and Nelly Furman. New York: Praeger, 1980.

Gregory, Stewart. "Further Notes on the Text of Béroul's *Tristan*." *French Studies* 42, 1 (1988): 1–19; 42, 2 (1988): 129–49.

Greimas, A. J. *Dictionnaire de l'ancien français*. Paris: Larousse, 1969.

Grosz, Elizabeth A. *Jacques Lacan: A Feminist Introduction*. London/New York: Routledge, 1990.

————. "Luce Irigaray and the Ethics of Alterity." In *Sexual Subversions: Three French Feminists*. Sydney: Allen and Unwin, Winchester, Mass.: Unwin Hyman, 1989.

Guiraud, Pierre. *Dictionnaire érotique*. Paris: Payot, 1978.

Harrison, Robert L., trans. *Gallic Salt: Eighteen Fabliaux Translated from the Old French*. Berkeley: University of California Press, 1974.

Heilbrun, Carolyn. *Hamlet's Mother and Other Women*. New York: Columbia University Press, 1990.

Hite, Molly. "Writing—and Reading—the Body: Female Sexuality and Recent Feminist Fiction." *Feminist Studies* 14, 1 (1988): 121–42.

Horney, Karen. *Feminine Psychology*. New York: Norton, 1967.

Huchet, Jean Charles. *L'amour discourtois: La "Fin'amours" chez les premiers troubadours*. Paris: Privat, 1987.

————. "Un Entretien avec Georges Duby sur la littérature courtoise." *Ornicar* 26–27 (1983): 179–95.

————. "Nom de femme et écriture féminine au Moyen Âge: Les *Lais* de Marie de France." *Poétique* 12 (1981): 407–30.

————. *Le Roman médiéval*. Paris: Presses Universitaires de France, 1984.

————. "La Voix d'Héloïse." *Romance Notes* 25, 3 (Spring 1985): 271–87.

Huot, Sylvia. "The Medusa Interpolation in the *Romance of the Rose*: Mythographic Program and Ovidian Intertext." *Speculum* 62, 4 (1987): 865–77.

———. "Seduction and Subliminations: Christine de Pisan, Jean de Meun, and Dante." *Romance Notes* 25, 3 (Spring 1985): 361–73.

Irigaray, Luce. "Ce Sexe qui n'en est pas un." In *Ce Sexe qui n'en est pas un*. Paris: Éditions de Minuit, 1977.

———. "La Différence sexuelle." In *Éthique de la différence sexuelle*. Paris: Éditions de Minuit, 1985.

———. *Spéculum de l'autre femme*. Paris: Éditions de Minuit, 1974.

———. *Speculum of the Other Woman*. Trans. Gillian C. Gill. Ithaca, N.Y.: Cornell University Press, 1985.

———. *This Sex Which Is Not One*. Trans. Catherine Porter. Ithaca, N.Y.: Cornell University Press, 1985.

Isidore of Seville. *Etymologies*. Ed. and trans. Marc Reydellet. Paris: Société des Éditions "Les Belles Lettres," 1984).

Jackson, W.T.H. "Problems of Communication in the Romances of Chrétien de Troyes." In *Medieval Literature and Folklore Studies: Essays in Honor of Francis Lee Utley*, ed. J. Mandel and Bruce A. Rosenberg. New Brunswick, N.J.: Rutgers University Press, 1970.

Jacobus, Mary. "Is There a Woman in This Text?" *New Literary History* 14 (Fall, 1982): 117–41.

———. *Reading Woman: Essays in Feminist Criticism*. New York: Columbia University Press, 1986.

Jardine, Alice. "Gynesis." *Diacritics* (Summer 1982): 54–65.

———. *Gynesis: Configurations of Women and Modernity*. Ithaca, N.Y.: Cornell University Press, 1985.

Jed, Stephanie. *Chaste Thinking: The Rape of Lucretia and the Birth of Humanism*. Bloomington: Indiana University Press, 1989.

Johnson, Leslie. "Women on Top: Antifeminism in the Fabliaux?" *Modern Language Review* 78, 2 (1983): 298–307.

Jones, Anne Rosalind. "Writing the Body: Toward an Understanding of *l'écriture féminine*." In *New Feminist Criticism: Essays on Women, Literature, and Theory*, ed. Elaine Showalter. New York: Pantheon, 1985.

Jones, Nancy. "The Daughter's Text and the Thread of Lineage in the Old French *Philomena*." Manuscript.

Jonin, Pierre. *Les Personnages féminins dans les romans français de Tristan au 12e siècle: Étude des influences contemporaines*. Aix en Provence: Gap, 1958.

Joplin, Patricia Klindienst. "The Voice of the Shuttle is Ours." *Stanford Literature Review* 1, 1 (1984): 25–53.

Justice, Steven. "The Authority of Ritual in the *Jeu d'Adam*." *Speculum* 62, 4 (1987): 851–64.

Kamuf, Peggy. *Fictions of Feminine Desire: Disclosures of Heloise*. Lincoln: University of Nebraska Press, 1982.

———. "Replacing Feminist Criticism." *Diacritics* (Summer 1982): 42–47.

———. *Signature Pieces: On the Institution of Authorship*. Ithaca, N.Y.: Cornell University Press, 1988.

Kay, Sarah. "The Tristan Story as Chivalric Romance, Feudal Epic, and Fabliau." In *The Spirit of the Court: Selected Proceedings of the Fourth Congress of the International Courtly Literature Society, Toronto, 1983*, ed. Glyn Burgess and Robert Taylor. Woodbridge, Suffolk/Dover, N.H.: D.S. Brewer, 1985.

———. *Subjectivity in Troubadour Poetry*. Cambridge/New York: Cambridge University Press, 1990.

Kelly, Douglas. *Sens et conjointure in the* Chevalier de la Charrette. The Hague: Mouton, 1966.

———. "The Source and Meaning of *Conjointure* in Chrétien's *Erec*." *Viator* 1 (1970): 179–200.

Kennedy, Angus. *Christine de Pizan: A Bibliographical Guide*. London: Grant and Cutler, 1984.

Kern, Fritz. *Kingship and Law in the Middle Ages*. Trans. S. B. Chrimes. Oxford: Basil Blackwell, 1939. Reprint Westport, Conn.: Greenwood Press, 1985.

Kofman, Sarah. *L'Enigme de la femme: La femme dans les textes de Freud*. Paris: Galilée, 1980.

———. *The Enigma of Woman: Woman in Freud's Writings*. Trans. Catherine Porter. Ithaca, N.Y.: Cornell University Press, 1985.

Kristeva, Julia. "Woman Can Never be Defined." In *New French Feminisms: An Anthology*, ed. Elaine Marks and Isabelle de Courtivron. Amherst: University of Massachusetts Press, 1980.

———. "Women's Time." Trans. Alice Jardine and Harry Blake. *Signs* 7, 1 (1981): 13–35.

Krueger, Roberta L. "Desire, Meaning, and the Female Reader: The Problem in Chrétien's *Charrette*." In *The Passing of Arthur: New Essays in the Arthurian Tradition*, ed. Christopher Baswell and William Sharpe. New York: Garland, 1988.

———. "Double Jeopardy: The Appropriation of Woman in Four Old French Romances of the 'Cycle de la Gageure.'" In *Seeking the Woman in Late Medieval and Renaissance Writings: Essays in Feminist Contextual Criticism*, ed. Sheila Fisher and Janet E. Halley. Knoxville: University of Tennessee Press, 1989.

———. *Women Readers and the Ideology of Gender in Old French Romance*. Cambridge: Cambridge University Press, forthcoming.

———. "Love, Honor, and the Exchange of Women in *Yvain*: Some Remarks on the Female Reader." *Romance Notes* 25, 3 (Spring 1985): 302–17.

———. "Loyalty and Betrayal: Iseut and Brangien in the *Tristan* Romances of Béroul and Thomas." In *Sisterhood Surveyed: Proceedings of the Mid-Atlantic Women's Studies Association*, ed. Anne Dzamba Sessa. West Chester, Pa.: West Chester University, 1983.

Lacan, Jacques. *Séminaire XX, Encore*. Paris: Éditions de Seuil, 1975.

Lacy, Norris J. "Deception and Distance in Béroul's *Tristan*: A Reconsideration." *Journal of the Rocky Mountain Medieval and Renaissance Association* 6 (January 1985): 33–39.

———. "Fabliau Women." *Romance Notes* 25, 3 (1985): 318–27.

———. "Narrative Point of View and the Problem of Erec's Motivation." *Kentucky Romance Quarterly* 18 (1971): 355–62.

Lanfors, A., ed. "Le Fabliau du Moine." *Romania* 44, 3 (1915–17): 559–63.

Lange, Lynda. "Woman is Not a Rational Animal: On Aristotle's Biology of Reproduction." In *Discovering Reality: Feminist Perspectives on Epistemology, Metaphysics, Methodology, and Philosophy of Science*, ed. Sandra Harding and Merrill B. Hintikka. Dordecht/Boston: D. Reidel, 1983.

Laqueur, Thomas W. *Making Sex: Body and Gender from the Greeks to Freud*. Cambridge, Mass.: Harvard University Press, 1990.

Lauretis, Teresa de. "The Female Body and Heterosexual Presumption." *Semiotica* 67, 3–4 (1987): 259–79.

———. "Feminist Studies/Critical Studies: Issues, Terms, and Contexts." In *Feminist Studies, Critical Studies*, edited by Teresa de Lauretis. Bloomington: Indiana University Press, 1986.

———. *Technologies of Gender: Essays on Theory, Film, and Fiction*. Bloomington: Indiana University Press, 1987.

———. "Through the Looking Glass." In *The Cinematic Apparatus*, ed. Teresa de Lauretis and Stephen Heath. London: Macmillan; New York: St. Martin's Press, 1980.

———. "Upping the Anti(sic) in Feminist Theory." In *Conflicts in Feminism*, ed. Marianne Hirsch and Evelyn Fox Keller. New York: Routledge, 1990.

Lea, Henry Charles. *The Ordeal* Published 1866 as Part III, *Superstition and Force*. Reprint. Philadelphia: University of Pennsylvania Press, 1973.

Lederer, Wolfgang. *Fear of Women*. New York: Grune and Stratton, 1968.

LeDoeuff, Michèle. "Women and Philosophy." In *French Feminist Thought: A Reader*, ed. Toril Moi. Oxford: Basil Blackwell, 1987.

Lemaire, Ria. *Passions et positions: Contributions à une sémiotique du sujet dans la poésie lyrique médiévale en langues romanes*. Amsterdam: Rodopi, 1988.

Lemay, Helen Rodnite. "Human Sexuality in Twelfth- Through Fifteenth-Century Scientific Writings." In *Sexual Practices and the Medieval Church*, ed. Vern L. Bullough and James Brundage. Buffalo, N.Y.: Prometheus Books, 1982.

———. "Some Thirteenth- and Fourteenth-Century Lectures on Female Sexuality." *International Journal of Women's Studies* 1, 4 (1978): 391–400.

Leupin, Alexandre. *Barbarolexis: Medieval Writing and Sexuality*. Cambridge, Mass.: Harvard University Press, 1989.

———. "La Compromission: Sur *Le Voyage de Charlemagne à Jérusalem et à Constantinople*." *Romance Notes* 25, 3 (1985): 222–38.

———. *Le Graal et la littérature: Étude sur la vulgate arthurienne en prose*. Geneva: L'Âge d'homme, 1982.

Lévi-Strauss, Claude. *The Elementary Structures of Kinship*. Trans. James Harle Bell, John Richard von Sturmer, and Rodney Needham. Boston: Beacon Press, 1969.

Livingston, Charles H. *Le Jongleur Gautier le Leu: Études sur les fabliaux*. Cambridge, Mass.: Harvard University Press, 1951.

Lorcin, Marie-Thérèse. *Façons de sentir et de penser: Les fabliaux français*. Paris: Champion, 1979.

Lugones, Maria C. and Elizabeth V. Spelman. "Have We Got a Theory For You! Feminist Theory, Cultural Imperialism, and the Demand for 'the Woman's Voice'." *Women's Studies International Forum* 6, 6 (1983): 573–81.

Maddox, Donald. *Structure and Sacring: The Systematic Kingdom in Chrétien's* Erec et Enide. Lexington, Ky.: French Forum Publishers, 1978.

Marchello-Nizia, Christine. "Amour courtois, société masculine et figures de pouvoir." *Annales E.S.C.* 36 (1981): 969–82.

Marcus, Jane. "Still Practice, A/Wrested Alphabet: Toward a Feminist Aesthetic." In *Feminist Issues in Literary Scholarship*, ed. Shari Benstock. Bloomington: Indiana University Press, 1989.

Maclean, Ian. *The Renaissance Notion of Woman: A Study in the Fortunes of Scholasticism and Medical Science in European Intellectual Life.* Cambridge: Cambridge University Press, 1980.

McLaughlin, Eleanor Commo. "Equality of Souls, Inequality of Sexes: Woman in Medieval Theology." In *Religion and Sexism*, ed. Rosemary Radford Ruether. New York: Simon and Schuster, 1974.

McLaughlin, Mary Martin. "Abelard and the Dignity of Women." In *Pierre Abélard, Pierre le Vénérable: Les courants philosophiques, littéraires et artistiques en Occident au milieu du XIIe siècle.* Paris: Centre National de la Recherche Scientifique, 1975.

McNamara, Jo Ann and Suzanne Wemple. "Sanctity and Power: The Dual Pursuit of Medieval Women." In *Becoming Visible: Women in European History*, ed. Renate Bridenthal and Claudia Koonz. Boston: Houghton Mifflin, 1977.

Méla, Charles. *La Reine et le Graal: La conjointure dans les romans du Graal de Chrétien de Troyes au "Livre de Lancelot."* Paris: Éditions de Seuil, 1984.

Ménard, Philippe. *Les fabliaux: Contes à rire du Moyen Âge.* Paris: Presses Universitaires de France, 1983.

———. *Le Rire et le sourire dans le roman courtois en France au Moyen Âge.* Geneva: Droz, 1969.

Meun, Jean de. *Le Roman de la Rose.* Ed. Daniel Poirion. Paris: Garnier-Flammarion, 1974.

Miles, Margaret. *Carnal Knowing: Female Nakedness and Religious Meaning in the Christian West.* Boston: Beacon Press, 1989.

Miller, Nancy K. "Arachnologies: The Woman, the Text, and the Critic." In *The Poetics of Gender*, ed. Nancy K. Miller. New York: Columbia University Press, 1980.

———. "Changing the Subject: Authorship, Writing and the Reader." In *Feminist Studies, Critical Studies*, ed. Teresa de Lauretis. Bloomington: Indiana University Press, 1986.

———. *Subject to Change: Reading Feminist Writing.* New York: Columbia University Press, 1988.

———. "Rereading as a Woman: The Body in Practice." *Poetics Today* 6, 1–2 (1985): 291–99.

———. "The Text's Heroine: A Feminist Critic and Her Fictions." *Diacritics* (Summer 1982): 48–53.

Miller, Nancy K. and Peggy Kamuf. "Parisian Letters: Between Feminism and Deconstruction." In *Conflicts in Feminism*, ed. Marianne Hirsch and Evelyn Fox Keller. New York: Routledge, 1990.

Moi, Toril. "Patriarchal Thought and the Drive for Knowledge." In *Between Femi-*

nism and Psychoanalysis, ed. Teresa Brennan. London/New York: Routledge, 1989.

———. *Sexual/Textual Politics: Feminist Literary Theory*. London/New York: Methuen, 1985.

———. "'She Died Because She Came Too Late': Knowledge, Doubles and Death in Thomas's *Tristan*." *Exemplana* 4, 1 (1992): 105–33.

Montaiglon, Anatole de and Gaston Raynaud. *Receuil général et complet des fabliaux*. 6 vols. Paris: Librairie des Bibliophiles, 1872–1890.

Morris, Meghan. "In Any Event . . ." In *Men in Feminism*, ed. Alice Jardine and Paul Smith. London/New York: Methuen, 1987.

Morrison, Toni. *Beloved*. New York: Knopf, 1987.

Munich, Adrienne. "Notorious Signs, Feminist Criticism and Literary Tradition." In *Making a Difference: Feminist Literary Criticism*, ed. Gayle Greene and Coppelia Kahn. London/New York: Methuen, 1985.

Muscatine, Charles. *The Old French Fabliaux*. New Haven, Conn.: Yale University Press, 1986.

Musseter, Sally. "The Education of Enide." *Romanic Review* 73, 2 (1982): 151–52.

Nichols, Stephen G. "Medieval Women Writers: Aisthesis and the Powers of Marginality." *Yale French Studies* 75 (Fall 1988): 77–94.

———. "Rewriting Marriage in the Middle Ages." *Romanic Review* 79, 1 (1988): 42–60.

———. "Working Late: Marie de France and the Value of Poetry." *Stanford French and Italian Studies* 58 (1988): 7–16.

Noomen, Willem, ed. *Le Jeu d'Adam*. Paris: Champion, 1971.

Noomen, Willem and Nico Van den Boogaard. *Nouveau recueil complet des fabliaux (NRCF)*. 6 vols to date. Assen, the Netherlands: Van Gorcum, 1984–91.

Nykrog, Per. *Les Fabliaux*. Geneva: Droz, 1973.

O'Flaherty, Wendy Doniger. *Tales of Sex and Violence: Folklore, Sacrifice, and Danger in the Jaimiṇīya Brāhmaṇa*. Chicago: University of Chicago Press, 1985.

———. *Women, Adrogynes, and Other Mythical Beasts*. Chicago: University of Chicago Press, 1980.

Ovid. *Metamorphoses*. Trans. Rolfe Humphries. Bloomington: Indiana University Press, 1968.

Paden, William, ed. *The Voice of the Trobairitz: Perspectives on the Women Troubadours*. Philadelphia: University of Pennsylvania Press, 1989.

Pagels, Elaine. *Adam, Eve, and the Serpent*. New York: Random House, 1988.

Paris, Gaston. "Lai du Lecheor." In "Lais inédits." *Romania* 8 (1979): 64–66.

Parker, Patricia. "Coming Second: Woman's Place." In *Literary Fat Ladies: Rhetoric, Gender, Property*. London/New York: Methuen, 1987.

Patterson, Lee. "Virgil and the Historical Consciousness of the Twelfth Century: The *Roman d'Enéas* and *Erec et Enide*." In *Negotiating the Past: The Historical Understanding of Medieval Literature*. Madison: University of Wisconsin Press, 1987.

Payen, Jean Charles. "Lancelot contre Tristan: La conjuration d'un mythe subversif." In *Mélanges le Gentil*. Paris: SEDES, 1973.

Payer, Pierre. *Sex in the Penitentials: The Development of a Sexual Code 550–1150.* Toronto: University of Toronto Press, 1984.

Perret, Michèle. "Travesties et transsexuelles: Yde, Silence, Grisandole, Blanchandine." *Romance Notes* 25, 3 (1985): 328–40.

Pfeffer, Wendy. *The Change of Philomel.* New York: Peter Lang, 1985.

Picot, Émile and Christophe Nyrop, eds. *Nouveau recueil de farces françaises des XVe et XVIe siècles.* Paris: Damascène Morgand and Charles Fatout, 1880.

Plato. *Timaeus.* Ed. and trans. John Warrington. London: Dent, 1965.

Plummer, John F. "*Bien dire* et *Bien aprandre* in Chrétien de Troyes's *Erec et Enide.*" *Romania* 95 (1974): 380–94.

———, ed. *Vox Feminae: Studies in Medieval Women's Song.* Kalamazoo, Mich.: Medieval Institute Publications, 1981.

Poovey, Mary. "Feminism and Deconstruction." *Feminist Studies* 14, 1 (1988): 51–65.

Prusak, Bernard P. "Woman: Seductive Siren and Source of Sin? Pseudepigraphical Myth and Christian Origins." In *Religion and Sexism: Images of Woman in the Jewish and Christian Traditions,* ed. Rosemary Radford Reuther. New York: Simon and Schuster, 1974.

Rabine, Leslie. "The Establishment of Patriarchy in Tristan and Isolde." *Women's Studies* 7 (1980): 19–38.

———. "A Feminist Politics of Non-Identity." *Feminist Studies* 14, 1 (1988): 11–31.

Radice, Betty, trans. and ed. *The Letters of Abelard and Heloise.* Baltimore: Penguin, 1974.

Regalado, Nancy F. "Tristan and Renart: Two Tricksters." *Esprit Créateur* 16 (1976): 30–38.

———. "Vos Paroles ont mains et pies": Woman's Wary Voice in the *Response au Bestiaire d'Amors de Maître Richard de Fournival,* Kentucky Romance Language Conference, 1986.

Rémy, Paul. "La Lèpre, thème littéraire au Moyen Âge: Commentaire d'un passage du roman provençal de *Jaufré.*" *Le Moyen Âge* 52, 2 (1946): 195–242.

Renaud de Lage, G. *Trubert.* Geneva: Droz, 1974.

Reuther, Rosemary Radford. "Mysogynism and Virginal Feminism in the Fathers of the Church." In *Religion and Sexism: Images of Woman in the Jewish and Christian Traditions,* ed. Rosemary Radford Reuther. New York: Simon and Schuster, 1974.

Rey-Flaud, Henri. *La Nevrose courtoise.* Paris: Navarin, 1983.

Rich, Adrienne. *Of Woman Born: Motherhood as Experience and Institution.* New York: Norton, 1976.

Richards, Peter. *The Medieval Leper and His Northern Heirs.* Cambridge: D. S. Brewer, 1977.

Rigolot, François. "Valeur figurative du vêtement dans la *Tristan* de Béroul." *Cahiers de Civilization Médiévale* 10, 3–4 (1967): 447–53.

Riley, Denise. *Am I That Name? Feminism and the Category of "Women" in History.* Minneapolis: University of Minnesota Press, 1988.

———. *War in the Nursery.* London: Virago Press, 1983.

Robertson, Elizabeth. *Early English Devotional Prose and the Female Audience.* Knoxville: University of Tennessee Press, 1990.

Rubin, Gayle. "The Traffic in Woman: Note on the Political Economy of Sex." In *Toward an Anthropology of Woman*, ed. Rayna R. Reiter. New York: Monthly Review Press, 1975.

Rychner, Jean. *Contribution à l'étude des fabliaux*. Geneva: Droz, 1960.

Sargent, Barbara Nelson. "Medieval *Rire, Ridere*: A Laughing Matter?" *Medium Aevum* 43, 2 (1974): 116–32.

Sargent-Baur, Barbara Nelson. "Between Fabliau and Romance: Love and Rivalry in Béroul's *Tristan*." *Romania* 105 (1984): 292–311.

———. "La Dimension morale dans le *Roman de Tristan* de Béroul." *Cahiers de Civilization Médiévale* 31 (1988): 49–56.

———. "Erec's Enide, 'sa fame ou s'amie'?" *Romance Philology* 33, 3 (1980): 373–87.

Schenck, Mary Jane Stearns. *The Fabliaux: Tales of Wit and Deception*. Amsterdam/Philadelphia: John Benjamins, 1987.

Schor, Naomi. "Dreaming Dissymetry: Barthes, Foucault, and Sexual Difference." In *Men in Feminism*, ed. Alice Jardine and Paul Smith. London: Methuen, 1987.

———. "This Essentialism Which Is Not One." *Differences* 1, 2 (Summer 1989): 38–58.

Schulze-Busacker, Elisabeth. "Philomena: Une révision de l'attribution de l'oeuvre." *Romania* 107 (1986): 459–85.

Scully, Terence. "The *Sen* of Chrétien de Troyes's *Joie de la Cort*." In *The Expansion and Transformation of Courtly Literature*, ed. Nathaniel B. Smith and Joseph T. Snow. Athens: University of Georgia Press, 1980.

Sedgwick, Eve K. *Between Men: English Literature and Male Homosocial Desire*. New York: Columbia University Press, 1985.

Seidler, Victor. "Reason, Desire, and Male Sexuality." In *The Cultural Construction of Sexuality*, ed. Pat Caplan. London: Tavistock Publications, 1987.

Shahar, Shulamith. *The Fourth Estate: A History of Women in the Middle Ages*. Trans. Chaya Galai. London: Methuen, 1983.

Showalter, Elaine. *A Literature of Their Own: British Women Novelists from Brontë to Lessing*. Princeton, N.J.: Princeton University Press, 1977.

———. "Toward a Feminist Poetics." In *Women Writing and Writing About Women*, ed. Mary Jacobus. London: Croom Helm, 1979.

Silverman, Kaja. *The Acoustic Mirror: The Female Voice in Psychoanalysis and Cinema*. Bloomington: Indiana University Press, 1988.

———. "*Histoire d'O*: The Construction of a Female Subject." In *Pleasure and Danger: Exploring Female Sexuality*, ed. Carole S. Vance. Boston: Routledge and Kegan Paul, 1984.

Solterer, Helen. "Dismembering, Remembering, and the Chastelain de Coucy." *Romance Philology*, 46, 2 (1992).

———. *The Master and Minerva: Disputing Women in Late Medieval French Culture*. Forthcoming.

———. "Seeing, Hearing, Tasting Woman: The Senses of Medieval Reading." In *Medieval Texts and Contemporary Readers*, ed. Anne Berthelot. Ithaca, N.Y.: Cornell University Press, 1987.

Spelman, Elizabeth. "Woman as Body: Ancient and Contemporary Views." *Feminist Studies* 8, 1 (Spring 1982): 109–31.

Spivak, Gayatri. "Displacement and the Discourse of Woman." In *Displacement: Derrida and After*, ed. Mark Krupnick. Bloomington: Indiana University Press, 1983.

Stanbury, Sarah. "Feminist Film Theory Seeing Chrétien's *Enide*," *Literature and Psychology* 36, 4 (1990): 47–66.

Stanton, Domna. "Difference on Trial: A Critique of the Maternal Metaphor in Cixous, Irigaray, and Kristeva." In *The Poetics of Gender*, ed. Nancy K. Miller. New York: Columbia University Press, 1986.

Steenberghen, Fernand van. *La Philosophie au 13e siècle*. Louvain: Publications Universitaires, 1966.

Sturm-Maddox, Sara and Donald Maddox. "Description in Medieval Narrative: Vestimentary Coherence in Chrétien's *Erec et Enide*." *Medioevo Romanzo* 9, 1 (1984): 51–64.

Suleiman, Susan. *The Female Body in Western Culture: Contemporary Perspectives*. Cambridge, Mass.: Harvard University Press, 1986.

———. *Subversive Intent: Gender, Politics, and the Avant-Garde*. Cambridge, Mass.: Harvard University Press, 1990.

Tissier, André. *Recueil de Farces (1450–1550)*. Vol. 1. Geneva: Droz, 1986.

Tuska, Jon. *The Films of Mae West*. Secaucus, N.J.: Citadel Press, 1973.

Vance, Eugene. *From Topic to Tale: Logic and Narrativity in the Middle Ages*. Minneapolis: University of Minnesota Press, 1987.

———. *Mervelous Signals: Poetics and Sign Theory in the Middle Ages*. Lincoln: University of Nebraska Press, 1986.

Várvaro, Alberto. *Béroul's "Romance of Tristan."* Trans. John C. Barnes. Manchester: Manchester University Press; New York: Barnes and Noble, 1972.

Vickers, Nancy J. "Diana Described: Scattered Woman and Scattered Rhyme." *Critical Inquiry* 8, 2 (Winter, 1981): 265–79.

Weed, Elizabeth. "A Man's Place." In *Men in Feminism*, ed. Alice Jardine and Paul Smith. London: Methuen, 1987.

Wetherbee, Winthrop. *Platonism and Poetry in the Twelfth Century: The Literary Influence of the School of Chartres*. Princeton, N.J.: Princeton University Press, 1972.

White, Sarah Melhado. "The Old French *Jeu d'Adam*: Latin *ordo*, Vernacular Play." Manuscript.

———. "Sexual Language and Human Conflict in Old French Fabliaux." *Comparative Studies in Society and History* 24, 1 (1982): 185–210.

Whitford, Margaret. *The Irigaray Reader*. Oxford/Cambridge, Mass.: Basil Blackwell, 1991.

———. "Rereading Irigaray." In *Between Feminism and Psychoanalysis*, ed. Teresa Brennan. London/New York: Routledge, 1989.

Willard, Charity Cannon. *Christine de Pizan: Her Life and Works*. New York: Persea Books, 1984.

Willis, Sharon. *Marguerite Duras: Writing on the Body*. Urbana: University of Illinois Press, 1987.

Wilson, Katharina M., ed. *Medieval Women Writers*. Athens: University of Georgia Press, 1984.

Wright, Laurence. "Burning and Leprosy in Old French Literature." *Medium Aevum* 56, 1, (1987): 101–11.

Yenal, Edith. *Christine de Pisan: A Bibliography of Writings by Her and About Her.* Metuchen, N.J./London: Scarecrow Press, 1982; supplement, 1989.

Zink, Michel. *Les Chansons de toile.* Paris: Champion, 1977.

Zumthor, Paul. *Essai de poétique médiévale.* Paris: Éditions de Seuil, 1972.

———. "Le texte-fragment." *Langue Française* 40 (1978): 75–82.

Index

Aaron, 98

Abduction: in courtly literature, 14; in *Philomena*, 117

Abelard, 77, 103 n.11

Accarie, Maurice, 105 n.30

Adam, 71–73, 75, 83, 91; in the Fall, 75–76, 78–83, 92, 95–96, 105 n.37; in *Jeu d'Adam*, 98–102

Adultery, 15–16, 112, 205–6, 208–9, 211, 213–14, 215, 218, 220, 231, 233, 236–37, 238 n.11, 246

Agency, female; 36; in *Philomena*, 117, 118, 123, 132;

Allen, Peter L., 249 n.3

Allen, Prudence, 103 n.6, 106 n.50

Allen, Robert C., xiii n.8

Ambrose, 73

Anatomy, female: and reading, xii; and desire, 110; and identity, 244; and male anatomy, 247; catalogued, 115; constructed, 203; fictive, 62; gendered, viii; denunciation of, 56; Galen's view of, 85; gaze on, 208; in fabliau, 248; in *Roman de Silence*, 244; medieval man's failure to understand, 34, 40; sexualized, 229

Anatomy, male: restructuring of 62–63

Antifeminism, 13, 16, 45, 65 n.1, 242

Anus, 48, 69 n.50, 74–5

Aquinas, Thomas, 77, 102 nn.3–4

Aristotle, 35, 66 n.16, 72, 77, 85, 86, 89–90, 98, 241

Arthur, King, 212, 213, 220, 224, 226, 233, 237, 238 n.17

Arthurian Vulgate Cycle, 15, 21 n.39

Ass, 66 n.11; in "Berangier," 39–40, 43; compared to vagina, 43; in farce, 31, 33–37, 41, 77; speech of, 58

Asshole, in Augustine, 73–76, 93

Atkinson, Ti-Grace, 244

Auerbach, Nina, xii n.2, 20 n.29, 67 n.18

Augustine, 72–76, 78–79, 83–86, 90, 96, 99, 102, 102 n.2, 104 nn.22–24

Author, 38; absent, 12; female, 19 n.18; male, 16

Authority, 248

Authorship: female, 9; in *Erec et Enide*, 195

Bal, Mieke, 91, 105 n.37

Barons: in *Roman de Tristan*, 218–20, 230, 232, 234

Barthes, Roland, xii n.2

Bauer, Barbara Nelson Sargeant, 201 n.41, 202 n.43

Beauty, erotic, of Philomena's tapestry, 118; of Itys, 141

Beauty, female, 16, 242; and knowledge, 147, 149 n.16; and speech, 234; catalogue of in *Philomena*, 119, 125; catalogue of in *Roman de Tristan*, 221; constructed, medieval, 131; descriptions of, 127, 220–21; ideal, 87; in courtly romance, viii, 106, 112, 117; in *Erec et Enide*, 184; linked to Nature and God, 118; medieval conception of, viii, 109, 204, 208; of Enide, 176; of eroticized female body, 146; of Iseut, 223–24, 226, 230, 233–35; of Philomena, 118–19, 121, 145; of Philomena's knowledge, 121; shift of in *Philomena* to knowledge, 146; source of, 192

Bedchamber, 171, 210, 232

Bedsheets, 231–33

Bédier, Joseph, 65 n.4

Beck, Jonathan, 104 n.23

Beloved (Toni Morrison), 140, 150 n.31

Belsey, Catherine, xi, 68 nn.35–36

"Berangier au long cul," 39–43, 45–46, 66 n.12

Berg, Elizabeth, 238 n.10

Béroul, 204, 206, 208–09, 214, 220, 224, 228–29, 237 nn.5–6, 238 nn.7, 11, 16, 239 n.26

"Black Balls," 56–57, 60–61, 69 n.45

University of Pennsylvania Press
NEW CULTURAL STUDIES
Joan DeJean, Carroll Smith-Rosenberg,
and Peter Stallybrass, Editors

Jonathan Arac and Harriet Ritvo, editors. *Macropolitics of Nineteenth-Century Literature: Nationalism, Exoticism, Imperialism.* 1991.

John Barrell. *The Birth of Pandora and the Division of Knowledge.* 1992.

Bruce Thomas Boehrer. *Monarchy and Incest in Renaissance England: Literature, Culture, Kinship and Kingship.* 1992.

E. Jane Burns. *Bodytalk: When Women Speak in Old French Literature.* 1993.

Julia V. Douthwaite. *Exotic Women: Literary Heroines and Cultural Strategies in Ancien Régime France, 1670–1784.* 1992.

Barbara J. Eckstein. *The Language of Fiction in a World of Pain: Reading Politics as Paradox.* 1990.

Katherine Gravdal. *Ravishing Maidens: Writing Rape in Medieval French Literature and Law.* 1991.

Jayne Ann Krentz, editor. *Dangerous Men and Adventurous Women: Romance Writers on the Appeal of the Romance.* 1992.

Linda Lomperis and Sarah Stanbury, editors. *Feminist Approaches to the Body in Medieval Literature.* 1993.

Karma Lochrie. *Margery Kempe and Translations of the Flesh.* 1991.

Alex Owen. *The Darkened Room: Women, Power and Spiritualism in Late Victorian England.* 1990.

Jacqueline Rose. *The Case of Peter Pan.* 1992.

This book has been set in Linotron Galliard. Galliard was designed for Mergenthaler in 1978 by Matthew Carter. Galliard retains many of the features of a sixteenth-century typeface cut by Robert Granjon but has some modifications that give it a more contemporary look.

Printed on acid-free paper.